C000245785

The British Sociological Association

A sociological history

Jennifer Platt

Published by:
sociologypress
[Registered office: Department of Sociology and Social Policy,
University of Durham, 32 Old Elvet, Durham, DH1 3HN
Or http://www.sociologypress.co.uk]

sociologypress is supported by the British Sociological Association. It furthers
the Association's aim of promoting the discipline of sociology and disseminating
sociological knowledge.

© Jennifer Platt 2003

All rights reserved. Except for the quotation of short passages for the purposes of criticism
and review, no part of this publication may be reproduced, stored in a retrieval system,
or transmitted in any form, or by any means, without the prior permission of the publisher.

This book may not be circulated in any other binding or cover and the same condition
must be imposed on any acquiror.

British Library Cataloguing in Publication Data
A CIP catalogue record for this book is available from the British Library

ISBN 1 903457 06 8

Cover: The image on the front cover is from a photo image disk called Model Released
Crowds from Image 100 Ltd, for which copyright assignment has been obtained by the
British Sociological Association.

Printed and bound by:
York Publishing Services, 64 Hallfield Road, Layerthorpe, York YO31 7ZQ

Contents

List of tables iv

Abbreviations used v

Preface vi

1 Introduction 1

2 Prehistory and foundation of the BSA 5

3 The changing structure and functions of the Association 27

4 The BSA and intellectual life 47

5 Membership and activists 69

6 'For women only'? 89

7 Affairs of the head: conflict and defence 108

8 How the organisation has run 124

9 The BSA in its organisational context 139

10 The BSA's trajectory: an overview 160

Notes on sources 173

Appendix 177

Bibliography 193

Index to content 204

Index to references 211

List of tables

Table 1   Sponsors, their membership of the PEC and of the Association   20
Table 2   Numbers of members from different groups, October 1951   22
Table 3   Highest qualification in sociology, holders of jobs in sociology
           (%), *Register*   35
Table 4   Topics and attendance at non-teaching meetings of the
           Teachers' Section   48
Table 5   Conferences   49
Table 6   Changes in conference pattern   53
Table 7   Ratio of non-plenary papers to attendance   53
Table 8   Number of study groups, related to membership   55
Table 9   Proportion of women authors   63
Table 10   Gender composition of editorial boards: proportion female   64
Table 11   Number of pages in *Sociology*   65
Table 12   BSA membership as reported to Annual General Meetings   70
Table 13   Rates of BSA membership among sociologists listed in the
           CUYB   71
Table 14   BSA membership among 1972 and 1976 CUYB
           sociologists, 1973 and 1977   71
Table 15   Sex of BSA membership   76
Table 16   Among sociologists listed in the CUYB, the proportions of
           men and of women who were BSA members   76
Table 17   Proportion of departments with at least eight sociologists
           where at least half of those listed were BSA members   76
Table 18   EC membership (presidents omitted) by rank, percentages   79
Table 19   Average age of EC members   81
Table 20   Sex of EC members   81
Table 21   EC membership-years from (former) polytechnics   81
Table 22   Departments with at least three different (near-)consecutive
           EC members   84
Table 23   In departments of at least eight, the number providing at least
           one EC member/year   85
Table 24   In departments of at least eight, the average number of EC
           member/years provided   85
Table 25   Caucus/EoS/BSA events and publications on topics related to
           gender issues   97
Table 26   Major components of BSA income   129
Table 27   Overall financial situation at 1985 prices   129
Table 28   British ISA EC members and their main BSA roles   141
Table 29   BSA as 'professional association': characteristics present   168
Table A1   Members of the Executive Committee   177
Table A2   Editors of *Sociology*   186
Table A3   Editors of *Work, Employment and Society*   186
Table A4   Study groups: dates active   187
Table A5   BSA annual accounts   191

Abbreviations used

AGM	Annual General Meeting
ALSISS	Association/Academy of Learned Societies in the Social Sciences
ASA	American Sociological Association
ATCDE	Association of Teachers in Colleges and Departments of Education
ATSS	Association for the Teaching of the Social Sciences
AUT	Association of University Teachers
BAAS	British Association for the Advancement of Science
BJS	*British Journal of Sociology*
BLPES	British Library of Political and Economic Science
BPS	British Psychological Society
BSA	British Sociological Association
CNAA	Council for National Academic Awards
COS	Charity Organisation Society
CUYB	*Commonwealth Universities Year Book*
DSIR	Department of Scientific and Industrial Research
EC	Executive Committee
EoS	Equality of the Sexes Subcommittee
ESRC	Economic and Social Research Council
ESA	European Sociological Association
HoDs	Heads of Departments
ISA	International Sociological Association
LSE	London School of Economics
HEFCE	Higher Education Funding Council for England
NATHFE	National Association of Teachers in Higher and Further Education
PEP	Political and Economic Planning
PHoDs	Professors and Heads of Departments
PIC	Population Investigation Committee
PSA	Political Studies Association
RAE	Research Assessment Exercise
RSS	Royal Statistical Society
SCASS	Standing Conference of Arts and Social Sciences
SCOS	Standing Committee of Sociologists
SHAFE	Sociology Heads in Advanced Further Education
SIP	Sociologists in Polytechnics
SPA	Social Policy Association
SR	*Sociological Review*
SSRC	Social Science Research Council
UNESCO	United Nations Educational, Scientific and Cultural Organisation
WCN	*Women's Caucus Newsletter*
WES	*Work, Employment and Society*

Preface

This book was commissioned by the British Sociological Association (BSA), which funded the research on which it is based. The BSA's aim was to mark the fiftieth anniversary of its founding, an appropriate occasion for celebration. I was very pleased to receive the commission, because the work fitted well with my research interests, and I was happy to develop them further in this direction. The Association has been a model funding body, in the sense that it has set no constraints on the way in which I have carried out the commission, and there has been no pressure to write in a purely celebratory style. Moreover, much practical help has been received from the office. I acknowledge with gratitude all this support and assistance.

There are also a large number of individuals, in addition to those interviewed, to thank for their contributions to the work. Bev Barstow acted as research assistant on the project, and made important contributions to the data. Next, the members of the steering committee appointed by the BSA: Sheila Allen, Joe Banks and John Westergaard; their advice and support was invaluable. Others who have played a variety of helpful roles include Caroline Baggaley, Olive Banks, Michael Banton, Jim Beckford, Nicola Boyne, Richard Brown, Robert Dingwall, Anne Dix, Jacquie Gauntlett, Charles Goldie, Chelly Halsey, Gayle Letherby, David Mills, Jo Moran-Ellis, Judith Mudd, William Outhwaite, Geoff Payne, Kit Platt, John Rex, John H. Smith and W. M. Williams.

Chapter 1
Introduction

A history of the British Sociological Association (BSA) is inevitably to some extent also a history of British sociology, and of some of the major changes in the social context within which that has developed. The BSA has had its internal dynamics, but it has also responded to and been affected by many external factors, ranging from government policies to the rise of feminism. It has both contributed to the intellectual development of sociology, and been affected by that; in addition, it has been influenced by movements intellectual and social arising outside sociology. An intellectual history of British sociology remains to be written, however, although material relevant to that appears here, and is sometimes used to account for developments within the BSA. (Here intellectual currents are treated as factors affecting developments within the Association; if an intellectual history were written sociologically, its focus of interest would tend to reverse these roles of independent and dependent variables.)

Learned societies such as the BSA are a vital part of the social structure of academic life; not every eligible person belongs to one, but nonetheless all are affected by them. However, the topic is one that has usually been neglected in general historical work on academic disciplines. That often focuses on disembodied ideas or, at most, uses social units such as schools of thought, departments or educational institutions. Learned societies deserve better than to be confined to the ghetto of commissioned anniversary organisational histories. They cut across the boundaries of those conventional historical units, organising conferences, promoting the professional development of their members, creating networks and publishing journals and books which are important to the intellectual life of the discipline. They also represent the discipline to the outside world, whether in the large political arena of major governmental decisions on education and research, or in the many smaller arenas of funding bodies, exam boards and governing bodies in higher education. More broadly, the BSA can be looked at as one part of the institutional structure of the social sciences, both national and international; it is a disciplinary association which can usefully be compared with the associations of other disciplines, and a national sociological association which can be compared with those of other nations (cf. Platt, 2002). Perhaps its form can be understood better in terms of that context, as well as of its internal and disciplinary characteristics.

I hope that this book will be regarded as a work of sociology as well as an organisational history, though the basic needs of a history of the organisation have taken some priority, and that it can be fruitfully read by people who do not have a special interest in the BSA as such. (Those readers who do, and who feel already familiar with the BSA's story, will find that not all the widely shared understandings of that are supported by the data adduced.) Here, the narrative history is largely confined to the first two main chapters, and later chapters add some more analytical description and discussion of the causes of events and patterns, and pursue those with further data wherever possible. Some of the book's claim to a sociological character rests on its concern, within this context, with traditionally sociological matters such as stratification (here mainly by academic rank and gender), the social impact of population composition (in this case the changing demography of academia), the effects of increasing size on organisational structure, and the tension between the provision of public and private goods in the maintenance of an organisation from whose efforts many can benefit as free riders. It is also related to aspects of the sociology of higher education, and of the women's movement. The most general theme explicitly raised is the concluding one of the idea of a professional association, and how well the BSA has fitted that; it does not fit very well, in that it is neither a 'professional association' like the classic cases of the type nor, in so far as that is contrasted with 'learned society', is it simply a learned society. This opens up issues of the relevance of current ideal types, and the possible need for an extended typology, which are equally applicable to many other associations.

Because the material is arranged by substantive topic as it arises from the history of the BSA, such themes are usually touched on as they are raised by the topic in hand, rather than dealt with in one place. The total picture painted is one in which the BSA as an organisation acts in changing historical circumstances which depend, on the one hand, on the personal agendas of its members, and on the other hand on the challenges, constraints and opportunities provided by the broader social environment; the forms which its action has taken have also depended on its internal structure and traditions. Individual members bring to it their intellectual and career agendas, sometimes ones which are shared by self-conscious, even organised, groups, and such agendas of course affect whether they become and remain members and what roles they play within the organisation. Personal networks, often but not only departmentally based, affect the salience of the BSA as a forum; those who are drawn into more active roles develop associational networks and careers, and recruit others to them. The BSA needs to respond to the agendas of current and potential members in order to maintain its financial base, but it has sometimes been difficult for it to reconcile that practical need with the ideological priorities of its members. The broader social environment has provided challenges ranging from the early expansion of universities and sociology departments, through the periods of student unrest, the women's movement, high levels of inflation, Thatcher Government university cuts and changes in the roles played by polytechnics, to the more recent governmental pressures for accountability in teaching and research and changes in charity legislation. All of those have had consequences for the BSA, and it has responded to them, if not always with complete success.

The data used come from a variety of sources, mainly documentary. First, there is a collection of BSA office papers in the archives section of the British Library of Political and Economic Science (BLPES) at the London School of Economics. Most of those were deposited when the office moved to Durham in 1992; they represent not materials deliberately collected for social-scientific archival purposes, but what the office held for office purposes and deemed not to be needed for the future. These have been supplemented, to update key sources such as Executive Committee minutes, conference programmes and Annual Reports, by copies of papers now held at the Durham office. Some of those papers deal with the internal running of the Association and were not for circulation, while others are its publications. These collections have been further supplemented at some points by similar documents which I had myself kept, and a number of valuable donations have been made by colleagues who had saved papers not in the public archives, or sometimes were solicited from participants as the need arose. Use has also been made of the *Commonwealth Universities Year Book* (CUYB) to provide data on sociologists employed in universities. (For more detail on the range of available sources, and their strengths and limitations, see the Note on Sources.)

In addition, 35 interviews have been carried out. Those interviewed have not been a systematic sample in the usual sense, but have been selected for the roles they have played in relation to the BSA. Inevitably, the earliest cohort of more senior activists is not represented, because they had died before the research started, but a number of the more junior people who were involved at the earliest stages are fortunately still with us. That constraint apart, a key aim was to select respondents who had played active roles of different kinds, at different periods, on which they could be used as informants. Since most of these people had played more than one role, we cannot characterise each by one label, but they included eight presidents, six Executive Committee Chairs, six secretaries, seven treasurers, several conference organisers and study-group convenors, three journal editors, several people prominent in the early Teachers' Section or the Sociologists in Polytechnics group, several active in BSA Scotland, some summer school directors, members of subcommittees such as those for Equality of the Sexes and Publications and of journal editorial boards, and those responsible for organising a number of ad hoc activities. In addition, a special effort was made to represent 'the other side', by seeing some people who, from outside BSA office-holding, had played a prominent role in particular important episodes, had been involved in controversy with the Association or had publicly criticised it or resigned from it. In most cases, the opportunity was taken to ask also about the personal career of the respondent in relation to the Association. Some interview data which came from what were formally other sources has also occasionally been drawn on: Bev Barstow, the research assistant on the BSA project, also interviewed a number of people for her dissertation on the Women's Caucus, and each of us carried out interviews for a project on 'Gender and the Sociological Labour Market', funded by the Leverhulme Foundation. Drafts of chapters have been circulated for comment to some of those with relevant experience, and their responses have sometimes added fresh information.

These are rich sources, but on some points their coverage is very uneven, and there are certainly topics which could have been developed much further if more had been documented in the papers available. For instance, the material on study groups depends heavily on the efficiency, and the sense of obligation to the central organisation, of individual convenors, and is often very incomplete, varying over time and sometimes almost completely absent. Different secretaries have followed different formulae in the production of annual reports, so that when the secretaryship changes hands a chronological series of data may be broken. And so on …

Among the data drawn on have been some from myself. I have been active in the BSA for many years, in a number of roles. Writing this book has, thus, related to my personal experience and, as it will for many of my readers too, has offered an opportunity to reflect on the context in which that has taken place in a more systematic way than I would otherwise have done. It seemed foolish, even potentially misleading, to ignore what this meant that I could contribute, and to write as if I had not had any involvement, though important that the story should not be told from a personal perspective. I have, therefore, permitted myself the occasional anecdote from my own experience, in the same way as I have drawn on interviews with others, but have tried not to give those any special weight. Where I have direct knowledge of a particular episode or period, my account is also inevitably informed by that, though I have aimed to represent others' versions too wherever there is reason to believe that there were different perspectives on the matter and where data on those are available.

The first two substantive chapters give a general historical overview, starting with the range of predecessor organisations from which the BSA eventually emerged, and going on to how it came to be founded, the major changes in educational policy and structures which have formed much of the context for its activities, and the ways in which it has, in response to both internal and external pressures, changed over time. Those chapters could be read on their own as a historical story. Against that background, the following chapters each take up a number of more detailed or analytical themes as they have developed across the whole time span. First, there is an account of the BSA's role in intellectual life: conferences, study groups, journals. This is followed by material on the membership and its fluctuations, and on the characteristics of executive members and how they have been drawn into activism. The women's movement has been very consequential on both those fronts, and the role it has played is described next. The Association has often concerned itself with political issues and personal cases; there have been several episodes of particular importance both in revealing alternative conceptions of its role and in showing the limits to its powers, and these are described. As well as being an intellectual and a political actor, the BSA has to maintain itself as a working body, so how this has been done in formal legal status, the provision and organisation of an office, the committee structure and financial policies is sketched. The Association is then placed in the context of the other associations, whether other groups of sociologists or governmental bodies, with which it has had relationships. Finally, some general conclusions are drawn about its character and the particular directions in which it has developed, and these are related to ideas about professionalism and professional associations.

The BSA has changed even as the work on this history has been in progress, and it will surely change again in response to new historical circumstances both internal and external; the history continues.

Chapter 2
Prehistory and foundation of the BSA

To understand the way in which the BSA emerged, why it was set up when it was and the form which it took, we need to look at the prehistory of academic sociology and of associations related to sociology. The BSA did not spring forth without precedent; there were earlier associations which could be seen as predecessors. In this chapter, we describe these and the intellectual and practical concerns which they represented, and show how it emerged against that background.

Development of early institutions

From the 1830s onwards, a variety of bodies existed which in one way or another had some claim to sociological relevance, although they were strongly associated with practical policy concerns and did not always have any real scientific basis.[1] Some, but not all, had 'sociology' in their names, but this did not distinguish between those which we might now be more and less inclined to treat as truly sociological in a sense that we would recognise. Initially at least, they were part of the response to the major social upheavals of early industrialisation; they were especially concerned with the condition of the working classes in towns, but also dealt with many other topics. Some of these bodies long preceded the first university posts and courses although, as those emerged, there were many connections with the network of voluntary activity. They are considered below in rough chronological order.

Royal Statistical Society

In 1833, a statistical section of the British Association for the Advancement of Science (BAAS) was formed, and from this arose other statistical societies, such as the Manchester one. In 1834, a London society was set up, proposed by Malthus. This became the Royal Statistical Society (RSS) in 1887; its social cachet is shown by the fact that successive monarchs have been its 'patron'; all its early presidents, and a fair sprinkling of later ones, were members of the nobility. At this period, it was taken for granted that the statistics in question were social data, rather than an abstract mathematical technique. Its declared goal was 'the collection and classification of all facts illustrative of the present condition and prospects of society … ' (Kent, 1981: 20). Their concern was to provide useful data to inform policy, and they put forward a conception of pure facts showing the way. (In practice, the 'facts' did not, of course, give unambiguous guidance.) Of the papers presented to it in 1863–84, the great majority were on social topics, though that included economic as well as more sociological ones. For 1884–1909, the papers read were again mainly social, classified by the society's historian into such categories as Vital Statistics, Moral and Social Statistics (including several papers by Charles Booth), Political Statistics, Commercial Statistics, Financial Statistics, Statistics of Production, Consumption, Wealth and Income (Royal Statistical Society, 1934: 122, 163).

By the 1870s, there was active discussion of the desirability of making some use of hypotheses so that the relation of fact and opinion could be considered, and a division grew up between those who moved into the technicalities of the mathematical treatment of statistics and those who were primarily concerned with bringing data to bear on social questions, including most of those who defined themselves as sociologists, who developed alternative approaches outside the society (Abrams, 1968: 20–30). However, the RSS for a long time played a key role in relation to empirical social research, providing the main forum in which results could be presented. Quantitative researchers of all kinds, including those carrying out governmental research and producing official statistics, presented papers at its regular meetings, and this role continued at least until after the Second World War and is to some extent retained to the present day.

National Association for the Promotion of Social Science

The National Association for the Promotion of Social Science was an association of reform groups, founded in 1857. It had departments for jurisprudence, education, punishment and reformation, public health and social economy, and discussed subjects ranging from the education of girls to sanitary arrangements in Indian barracks. '[T]he belief that held it together was that for every social problem there was an optimal ameliorating measure which could be scientifically arrived at by investigation and by patient discussion between all interested parties' – and this should then lead to proposals to go to Parliament. It held large and successful congresses in which many distinguished people took part, and had a considerable influence on legislation. Abrams commented that its approach gave almost no attention to the development of theoretical understanding or the intellectual development of social science (1968: 44–7), and that is not surprising. But interest in it gradually declined. Perris (1913: 164) suggested that 'with a thousand elementary tasks of social reform pressing for accomplishment, in the infancy of evolutionary thought, a Sociological Society, such as we now have [on which see below], could not be attempted ... '; when 'sociological thought was ripening to the dignity of an acknowledged science', and a more democratic era opened, its time was past, and by 1886 it had ceased to exist.

London School of Economics

In 1903, lectures in sociology started at the London School of Economics and Political Science (LSE), funded by a private benefaction from Martin White, a wealthy landowner and former Liberal MP with a strong interest in the subject.[2] The LSE is a college of London University, in whose foundation the leading role was played by the Fabian socialists Sidney and Beatrice Webb. The Fabian Society, founded in 1883, was strongly oriented to fact-finding research and, when in 1895 it received a legacy from a supporter to be used for its purposes, the decision was made, at Sidney Webb's instance, to apply this money to the foundation of what became the LSE, a specialist institution for the social sciences. Its prospectus stated that 'the special aim of the School will be ... the study and investigation of the concrete facts of industrial life and the actual working of economic and political relations as they exist or have existed ... ' (Dahrendorf, 1995: 20). A memorandum defined the aims of the sociology lectures:

(1)   *To promote the application of scientific method to sociological studies.*

(2)   *To encourage the study of the more general and philosophical aspects of sociological science.*

(3)   *To demonstrate the present possibility of an approximate synthesis of sociological knowledge.*

(4)   *To encourage the study, and to promote the correlation, of the more recently established departments of sociological investigation, like Anthropology, Social Psychology etc.*

(5)   *To show that the special sciences of Man and the general or philosophical studies of Humanity will each and all gain by being brought into more direct relation with each other.*

(6)   *To aid in establishing the academic status of Sociology in the Universities of this country in general and more particularly in that of London, and to create a body of academic opinion in favour of re-organising the curricula of social studies in Universities, on a basis which more adequately recognises synthetic sociological conceptions.*
(Branford, 1928: 340)

Whether or not these stated aims provided specific guidance in the making of appointments or the subjects of the lectures given is not known, but the document is of some interest in itself. A Finnish anthropologist or ethnologist, Edward A. Westermarck, became the first lecturer; he was joined the following year by Leonard T. Hobhouse, whose background was in philosophy and journalism. The country's first university professorship in sociology was created at the LSE in 1907, also funded by White (as was Westermarck's lectureship); Hobhouse, who shared many views with the Webbs, was appointed to it.[3]

The Charity Organisation Society (COS), set up in 1869, represented an important strand of social reform; it was concerned with encouraging self-help, and giving charitable assistance only to the deserving poor, identified as such by scientific investigation, while the undeserving would be offered relief on unattractive terms. It 'aimed at helping the poor by direct and practical action rather than by political agitation and institutional change'. In this, it differed from the Fabian socialists, who were more concerned with political solutions to what they saw as social rather than individual problems than with education for direct action by social workers (Dahrendorf, 1995: 95). The COS tried to copy the success of the LSE by setting up the London School of Ethics and Social Philosophy. This failed, but it was succeeded around 1903 by the School of Sociology and Social Economics, led by Urwick (previously at the first social settlement, Toynbee Hall[4]), which provided professional training for social workers. Nine years later, this was failing, and merged with the LSE, becoming its Department of Social Science (Dahrendorf, 1995: 95) – separate from the Department of Sociology – and continuing to train social workers.

The Sociological Society

The idea of a British Sociological Society was initiated by Victor Branford, as a forum to spread knowledge of developments in social studies and to promote Patrick Geddes' ideas. Who was Geddes?[5] He was a biologist by training, but a man of wide and eclectic interests. He became a follower of Le Play, but for him the strength of Le Play's trio of *Lieu, Travail, Famille* was its emphasis on the interaction between man and environment, and this became a primary concern with what he called 'civics' and, in its practical manifestation, what later generations have known as town planning. He saw social surveys as a necessary stage in the development of satisfactory town plans. He was actively involved in making plans and recommendations for the improvement of cities, especially his native town of Edinburgh, in the 1880s living himself with his family among the working class, buying and managing decent housing for the poor, and setting up self-managing student halls of residence. In 1892, he also set up there the 'Outlook Tower' in an old astronomical observatory, and this became known as a sociological museum or laboratory (Zueblin, 1899) and survived until 1914. It contained an exhibition which led the visitor from floor to floor in a sequence from the local to the regional, national and global – finishing with a camera obscura on the top floor, from which the town and its region could be viewed.

Geddes had given lectures in a variety of contexts, some on the application of the idea of evolution in social studies. In 1890–5, he organised summer schools in Edinburgh with lectures on philosophy, social science history, geography and natural science. His own lectures worked through great past world civilisations and their social evolution, finishing with discussion of the present. The largest attendance was about 120 people in 1893, but through this a core of committed supporters was recruited, including Branford, an accountant and businessman, who became his long-term collaborator.

The Sociological Society was founded in 1903 (again with financial support from Martin White, who acted as its treasurer from 1903 to 1923). Its first president, a Member of Parliament, offered as a reason why it was needed that:

> *where various branches of investigation have been studied and developed as special departments of the so-called social sciences, there ... does not between them exist that intimate relation which ought to exist for the common benefit of all ... by having one society to which the other more specialised societies may send communications that are of general interest for all or many departments of human study, a more rapid advance may be made towards the correlation and unification of all forms and kinds of knowledge bearing on Man.*
> (Bryce, 1904: xv–xvi)

A statement of the society's purposes says that:

> The aims of the Sociological Society are scientific, educational and
> practical. It seeks to promote investigation, and to advance education in
> the social sciences in their various aspects and applications. Its field
> covers the whole phenomena of society ... the Society affords the
> common ground on which workers from all fields and schools may
> profitably meet – geographer and naturalist, anthropologist and
> archaeologist, historian and philologist, psychologist and moralist, all
> contributing their results towards a fuller Social Philosophy ... physician
> and the alienist, the criminologist and the jurist, have here again their
> common meeting ground with hygienist and educationist, with
> philanthropist, social reformer and politician, with journalist and cleric.[6]
> (Galton et al., 1904: 284)

Both these statements, in their different ways, show the grand synthetic
conception of sociology as the master social science, which was also held by the
leading early academic sociologists.

The society had a large membership drawn from many areas of public life.
It was certainly not limited to members whose primary intellectual or
occupational identification was with sociology, however defined. In addition
to the tiny number of recognised academic sociologists such as Westermarck
and Hobhouse, it drew on other established constituencies such as eugenicists
and the 'civics' group, as well as social workers, the survey movement and
practical social reformers and men of affairs. Important foreign sociologists
such as Durkheim, W. I. Thomas and Tönnies contributed in writing to the
society's discussions, and there were wide international contacts. It held regular
meetings at the LSE, with a large attendance, at which papers were given by
distinguished contributors.

The dominant conception of sociology in the society is indicated by the
fact that in the first volume of its *Sociological Papers* – which published as
books papers given at its meetings – the only one on a contemporary empirical
topic ('Life in an agricultural village in England'), which presented data on
incomes and poverty, merits a footnote explaining its appearance in 'a volume
explicitly sociological'; there was hesitation whether it was appropriate to include
anything so 'internal and technical' to economics (Galton *et al.*, 1904: 163).
More typical papers covered such topics as the role of eugenics (Galton), and
'The position of woman in early civilization' (Westermarck). The Papers ceased
publication after three issues (1904, 1905 and 1906), and in 1907 were replaced
by the *Sociological Review* (SR). It might have been expected that the RSS and
the Sociological Society would have had much in common; however, Abrams
(1968: 128) points out that, by 1914, they had almost no overlap of membership
– only four people belonged to both. A division had grown up between the
statistical style of work and the Geddes style, prominent within the Sociological
Society, and each had some claim to the name of 'sociologist'.

The eugenicists withdrew from the society in 1907 and set up the Eugenics
Education Society, which in 1909 established its own journal, the *Eugenics
Review*. By 1913, the British Medical Association had formed a 'Medical
Sociology' section whose main interest was in eugenic issues, and the main

interests of the eugenicists became medical ones, such as the heritability of disease (Halliday, 1968: 394).[7] The civics group set up a separate Cities Committee within the Sociological Society in 1907–8, and increasingly evangelised on behalf of Geddes' ideas; it had most influence within geography and town and country planning, advocating city surveys as a basis for planning.

In 1920, the Civics group of the Sociological Society founded Le Play House, as a centre for regional and civic sociology, and this involved leading figures from the Geographical Association and the Town Planning Institute and offered advice and encouragement on regional surveys. Dorothea Farquharson, who was closely involved in its activities, saw this as adding an important dimension to the work of the Sociological Society: 'field work was henceforth combined with sociological theory' (1955: 168). One of its most popular activities was the 'educational tour', in which participants carried out fieldwork using regional survey techniques; this followed on from the International Visits Association which had been run by the Sociological Society. By 1930, the Le Play House group had become dissatisfied with the Sociological Society, and broke away.

The society was reconstituted as the Institute of Sociology, still sponsoring the SR, which now had an editorial board which included Morris Ginsberg of the LSE as a member.[8] Monthly meetings were held at which there were some distinguished speakers, such as von Wiese and Znaniecki. It was also responsible for some useful conferences, in which academics from various disciplines participated, on the relation between sociology and other disciplines. One book of some significance (Marshall, 1938), addressing the issues of social stratification which were for a long time central to later British sociology, resulted from these. Another of less long-term significance, but of considerable interest in relation to contemporary conceptions of sociology, was on relations between the social sciences (Marshall, 1936).

Eugenics Society

This society was founded in 1907. As Mazumdar (1992) points out, it drew on the same constituency of the educated middle classes concerned about the condition of the working class as such bodies as the Charity Organisation Society and the Sociological Society, though its preferred explanations and solutions were in terms of biological heredity, and it was especially preoccupied with class differentials in fertility and their presumed relation to degeneration in population quality. As many writers have shown, these were common themes of the time, and eugenics was a common interest of reforming intellectuals on both left and right. In 1929, the society founded the British Population Society; this initially had a membership of 20, which included Keynes, Beveridge and the anthropologists Pitt-Rivers and Malinowski, as well as Carr-Saunders (who had published at least two books on population, and is characterised by Grebenik (1986: 13) as then the leading British expert on population). The Eugenics Society set up a joint Population Policies Committee with Political and Economic Planning (PEP) (on which see below), aimed at providing evidence for a Royal Commission on the birth rate, whose membership overlapped with that of the other groups; this was disbanded in 1940 (Grebenik, 1986: 20). In 1936, the Population Investigation Committee was founded, with Carr-Saunders in the chair, and David Glass as the research secretary, and funded by the Eugenics Society. This was based in the Eugenics Society's premises, until it moved to the LSE when, in 1945, Glass was appointed to a readership in demography in the Department of Sociology. There were, thus, many connections with what became academic sociology.

LSE Sociology Club

There was also a 'Sociology Club' based at the LSE, which met in the inter-war period and continued to exist for a while after the Second World War.[9] It was initiated in 1923. Hobhouse was the first president, and Ginsberg the secretary – succeeding to the presidency when he succeeded to the LSE chair – but it was not a purely departmental club, and membership was open to people from outside the LSE. However, there was a limit on the total membership of 45 in London and 20 from elsewhere; London members absent from four consecutive meetings without satisfactory explanation ceased to be members. Papers were given to this club by members both of the Department of Sociology and of other departments, or from outside the LSE. The topics were by no means exclusively sociological; among the earliest papers were 'The implications of the Cambridge School of economics' and 'The social value of mental tests'. Some papers were on policy/political issues, as when Hugh Gaitskell (then a lecturer in economics, later leader of the Labour Party) spoke in 1932 on 'Some problems of the socialist economy'. Ginsberg gave papers which appear to have applied his distinctive theoretical/philosophical approach to issues of topical interest: 'Theories of the causes of war' in 1937, and 'The moral basis of present-day political conflict' in 1949. The club continued to meet until the late 1940s, but its last record is from 1953, when it is presumed to have lapsed. (Ginsberg retired in 1954.) Since the minutes of a Special General Meeting then say that it was decided to make the interdepartmental nature of the club clearer, one may perhaps infer that, as the social sciences became more specialised, members of other departments lost interest in it. In addition, it seems likely that the newly founded BSA had taken on some of its functions.

This club appears to have functioned partly as an internal seminar series, and partly as another place (analogous to the provincial 'literary and philosophical' societies) where academics and prominent figures outside academia could meet and exchange ideas.

Mass-Observation

Mass-Observation was a body of a quite different kind, with some of the characteristics of a social movement; it spoke to some of the concerns reflected in other developments of the period such as the Left Book Club. It was set up in 1937 by three young men, Charles Madge, Humphrey Jennings and Tom Harrisson. The aim was to create an 'anthropology of ourselves' – a study of the everyday lives of ordinary people. They set up a national panel of volunteers to reply to regular questionnaires on a variety of matters, and Harrisson and a team of observers initiated a project to make detailed observations of life and people in Bolton, while Madge remained in London to organise the writing of the volunteer panel. Harrisson's team went into a variety of public situations:

meetings, religious occasions, sporting and leisure activities, in the street and at work, and recorded people's behaviour and conversation in as much detail as possible. This caught the spirit of the times, and was immediately successful; it led to publications such as *Britain by Mass-Observation* (Madge and Harrisson, 1939). When the war started, Mass-Observation was one of the bodies drawn on for war-related research, shown for instance in *War Factory* (Mass-Observation, 1943). After the war, the organisation became a market research agency.[10] Charles Madge, originally a poet and journalist, moved in 1940 to the National Institute of Economic and Social Research, and then PEP. In 1950, he became Professor of Sociology at the University of Birmingham.

Political and Economic Planning

Political and Economic Planning (PEP) was an independent, non-party organisation, set up in 1931, and it described its own role as to act as

> *a bridge between research on the one hand and policy making on the other, whether in government, the social services or industry. Its aim is ... to study problems of public concern, to find out the facts, to present them impartially, and to suggest ways in which knowledge can be applied ...*
> (Lindsay, 1981: 9)

It represented part of the important current of opinion in favour of increased social planning, responding to the felt bankruptcy of political ideas in the face of the slump and the demise of the Labour government. It did not claim to be 'sociological', but nonetheless had a key role in the development of sociological organisation.

PEP set up working groups on topics of current concern, consisting of both experts and lay members, and they produced reports – published anonymously – which usually drew heavily on data provided by others; its 'working members' were such people as civil servants, businessmen, politicians and academics, and it included a striking number of those who were, or became, 'the great and the good'. It had a lunch room which was used as a club by members, and was significant in creating networks. [Leslie Wilkins (1987) described it as 'a powerhouse'.] Although it had no official responsibilities for anything beyond its own activities, its significance is suggested by the fact that Michael Young (then its Director, but who later played a whole range of prominent roles in sociology and social science more widely) suggested that, since there was in the late 1940s no official body for the social sciences, PEP might take on some of its functions, and publish an annual review of work in the social sciences – though this suggestion was not taken up. Raymond Goodman, for a time Director of PEP and the author of the relevant chapter in its history, who, despite then being employed in business rather than academia, became the first secretary of the BSA, remarks that 'social scientists did look to PEP as a natural (not to say neutral) meeting ground for those working on the practical and theoretical sides of their discipline'. A number of those who were, or later became, prominent sociologists were among its working members in the later 1940s (Goodman, 1981: 109–10).

Summary of pre-war situation

Though several of the organisations described above had 'sociology' in their titles, whether or not it appeared there did not correspond to the varying extent to which they were relevant to what became sociology. In practice, almost all had dominant representation from groups other than professional sociologists, and the initiative came from those groups. 'Sociology' was not clearly distinguished from practical concerns, or sociologists from practitioners, until quite a late date.

The LSE professorship remained the only professorship of sociology at any British university until after the Second World War, although Westermarck continued to lecture there part time alongside Hobhouse until 1930 while also holding a university post in Finland, and Hobhouse's 1929 successor, Ginsberg, had under him two other members of staff, T. H. Marshall and an assistant. Karl Mannheim joined the staff in 1933. Most 'sociology' courses set up in the inter-war period were, like the Liverpool University School of Social Science[11] of 1905, intended to train social workers, voluntary or professional, in the skills needed for their tasks (Halliday, 1968: 390). The degrees which did exist had few component courses with 'sociology' in the title, or which we would recognise as intrinsically sociological. The London university Sociology degree was the only specialist one in the country before the Second World War (Banks, 1989: 523), although by 1914 there were 19 universities besides Oxford and Cambridge, and it was not taken by many students. [Most of those taking it were reported in 1935 to come from the department of Sociology, Social Studies and Economics at Bedford College (a women's college), though that remained heavily involved in social-work training; no member of staff there held the title 'sociologist' until 1935,[12] though they were said to teach their special fields in a way designed to fit into a sociological course (Marshall, 1936: 30–1). A 1939 history of the college said that the department's 'numbers are growing and its work developing as a result of increasing demands for workers in the various social services.' (Tuke, 1939: 261), and it was described by its future head as in 1944 'a Department concerned with training social workers' (Wootton, 1967: 99).] More students took the option of specialising in Sociology within the degree in Economics, or took social work diplomas which included some sociology.

Even in the inter-war period, the majority of research with some claim to be sociological was not conducted within universities, and long-term funding for it was not available. There was a growing market research industry, but it had no connection with formal sociology in Britain, though there was knowledge of some of Lazarsfeld's early work (Platt, 1991: 347). Some interesting studies were carried out, but they were often done by foreigners (e.g. Bakke, 1933 – funded by the Pilgrim Trust) some of whom were refugees (e.g. Marie Jahoda), or by private organisations such as PEP, or the amateurs such as the group in Mass-Observation. Indeed, it is striking how much of the empirical research that was done came from people who could be almost anything but a British university sociologist (Platt, 1991: 352). Rowntree, an enlightened Quaker industrialist, carried on the tradition of Booth by conducting significant research on poverty at his own expense (Rowntree and Lasker, 1911, Rowntree, 1941).

There was a continuing tradition of local 'social surveys'; Wells (1935: 13, 18), in a review of the field, defined such a survey as 'a fact-finding study, dealing chiefly with working-class poverty and with the nature and problems of the community', and went on to characterise its aim as 'the collection of facts relating to social problems and conditions in order to assist the formulation of practical measures ...'. Such studies were funded on an ad hoc basis, sources including special local subscriptions (Wells, 1935: 59–60), and used much voluntary labour. (It is worthy of note that what has some claim to be the first British textbook on sociological research methods[13] – Bartlett *et al.* (1939) – is clearly designed for amateurs as much as for students.) The surveys were not wholly unconnected with universities but, of those which were connected, none was carried out by members of sociology staff, though some of those involved later became associated with sociology.[14]

Of course one reason for the shortage of university-based research was the shortage of university sociologists, but the lack of real interest in empirical research of those who were most prominent made a significant contribution. The background in philosophy of the first professors encouraged general system-building and armchair thinking rather than the creation of fresh data (though Westermarck did fieldwork – but on Morocco; the evolutionary perspective also encouraged a special interest in 'simpler' societies.) In addition, the grand synthetic approach made it necessary to draw on such a range of sources that it would clearly be impossible to carry out much of the work oneself. As late as 1936, Ginsberg was listing as sociological specialisms the comparative study of institutions, comparative morals and comparative religion, social statistics and demography, social geography, social psychology, social biology and social economics (Ginsberg, 1956: 257–8), though going on to argue that the development of separate specialised work in such fields was necessary for the progress of the ideal synthetic and generalising sociology.[15] It is interesting to note that a member of the older generation who approached the discipline from a quite different background and angle, and did not call herself a sociologist, Barbara Wootton, could still take a position which has something in common with this in the 1960s:

> Today a natural scientist must confine himself to astrophysics or microbiology or some other narrow specialism. So likewise will the social scientist one day learn to respect boundaries and to restrict himself to a particular discipline such as sociology, social psychology, anthropology, economics or psephology. That time, however, is not yet. For the application to social problems of such basic scientific tools as exact observation and empirical testing of hypotheses is still so new, and so little understood or appreciated, that there remains much to be done by those whose primary concern is with the method itself rather than with any of the particular fields in which it can be employed.
> (Wootton, 1967: 210)

Within the LSE in the inter-war period, most empirical research which could be seen as in some way sociological was actually carried out in other departments.[16]

It has been suggested that the conservatism of the university system, dominated by Oxford and Cambridge, meant that sociology needed to justify its claims to a place in terms that were acceptable, and an emphasis on distinctively and traditionally academic characteristics helped in that, so that those chosen for the few early academic posts were the philosophers and systematisers. However, if that was so, the conception of academic 'sociology' that they and many others held paradoxically made it harder for them to find a place within the system of disciplines as it was emerging, since they appeared to make claims on territory which other disciplines, often more securely established, also claimed.

Wartime and early post-war

Other strands which came to contribute to the post-war sociology emerging in the 1950s had entirely different origins, several of them arising from work responding to the special needs of the war effort.

The Wartime Social Survey, originally set up in 1940 for the Ministry of Information to investigate morale and public opinion, was led by Frederick Brown, a statistician who worked in the Department of Business Administration at the LSE; his colleague Sybil Clement Brown of the Department of Mental Health (which trained psychiatric social workers) was also involved, as was Ethel Lindgren, an anthropologist by training and contributor to – and co-editor with Ginsberg and others of – Bartlett *et al.* (1939). The staff also included Marie Jahoda, well known for her sociological/psychological research and later a professor of social psychology. Sample survey data were collected, but there also came to be a considerable emphasis on the collection of relatively rich qualitative material (for the collection of which psychiatric social workers were seen as the appropriate kind of interviewer) to be quantified. However, disagreements arose as a result of which the entire research team resigned in 1941, and that was the end of the more qualitative work (Platt, 1986). However, Louis Moss from the British Institute of Public Opinion was appointed in place of Brown (who had left a little earlier for America), and became responsible for an organisation now concerned with largely factual surveys of living conditions. This eventually became the Government Social Survey and continued long after the war as a major governmental research body; its members in particular have made valuable contributions to survey method, usually through the network of the RSS rather than academic sociology (for details of its history, see Moss, 1991). Other government departments also carried out their own research.

'Operational research', developed then for practical reasons to do with such matters as the design of aircraft controls and the promotion of productivity in manufacturing, later became an important contributor to the dominant empirical field of the 1950s, industrial sociology (Stansfield, 1981). (Ronald Stansfield himself, originally a physicist, became involved in operational research, and by that route a sociologist; he was an early BSA executive member, and the second convenor of the BSA's study group on industrial sociology.) T. T. Paterson's *Morale in War and Work* (1955) exemplifies one way in which such work developed; Leslie Wilkins, who later worked for the Government Social Survey before entering academic life as a criminologist, came into social research by a similar route from work on the causes of aircraft accidents (Wilkins 2001).

Research related to industry was important at this period. The Department of Scientific and Industrial Research (DSIR), founded in 1917, started to support social research in 1950 (Cherns and Perry, 1976: 72–4). After the war, the Marshall Plan and associated efforts from the USA aimed at encouraging post-war reconstruction and industrial productivity both funded significant research and created contacts with the more advanced and empirically active US social science.

During the Second World War, the Tavistock Clinic, which started in 1920 as an outpatient psychiatric clinic to give psychotherapy to those unable to afford private fees, came to focus on morale, leadership, selection within the military, and the mental health of enemy nations.[17] Thus it developed concern with more social matters and phenomena in larger groups, which after the war was carried over into civilian life. This was reflected in the journal *Human Relations* and the Institute of Human Relations, founded in 1946 and 1947; the journal was a joint venture with the new US Center for Group Dynamics. There were many US contacts, some of them with sociologists; these included joint wartime work in London with Edward Shils and Kimball Young. (This was not the only such contact made as a result of the war.) In the post-war period, then, 'the Tavi' was heavily involved in work such as that by Elliot Jaques, Eric Trist and A. K. Rice, initially in a programme set up by the Human Factors Panel of the Committee on Industrial Productivity, one of the predecessor bodies to the Social Science Research Council (Nicol, 2000: 47); some of this work was regarded as industrial sociology, even if other disciplinary claims might have been made on it (Dicks, 1970, passim). (The Institute came to include an Institute for Operational Research from 1963.) Bott's important *Family and Social Network* (1957) was a product of another branch.

During the war, there were many discussions about wartime issues of social policy such as evacuation, and social directions for the post-war period. Karl Mannheim was involved in a number of discussion groups,[18] and ministers of education from the allied countries were meeting in the discussions which eventually led to the creation of UNESCO and its range of social-scientific activities. Social research was also encouraged by the 1945 Labour Government, creating the welfare state as it embarked on post-war reconstruction. (A number of the most prominent figures in the post-war Labour Party had backgrounds in academic social science, including the Prime Minister, Clement Attlee, who for some years had held a post in the LSE Department of Social Science.) Michael Young went in 1945 from directing PEP to head the Research Department of the Labour Party until 1951; in 1953, he founded the Institute of Community Studies, which was responsible for a whole series of empirical studies related to policy issues. This was part of the response to a need felt more widely at the time, as was shown by several government reports. Nicol (2000) documents the long sequence of representations, committees and enquiries which led eventually to the founding in 1965 of the Social Science Research Council (later Economic and Social Research Council), under the chairmanship of the ubiquitous Michael Young.

Teaching of sociology continued in wartime; the LSE was evacuated to Cambridge, though student numbers were reduced and much more likely than before to be drawn from women and foreigners (refugees could be excluded from government work) – who in the circumstances of the time were less likely to be candidates for staff jobs.[19] Immediately after the war, the expansion of universities, and of work in sociology, commenced; a UNESCO report, based on work by Donald MacRae, summarises this, with details about courses and local situations. It points out that 'a great deal of work which, in other countries, would be called sociology, has been and is still being carried on under other names' (UNESCO, 1953: 91). Many of the courses which he lists are in departments not called 'sociology', and/or with substantial commitment to the training of social workers. It is clear that 'sociology' is still institutionally defined in a broadly inclusive way. Opportunities for postgraduate study were limited, but a cohort of students at the LSE (Halsey, 1985) was to play a crucial role in the future development of British sociology.

Ginsberg remained professor and head of department at the LSE from 1929 until his retirement in 1954. It followed from his intellectual approach that he did not see a first or higher degree in sociology as a necessary, or even the best, qualification for teaching it. This meant that the situation where those who held such posts were not formally qualified in the field lasted longer than it need have done.[20] The two other professors of sociology at the LSE after the war were T. H. Marshall, who had moved over from teaching history to trainee social workers to a senior post in sociology in 1930 (invited by Ginsberg to take over the Comparative Social Institutions course on the death of Hobhouse), and D. V. Glass, whose first degree was in geography but who soon became a demographer. Both worked in styles which have more in common with later styles of sociology than Ginsberg's. In 1948, it was still true that the only university staff listed as sociologists in the CUYB were at London University. The number of LSE staff expanded from five in 1945–6 to eight in 1946–7 and 11 in 1951–2, responding to the high levels of demand for sociology, especially from those returning from the war; numbers then stabilised until 1959–60.

The activities of the Institute of Sociology were very much weakened by the restrictions during the Second World War; after the war, the LSE staff on the editorial board withdrew, when their offer to take over the SR was refused, in favour of the *British Journal of Sociology* (BJS), which they founded in 1949. In 1952, it was agreed to transfer the SR and the Institute's library to the new University College of North Staffordshire (which did not at that stage have a department of sociology). In 1955, the Institute finally closed. It is questionable whether the Geddes/Le Play/Institute group's work led directly to future developments within British sociology, despite their close entanglement with some parts of its history. However, their organisational contribution surely did something to encourage development.

Thus, by the early 1950s, academic sociology, though still very small, was starting to expand; there was a demand for teaching and research, there was a broader community with diffusely 'sociological' interests, and a network of contacts and a number of organised bodies with some stake in sociological matters outside the universities.

Foundation of the BSA

The BSA was founded in 1951. How did this come about? The real initiative, unlike the formal one, apparently did not come either from the Institute of Sociology or from the LSE department as such, but from a group of 'sociologists, opinion survey practitioners and others [which] met regularly at PEP', which included some LSE staff; five of PEP's working members were elected to the first BSA executive (Goodman, 1981: 109–10). The archives of PEP show a rather different version of events from that normally mentioned in BSA sources:

> A group of people working in the social sciences continued to meet monthly at PEP throughout the year ... the idea has been put forward that a professional body for sociologists (the term being defined very broadly) should be established. A meeting of interested people is to be called at the LSE later in the autumn, and the Chairman or the Director of PEP will be asked to act as one of the sponsors. If this body is founded, it will owe its existence directly to the social scientists' lunch club and thus indirectly to PEP ...
> (PEP, Annual Report to the Executive Committee (EC) by the Director, 15 September 1950)

An additional factor in the eventual establishment of the BSA was probably the foundation of the International Sociological Association (ISA), in which Ginsberg, Glass and Marshall were all involved, for which a national association was required to qualify for membership, not then open to individuals. (A number of other national sociological associations were founded at the same period and, like the BSA, joined the ISA almost at once (Platt, 1998).)

Twenty-four 'sponsors' were formally responsible for calling a meeting in October 1950 to discuss the possibility of forming a British sociological association. The letter recruiting them said that the aim of the proposed association was

> to serve as a means of raising the standards of, and increasing interest in, sociology in this country ... it is not desirable, at least in the initial stages, to define the terms 'Sociology' and 'Sociologist' in a very strict way. It would in fact be better to offer membership of the Association to persons trained in a wide variety of fields. If a definition of the interests of the Association is needed, it should deliberately be made very broad, embracing such fields as contemporary, historical and comparative studies of social structure, morals and religion; sociological aspects of Law; social philosophy; social psychology; social-biological aspects of mankind; social aspects of urban and rural settlement; human geography; and methodological aspects of social investigation ... But while wishing to attract members from different fields, it maybe desirable to distinguish between those persons who are simply 'interested' in sociology, and those whose training or experience (or both) should qualify them to take a more active part in promoting sociological studies.

It added that 'It is obviously important that this meeting be convened by a representative group, so that it is apparent to all concerned that the intended organisation is a national one' (LSE 434/2 A); the letter was signed by the director of the LSE, Carr-Saunders, and LSE professors of sociology Ginsberg and Glass, with replies to be sent to Glass. All but two of those invited agreed to serve, although not all of those serving in the end themselves joined the Association. The list of sponsors had only three holders of posts formally described as in sociology, the LSE professors; three or four others might be regarded as sociologists, while the remainder came from other social-scientific fields or philosophy (then sometimes bracketed with psychology). All but Goodman of PEP were academics, and all of those professors or heads of department; a number of them held knighthoods. Twelve were based in London. The basis of recruitment is suggested by comparison with the *Yearbook of the Universities of the Commonwealth* (later CUYB) for 1949–50, which shows that only five of the full universities[21] of the time are not represented.

The meeting was held; invitations to it included several economists, members of departments of psychology/psychiatry, social medicine and statistics and of various government departments, the Eugenics Society, the National Institute of Economic and Social Research, the National Institute of Industrial Psychology, the Royal Anthropological Institute, the National Foundation for Educational Research and the Institute of Sociology – and others. Of the 70 people recorded as actually attending (LSE 434/2 A), 20 were from the LSE (seven not from sociology), eight from other branches of London University, and 13 (of whom six were or shortly became formally sociologists) from other universities. Eight members of the Government Social Survey came, as did a wide sprinkling of members of groups such as the others listed above. Thus less than a third of the attendance was of 'sociologists'.

At this meeting, a provisional executive committee (PEC) was set up to initiate activity. A letter to *The Times* was published in May 1951 which announced the formation of the Association. This declared that

> *Social and legislative changes in recent years have made much sharper the need for study and research in sociological fields. In particular, the extension of planning since the war demands an understanding both of the sociological basis of planning and of its impact on society. The new association believes that it can play its part on the practical and on the theoretical side by providing opportunities for discussion of fundamental and technical questions and by promoting the comparability and closer coordination of research. We hope that by such means the results of individual investigations will become cumulative and lead to a systematic science of society.*
> (LSE 434/2 A)

The letter had 13 signatories, the members of the PEC. Of the 13, only the three LSE professors held university posts named as in sociology, though another three or four might be regarded as sociologists. Table 1 shows the names and positions of those involved at various stages in this procedure.

The BSA was not formally tied to the LSE, although in the earliest stages it certainly was tied to it practically. An office was provided for it by the LSE, staffed by a secretary paid by them, and there was effectively a hidden subsidy for many years in the form of such things as postage and photocopying costs, as well as free or low rent for premises conveniently located in central London.

Table 1 Sponsors, their membership of the PEC and of the Association

Sponsor	Rank and field	Institution	PEC	Member
Frederick Bartlett	Prof., Psychology	Cambridge		
Cyril Burt	Prof., Psychology	University College, London		
Alexander Carr-Saunders	Sociologist?; Director, LSE	LSE	×	×
Gordon Childe	Prof., Archaeology	Institute of Archaeology, London	×	×
G. D. H. Cole	Prof., Social and Political Theory	Oxford		
G. C. Field	Prof., Philosophy and Psychology	Bristol		×
Raymond Firth	Prof., Social Anthropology	LSE	×	×
P. Sargant Florence	Prof., Commerce	Birmingham		×
Percy Ford	Prof., Economics	Southampton		
Meyer Fortes	Prof., Social Anthropology	Cambridge	×	×
Morris Ginsberg	Prof., Sociology	LSE	×	×
David Glass	Prof., Sociology	LSE	×	×
Raymond Goodman	Director, PEP		×	×
H. J. Habakkuk	Prof., Economic History	Oxford		
Henry Hamilton	Prof., Political Economy	Aberdeen		×
Sir Hector Hetherington[22]	Philosopher; Chair, CVCP (a full-time job)	(formerly Glasgow)		×
C. A. Mace	Prof., Psychology	Birkbeck, London		×
Thomas H. Marshall	Prof., Sociology	LSE	×	×
T. H. Pear[23]	Prof., Psychology	Manchester	×	×
T. S. Simey	Prof., Social Science	Liverpool	×	×
W. O. Lester Smith	Prof., Education	Institute of Education, London		×
Walter J. H. Sprott	Prof., Philosophy	Nottingham	×	×
Brinley Thomas	Prof., Economics and Social Science	Cardiff		
Godfrey Thomson	Prof., Education	Edinburgh		
Richard Titmuss	Prof., Social Administration	LSE	×	×
Roger Wilson	Head, Dept. of Social Study	Hull		×
Barbara Wootton	Prof., Social Studies and Economics	Bedford, London	×	×

(For the first six years, it also received an unconcealed subsidy in the form of a grant from the Nuffield Foundation.) Of the PEC, six were on the staff of the LSE. [However, in a letter to Carr-Saunders on 19 March 1951, gratification is expressed that the Director of the LSE allows his name to be used, but it is indicated that he is not expected actually to attend meetings or bother with the papers (LSE 434/2 A).] Ginsberg of the LSE was the first chairman and, when the honorific office of president was introduced in 1955, became its first president. Marshall and Titmuss, also at the LSE, in 1954 and 1959 were the second and fourth chairmen. Interestingly, the first speaker meetings of the Association were held at PEP, as 'neutral ground' (PEC 25 April 1951), which suggests that there may have been some sensitivity about perceived LSE dominance.

The first annual general meeting (AGM) was held in March 1952, a date later than originally intended in order to allow time for ensuring that the constitution permitted the Association to be treated as a charitable body for tax purposes. At this meeting a new, non-provisional EC was elected – to which the only change from the PEC was the addition of Dr John Mogey, a lecturer in sociology appointed in 1949 at Oxford. The term of office appears to have been three years; the EC agreed among themselves to ensure that a third retired each year so that there would be renewal within continuity, and lots were drawn in January 1953 for the first to go: Carr-Saunders, Childe and Wootton. By March 1953, four nominations had been received for four vacancies: Ruth Glass (University College London), Charles Madge (Birmingham), John Madge (Building Research Station) and Ronald Stansfield (Department of Scientific and Industrial Research). The nominators, and the character of those nominated, suggest an attempt by the EC to broaden the constituency slightly, institutionally and geographically, and it is probably no coincidence that it was John Madge who succeeded Goodman as honorary general secretary at the next meeting (EC 16 March and 29 April 1953).

It was reported in May 1951 that 360 enquiries had been received so far in response to the letter to *The Times*. Early general membership, as well as the broad founding group, included many non-sociologists; this reflected not just the shortage of sociologists then, but also the broad conception of sociology. Many members were recruited from outside academia. It was suggested at an early EC meeting that approaches to potential members should be made to departments of economics, law and history (PEC, 25 May 1951). By October 1951, there were 324 members, of whom only 41% were university teaching staff or students and, of the staff, less than half were formally named as sociologists. Table 2 shows the details.

An interim report from the honorary general secretary summarised the position: 'not only are all the British universities well represented, but ... many people working in non-academic research bodies, in government departments and in the professions have also shown their interest in the study of society by joining ... ' (Goodman, 1951: 1). It could be speculated that people from other fields joined the BSA because they lacked a better alternative closer to their interests. However, given the dates of foundation of some of the potential alternative bodies (Royal Economic Society 1890, British Psychological Society (BPS) 1901, Association of Social Anthropologists 1946, Political Studies

Table 2 Numbers of members from different groups, October 1951

Social Studies and Sociology	51
Anthropology	11
Psychology	11
Economics	9
Other university fields	31
University research students (no fields given)	19
Non-university sociological, anthropological and economic research	29
Social services and public administration	49
Non-university teaching	29
Medicine, surgery, social medicine and psychiatry	23
Government departments	18
Commerce, industry and university administration	14
Other and not known	30

Source: This table is adapted from data provided to the EC by the secretary (LSE 434/2 A).

Association (PSA) 1950) that seems unlikely, except in the case of social policy/ social administration, whose Social Policy Association (SPA) was founded only in 1967.[24]

There was no restriction of membership, although at the PEC meeting of May 1951 a list was made of those categories of person suitable to be approached as potential members without vetting; these included members of university departments such as international relations, psychology, philosophy, anthropology, genetics and colonial administration, and also members of the Sociology Club, contributors to the BJS and those on a list of members of research stations provided by Ronald Stansfield. At first, a distinction was made between 'full' and 'associate' members, with the former intended to be 'either professionally trained as sociologists and working in that field, or else trained and working in cognate fields and making contributions to the development of sociology', while the latter were merely interested in the study of society. This was the earliest of several attempts to make some such distinction; it was rapidly abandoned, as it was found that the associates did not pay enough to cover the costs of their participation, some of them resented being classified in that category, and anyway it was difficult to decide where the borderline lay.[25] Similarly, the proposal to introduce a privileged category of 'Fellows' was not acted on. Since then, the only differences in formal membership category have been for such groups as student, emeritus and overseas members.

Monthly speaker meetings in London were the main initial activity, the first one reported to have had an audience of 90. The speakers were far from confined to sociologists. Early topics included, for instance, 'Social evolution in the light of archaeology' by an archaeologist, 'Impressions of social class and personality from speech and photographs' by a psychologist, and 'The need for a social philosophy' by a philosopher. The early membership was very much drawn from London; by 1958, it was noted that about 60% of the UK members were based in London or the immediately surrounding areas. (This may well have reflected the distribution of the constituency at the time.) Early attempts were, however, also made to organise 'provincial' groups and meetings, though these appear to have been relatively few.

Members received a reduced rate for subscriptions to the BJS (based at the LSE), and one was also negotiated, and additionally subsidised from Association funds, for the ISA's *International Bibliography of Current Sociology* (later just *Current Sociology*) and for the SR. Bibliographic matters were quite prominent in early affairs; there was also some demand for the provision of bibliographic guidance, and a subcommittee was set up to consider what could be offered. It was suggested that the Association might take over the provision of a regular list of sociological publications, before the war dealt with by the National Book League, but this was eventually rejected.

The Institute of Sociology approached the BSA in 1951 with various suggestions for activities in which it might engage, and the issue was raised of whether it might affiliate in some way or have corporate membership, for which no provision was made so far in the constitution. This issue was aired over several PEC meetings, and it was decided that corporate membership was not appropriate, but it would be appropriate to have some representation for the Institute, so that a proposal would be made to amend the constitution to include a representative of it on the EC. However, this does not appear to have been followed up, and no explanation is given in the minutes. (But Alexander Farquharson, its remaining leading figure, died in 1954, and the Institute closed in 1955.)

The first general conference of the BSA was held in 1953 (after that, conferences were, in principle, held every other year). It was on 'Social Policy and the Social Sciences', with a plenary address by Gunnar Myrdal and group discussions on health, physical planning and the social services. Several of the speakers were practitioners rather than academics. A policy that academic and practical emphases should alternate in conference topics had been adopted, with the latter chosen to start with because of its probable wider appeal. The report of the following AGM remarked that the themes covered 'had appealed to the very wide range of interest of members and had been regarded as stimulating and useful … the conference had shown that there is a place for social scientists among the men of affairs and for men of affairs among the social scientists … '. At this stage, one can see that the conception of sociology and its role was closely connected with the growth of the welfare state (in which a number of those from the LSE who were active in the early BSA had played an important advisory role). We may note the statement made that the Association's

> *objects are exclusively devoted to the promotion of sociology, that is the scientific study of society. They are therefore educational and, moreover, educational in a sphere peculiarly adapted to the promotion of public benefit since the purpose of sociology is to investigate the working of society in order to enable it to work better.*
> (EC 21 April, 1952)

– though perhaps, since the letter from which this passage comes was drafted with legal advice in support of the claim to exemption from tax, it may be taken with a pinch of salt as a full ideological position.

Even before then, the BSA had been approached by a Home Office official to ask if it could provide advice on the background to juvenile delinquency and other social problems; it was eventually decided to refer such enquiries to appropriate individual members. However, the PEC did act on behalf of the discipline in relation to government in sending a memorandum to the University Grants Committee, urging that further and better provision for social research should be made in the 1952–7 quinquennium.[26] It was also prepared to make a submission in support of the Government Social Survey, threatened by government economies; this was not done – it appears to have become unnecessary when the threat envisaged did not materialise.

A quite different area of activity related to the question of employment for sociologists. Graduate student members expressed anxiety about the future opportunities of what was the first significant cohort of trained postgraduate sociologists in Britain. (John H. Smith, a member of that cohort, reports that they were much concerned with professional identity; the student society held meetings on employment and on professional sociology in the USA.) Their anxiety was fuelled by Ginsberg's approach to sociology, which meant that he welcomed people trained in other social-science fields into it and, to indignation from his own students, appointed some of these to the few academic jobs available at the LSE; they were also, however, interested in the possibility of jobs in the Civil Service or in research related to social planning. A resolution was passed at the first AGM to set up a subcommittee to study the 'recruitment, training and employment of sociologists', and this collected and publicised extensive data, on which the first report was submitted in 1953 (Banks, 1958).[27]

Thus, by 1953, the BSA was well established. It had a constitution, an elected executive, an adequate short-term financial base, a substantial membership and appropriate activities for members, and an office with an Addressall machine. In addition, it was starting to take on the role of representing the discipline in various contexts.[28] However, in both personnel and style it had considerable continuity with predecessor bodies, and it was not yet unequivocally associated with professional sociologists.

Notes

1   There were also, of course, many earlier intellectual predecessors under such names as 'political arithmetic'.

2   For an obituary note, see Branford (1928).

3   White had hoped that Geddes – on whom see below – would be appointed to this and, when he was not, he funded a professorship of Botany for him at the University College of Dundee, with sufficiently few duties to enable him to maintain many other activities.

4   For more information on Toynbee Hall, see Bulmer et al. (1991).

5   This section draws heavily on Meller (1990).

6   Taylor (1994) has drawn attention to the continuing role of the clergy in social reform activities of the kind often associated with 'sociology'. This continued into the 1920s, when there were 'Anglo-Catholic Summer Schools of Sociology', and in 1931 a journal was started called *Christendom: a Journal of Christian Sociology.*

7   Interestingly, however, this did feed back into later sociology in one way. It was the Eugenics Education Society which, in response to wide concern about the birth rate and the lack of provision for study of population, set up in 1936 the Population Investigation Committee (PIC) at the LSE. David Glass, the PIC's research secretary until 1948, was largely responsible for establishing its reputation (Grebenik, 1986: 15) and, in due course, he became the country's third professor of sociology, after leading the work on the classic empirical study of *Social Mobility in Britain* (Glass, 1954) which inspired a generation of related studies in other countries.

8   In 1927, Ginsberg was asked on what terms he and his colleagues would be prepared to participate in the work of the Sociological Society, and replied that they would only do so if Geddes and Branford retired to purely honorary positions (Evans, 1983: 19–20).

9   All the information in this section comes from the Minute Book of the Club (Sociology Club, 1923–53). I am grateful to Gabriel Newfield for drawing my attention to this.

10   For a short general account of Mass-Observation, see Calder (1985). Its archive, and a continuing modern version of its panel of volunteers, are now based at the University of Sussex Library. (Details are available at http://www.sussex.ac.uk/library/massobs/homearch.html).

11   It was, however, to this department that Alexander Carr-Saunders was appointed as first professor in 1923. His training was in zoology, but he became a self-taught sociologist of a sort, joint author with his colleague Caradog Jones of *The Social Structure of England and Wales* (which became a standard source and went through several editions), and was responsible for obtaining a Rockefeller Foundation grant for the Social Survey of Merseyside, a major empirical work. T. S. Simey, who in 1939 succeeded him as Professor of Social Science, initially had responsibility for a diploma course in public administration aimed at local government officers, but in the post-war period became generally regarded as a sociologist (Kelly, 1981: 230–1).

12   In 1935, Henry Mess was given the title of Reader in Sociology and became head of the department.

13   This ignores the claims of the Webbs' *Methods of Social Study* (Webb and Webb, 1932).

14   Henry Mess was responsible for the survey of Industrial Tyneside (Mess, 1928), which followed from a conference on 'Christian Politics, Economics and Citizenship'; little if any of its data come from what would now be called a 'survey', and the fieldwork was done by volunteers. Caradog Jones, under the direction of his colleague in the Liverpool University department of Social Science Carr-Saunders, was responsible for the survey of Merseyside (Jones, 1934).

15   However, in his early career, Ginsberg carried out a piece of empirical research – quite out of character with the rest of his work – on social mobility, thus forming part of the long British tradition of work on stratification (Ginsberg, 1929). This actually used a questionnaire for some of its data, though with a sample derived from circulation via educational and trade union bodies.

16   *The New Survey of London Life and Labour* (Smith, 1930–5) was based at the LSE, and had several members of staff such as Bowley and Beveridge involved in its work – but none of them was in the sociology department. The shortlived (1930–7) Department of Social Biology under Lancelot Hogben – where Glass then worked – was also responsible for important social research in demographic areas (Dahrendorf, 1995: 249–65).

17   A 1930s staff member, the psychiatrist Emmanuel Miller, was a member of the LSE
     Sociology Club.

18   The book series he initiated in 1939, which became regarded as the main sociological
     outlet, was called 'The International Library of Sociology and Social Reconstruction'.

19   However, the war provided unexpected opportunities for some people. Betty Scharf
     (then Hinchliff) reports that, in 1944, she was summoned from a factory inspectorship to
     help out when the last member of staff got a wartime job and, with breaks for
     childrearing, she taught at the LSE for many years (Scharf, 1999).

20   A consequence of this, in combination with the small number of posts, was that
     excellent graduates such as Mark Abrams found careers elsewhere – in his case, in
     market research, where his firm eventually came to play a significant role in the data
     collection of British empirical sociology. Finally, he became the first Director of the Social
     Science Research Council's Survey Unit in the 1970s; he was one of the few people in
     the country qualified to hold such a post.

21   Other university institutions were 'university colleges', and three of those were also
     represented.

22   It is probably not irrelevant to his choice that he was also a trustee of the Nuffield
     Foundation.

23   Pear was a somewhat deviant psychologist, who had turned in the direction of social
     psychology and developed contacts outside his own discipline. He held office on the
     BSA EC in the 1950s. For more information on his position, see Costall (2001).

24   It is, of course, possible that some of those classified as non-sociologists may have held
     degrees in sociology, or among academics some have been in practice teachers of
     sociology though based in other departments, and those members not belonging to such
     categories may (like, for instance, Sargant Florence in economics?) have had interests
     which placed them at the margins of their formal fields. The real meaning of cross-
     disciplinary membership depends on such factors, which it is impossible to learn about
     from accessible sources without a disproportionate input of effort. It is wise, therefore,
     to be cautious about interpreting these figures.

25   The EC noted that, when the basis of membership was changed, the 203 existing
     associates were offered the choice of accepting full membership, becoming student
     members, or resigning; the response by the end of January 1953 had been that 107 had
     taken full membership, and 13 had resigned; 83 had not replied. One may infer that the
     net loss of members was greater than the numbers then known. (EC 30 January 1953)

26   The significance of the role of PEP in this may perhaps be suggested by the comment in
     the Annual Report of the Director to the EC of PEP that, 'One of the first acts of the new
     body has been to present a statement to the UGC [University Grants Committee] about
     the earmarked grant for the social sciences. This was one of the points dealt with in the
     first PEP broadsheet on Government aid for the social sciences' (PEP A/12/5).

27   This first study was followed up by later ones: Abbott (1969), Webb (1972). (The latter
     was funded by the SSRC.)

28   It was noted on the agenda papers for the EC meeting of 18 January 1952 that 'The
     Association is acquiring the status of a general information service on matters of
     sociological interest. Besides enquiries on such matters as how to get training for social
     welfare work etc., requests have been received from industrial organisations in this
     country and foreign universities on questions of research in this country' (LSE 434/2 B
     BSA).

Chapter 3

The changing structure and functions of the Association

In this chapter, we review the outlines of developments within the BSA over the rest of its history, relating them to changing external circumstances. This provides a background for many matters which are dealt with in more detail in later chapters.

Later 1950s

Some major changes in the British university system took place in the 1950s. The new university of Keele was founded in 1950, while Nottingham, Southampton, Leicester, Hull and Exeter, which had previously only offered London external degrees, became independent universities with their own degrees. From 1957 onwards, Colleges of Advanced Technology (CATs) were founded. Numbers of full-time university students had risen from 51,600 in 1945–6 to 85,400 in 1949–50, reflecting the presence of the returned servicemen and servicewomen who were given the opportunity to go to university; the total then fell back a little, but by 1959–60 had risen again to 104,000 (Stewart, 1989: 84–7, 268). The University Grants Committee (UGC) planned for expansion of the social sciences; the delay caused by a shortage of suitable teachers in some areas was helped by grants earmarked for the social studies from 1947 to 1952, recommended by a committee chaired by Sir John Clapham. From the 1940s onwards, there was a swing in teacher training colleges to more teaching on the sociological functions of education, at the same time as numbers of student in the colleges rose sharply (Stewart, 1989: 74, 77, 90). By the mid-1950s, the LSE and Leicester still had the only departments called 'sociology',[1] though there were at least three others (Birmingham, Liverpool, Bedford) which might have been deemed worthy of the title.

This was an important period of transition in staffing. As student numbers rose, so did the demand for teachers. The expansion was such that it was impossible to fill many posts, especially senior ones, with people formally qualified in sociology. The Director of the London School of Economics, reporting in its *Calendar* for 1948–9, had declared that the lack of expansion in staff since 1938, despite much increased student numbers, was due to a shortage of suitable candidates. In sociology, problems of recruitment were exacerbated by the high proportion of women students, at a time when relatively few of those were interested in academic careers (Platt, 2000). However, Banks' study of 1952 and 1953 graduates in sociology and anthropology (mostly sociology) showed that 45% of those with higher degrees and 11% of those with first degrees were employed in university teaching or research two and a half years after completing their studies (Banks, 1958: 277). Of the seven professors in 1955, one had no first degree, and of the six others only one had a first degree in sociology; two had no higher degree, and the only PhDs (in any field) were those of two of the LSE professors. By 1960, of the seven professors or other heads of department there were still only two with PhDs – though Ilya Neustadt could be deemed to increase the score by actually having two. Among their juniors, however, 28 out of 72 (39%) by then had PhDs, though not all in sociology.[2]

'My story begins with an external examiner who came to Queens' University in Belfast: I was a student in a programme called Economics, Economic History and Geography, and he sat in a student conference ... Some years later I was a beginning lecturer in Social Geography at Reading University ... Suddenly he appeared again, a fellow of Nuffield in Economics ... He had an offer of the lectureship at Oxford in Sociology in hand ... [which was accepted, and he started in 1949]. Six years later when I attended my first lecture in sociology given by somebody other than myself in Chicago, I still recall the delight that HE talked somewhat like I did.'
(Mogey, 2000)

It was a transitional period in relation to research and research funding too. The places in which 'sociological' research was done were by no means all departments of sociology, and funding for such work was limited. Discussions of a possible social science research council continued (Nicol, 2000: *passim*), but had come to nothing yet. However, from 1950, the DSIR had had two joint committees with the Medical Research Council concerned with efficiency and human relations in industry, supported financially by US Conditional Aid funds; these supported some social-scientific work. Those closed in 1958, but were succeeded by a Human Sciences Committee of the DSIR with funds for social-scientific research (Cherns and Perry, 1976: 72–3). The Nuffield Foundation (which in 1949 had initiated a policy of emphasis on biological and social research) and the Joseph Rowntree Memorial Trust were also prominent in funding social research. The LSE had had a longstanding relationship with the Rockefeller Foundation (Fisher, 1980), but money from US sources was now being directed more elsewhere. In part, but probably only in part, because of the pattern of funding, there was a strong tendency for research at this period to be directed towards generally recognised social problems such as juvenile delinquency rather than distinctively sociological topics (Cherns, 1963: 102–7; Glass and Gluckman, 1962). The Liverpool department of 'social science' was especially prominent in research, in particular in industrial sociology, owing to its use of the 1947 Clapham Award money to establish 'research lectureships' (Scott and Mays, 1960: 109). Also important was the Institute of Community Studies, founded in 1954, whose declared initial aim was 'to study the relationship between the social services and working-class family life' (Young and Willmott, 1961: 203); this was associated with social administration as much as sociology, but its many publications rapidly became widely used in the sociological literature.[3]

Goodman resigned from the EC and took a job in the USA in 1957; he had left PEP for Marks and Spencer's[4] in 1951, but this broke the last vestige of a link to PEP. At this period, it is still sufficiently unclear who should be counted as 'really' a sociologist for quantitative analysis not to be safe. However, there were other factors in the gradual change in the composition of the EC which lowered the number of those who formally were definite non-sociologists to four out of 13 in 1959–60 (the last of these were probably Richard Titmuss and the LSE anthropologist Maurice Freedman[5] in 1961–2), and correspondingly reduced the proportion of professors from the initial 92% to 53% in the second half of the decade. These changes should probably be taken as indicating the end of symbolic representation of the whole national social-science community as much as a shift in the understanding of how broadly to define sociology. The average age of EC members went down from the initial 51 to 47 for 1958–9: not a very large drop, but one which reflected an important change, the election to the EC in the latter part of the decade of post-war graduate students such as Asher Tropp, Joe Banks and A. H. Halsey.

By 1960, the total membership of BSA had reached 525, of whom 35 were student members; 43% of the students and 29% of the ordinary members were women. Of the non-students, only 60 (11%) of the total held jobs with 'sociology' in the title, though some of the others were in social science departments and were, then or later, regarded as sociologists (List of members, February 1960). The majority of the early members were based in London, and all meetings were held there. Early AGM reports show some dissatisfaction with this on behalf of those based too far away for convenient attendance. The question of regional groups was raised and, in 1955, a Scottish Branch was founded, leading immediately to an increase in membership in Scotland, and this branch has continued ever since,[6] while other, later, regional branches have come more fleetingly and gone. It was extremely active in organising regular meetings, and also established its own news-sheet *Sociology in Scotland*. The 1955 AGM report expressed the hope that more meetings would be held outside London, and offered the financial or other support of the EC 'to support the initiative of groups of members in provincial centres who wished to arrange suitable meetings or other activities... '. However, at the 1958 AGM it was reported that, of the UK members, about 60% were based in London or the Home Counties. In 1957, a *Bulletin*, under the editorship of Asher Tropp, started to keep members better informed, and seems to have received a very favourable response.

Conferences were held in 1955 ('Political Behaviour in Contemporary Democratic Society' – a topic chosen in part to permit cooperation with the PSA, with which it was jointly run) and in 1957 ('Sociology in Retrospect and Prospect'); a certain amateurishness is suggested by the collapse of plans for 1959 (and 1961). More specialist meetings were held by the 'study groups'. Those on Industrial Sociology and Urban Sociology were set up in 1955. Sociology of Education was soon added, and then Theoretical and Comparative Sociology in 1957. The first three all corresponded to areas of obvious current policy interest; the prominence of industrial sociology at this period certainly owes something to the much greater availability of research funding for work in that area. It is clear that the early groups included 'practitioners' as well as academic sociologists – neither of the first two convenors of the Industrial group then held academic posts, though both did later – and there were sometimes differences of interest between them. The first report on the Sociology of Education study group indicates some difference of opinion on aims, between those favouring a contribution to work on topics where insufficient work had been done and those more interested in getting information about work relevant to current issues of educational policy; this sounds like an academic/practitioner cleavage. A compromise solution had been reached to satisfy both parties, and it appears to have continued to work by setting itself a coherent programme of collective study, starting with the relation between occupation and education. Similar diversity is mentioned in the other groups; the Industrial one appears to have been particularly large and attractive to practitioners. It may be noted that almost all the earlier speakers at meetings of the very active Theoretical and Comparative Sociology group were of foreign origin, suggesting the significance of the contribution of refugees from countries with other intellectual traditions, and perhaps also less concern to respond to local policy issues.

Ad hoc meetings of a more specialised nature were also arranged from time to time. In 1954, a conference on interviewing for various purposes, including therapy and personnel selection, was held in York with the cooperation of the Acton Society Trust (an offshoot of the Rowntree Foundation), and to this only specialists were invited. At the 1955 AGM, T. J. Bishop, one of those who had proposed the study of graduate employment, presented a document called 'Functions of the Association, considered as a Professional Body'. This listed functions – ranging from 'talking shop', on which much was said to have been accomplished, through 'defining role of professional sociologist', on which nothing direct had been done, to 'promotion of research' and 'spokesman of British social scientists in their collective capacity' on which nothing at all was seen to have been done (despite a constitutional commitment to the former) – and made proposals for future activity under most heads. A general discussion resulted in the passing of a motion for the holding of a conference on 'The Present State and Development of Professional Sociology'; this took place in 1956. Unusually, it was not open to the whole membership, but attendance was by invitation only, and the invitations were addressed to 90 people, mainly university teachers and full-time research workers. This was said to have been felt by those present to be very successful, but its discussion was little publicised by the BSA; Banks (1967: 4) inferred that the EC believed 'professional sociology' to be of limited interest. Asher Tropp's (1956) paper on the conference reports concern about the poor standard of undergraduates and their common intention to become social workers rather than being interested in sociology as such, and the lack of funding for research. Employers expressed disappointment with the lack of preparation of graduates for empirical research, though there was ideological tension between those who wanted direct training for employment and those who saw this as threatening sociology's critical independence and its role in providing a broad humane education. (In a 1997 interview, one of those present put this less discreetly, saying that some, like David Glass, wanted a revolutionary discipline.)

At the 1957 AGM, the issue was raised, initially in relation to the potential submission of evidence on homosexuality to the Home Office, presumably in connection with the Departmental Committee on Homosexuality and Prostitution (Wolfenden, 1957), of whether the BSA should express views on public issues. Conflicting opinions were expressed, with some advocating the putting forward of research results, while others contrasted a learned society with a propaganda body. The resolution eventually passed instructed the EC merely to 'consider ways of making the views and special knowledge of members ... more readily available to public bodies ... ', and to report back. The report recommended that the aim should be pursued by attempting to get sociologists appointed to appropriate Royal Commissions and similar bodies. However, a 'substantial' statement, including support for the formation of a Social Science Research Council, was made in 1956 to the Heyworth Committee enquiry into 'Social Studies'.

There were also some other activities to promote sociology more generally. A pamphlet on university courses in sociology was produced for school leavers (and over the years it has been regularly revised and reissued). When in 1959 a Cambridge fellowship in sociology was advertised, which confined applications to graduates of Oxford or Cambridge, which meant that no sociology graduate could be eligible, a protest was made, though it was felt appropriate for this to be made individually rather than as from the BSA, and the protest was successful, as a revised advertisement removed the restriction. (A London graduate, John H. Goldthorpe, was appointed to it. His degree was in history, but he came from a post in the Leicester department of sociology.) Finally, steps were taken to press for the setting up of a Sociology Section of the BAAS. In October 1958, it was reported that the BAAS had decided, as a first step, to set up a 'sociological committee', on which the committees for geography, economics, anthropology and archaeology, psychology and education should be represented, with the aim of ensuring that sociological topics were included in their programmes. The Economics Section had – showing a more interdisciplinary spirit than has been common in more recent years from economists! – gone so far as to co-opt the BSA's honorary general secretary to its committee. But the existing sections felt they could not meet sociology's needs, and the BSA EC felt that a separate Sociology Section was still required; this was finally achieved in 1959 on the recommendation of a special 'committee of sociologists' (whose membership was not restricted to sociologists) (Macleod and Collins, 1981: 245) and, in the expectation that social anthropologists and social psychologists were likely to play an active part in it, it was proposed by the BSA EC – which appeared to have the power of decision – that one member from each of those should join three sociologists on a section committee (EC 12 October 1959).

The BSA's first secretary, Gwen Ayers, served it until 1963; she was joined in 1957 by Anne Dix, who took over the office and remained in charge until her retirement many years later. Both were initially, and remained, employed by the LSE, and also had some tasks to perform for the LSE. The LSE also in effect provided a substantial hidden subsidy, by charging little or no rent and providing central services such as postage and stationery. By 1956, it had been agreed that the LSE department's research funds should no longer support all the Association's secretarial costs, and up to £200 p.a. should be contributed towards those. Another important component of the early financial situation of the Association was an annual grant of £300 from the Nuffield Foundation, which ran until 1954 and was then tapered out. In 1957, it thus became necessary to raise the full annual subscription from £1-1-0 to £1-10-0, and then in 1959 to £2-2-0. In December 1957, a special EC subcommittee was set up to review the financial situation. It recommended various measures to improve the position, of which the most important was that future conferences should be held annually and planned to make a profit.

Towards the end of the decade, things were starting to stir in the wider society. This was the period of the Hungarian uprising and the invasion of Suez and the reactions to those, the foundation of the Campaign for Nuclear Disarmament and the *New Left Review*, the 'Angry Young Men' in literature, and realistic films about working-class life. The collective work *Out of Apathy* (Thompson, 1960) was the first New Left book, and four of its seven contributors were, or later became, sociologists; its original working title had been just *Apathy*, but it came to seem necessary to change that. Sociology had been becoming more widely institutionalised, and the BSA had been moving forward without radical change, but the increasing numbers of younger members of staff were becoming dissatisfied, and there were now enough of them to organise for change.

Expansion and change

Total numbers of university students increased from c.50,000 in 1945–6 to c.290,000 in 1984–5. The drift of policy had been towards expansion even before the Robbins report in 1963 recommended a significant planned further expansion. The sharpest increase took place in the later 1960s (Stewart, 1989: 268); the first 'new' university was founded in 1950, and then there were ten more in the 1960s. Within these totals, the social sciences played a significant role. The numbers of university teachers of all social sciences rose from 212 in 1938 to over 7,000 by the mid-1970s; from 1961 to 1966 alone, the numbers of undergraduates in social science increased by 181% and, over the period 1966–78, sociology was the most popular social science (Stewart, 1989: 111).

By 1960, university staff listed as sociologists in the CUYB appeared at 16 universities, but there were still only 54 teaching posts, of which 15 were at the LSE. A massive expansion of sociology, in connection with the development of the first cohort of new universities, took place through the 1960s, and transformed the situation; by 1968 there were 277 posts, and by 1972 there were 384. In 1962–3, 150 students graduated in sociology from universities; by the end of the 1960s, more than 1,000 were graduating each year, and sociology had become a major subject at A level. The number of higher degrees rose from 76 in 1965–6 to 330 in 1971–2.[7] The CATs were not intended to have a social-science role, but some social science grew up within their primarily technological framework; most of them became universities in the 1960s. The polytechnics were also meant to be oriented to technical and vocational fields but, in response to student demand, rapidly developed courses in the social sciences; they did not officially have the research function of universities but, despite a lack of the funding intended to support research, in many cases were eager to develop research too.

Jobs in sociology expanded in response to this demand, in both universities and other institutions. Until 1961, there were chairs of sociology in only five universities; between 1962 and 1969, 25 new established chairs were created –

and a further eight were added by 1974 (University Grants Committee, 1989: 10–11).[8] Robbins (1963: 10) showed that a rising percentage of home graduates three years earlier was entering university teaching as jobs increased; 'social studies' changed from being the faculty with the oldest staff in 1962 to that with the youngest in 1969, as new staff were recruited, and registrars reported finding it difficult to fill posts (Bibby, 1972: 26, 29). The 'conversion' MA course for graduates in other subjects became common, and produced many of those who took up teaching jobs. Higher degrees have not always been an essential initial qualification. Robbins (1963: 178) showed that, in the social studies, only 16% of those recruited to the profession in 1959–61 had a PhD, and a further 22% an MA.[9]

'Up to graduation I had no intention of becoming an academic, because I had met my husband ... I got a First, the best of my year I was told. It was the time of sociology expanding, and they wanted people for tutorial fellows, so I got a telegram [abroad] saying why don't you come home, there are these jobs. I did think about it, and it did seem that it would fit in with what we wanted to do so I came back and registered as a graduate student; I had no overall plan – an opportunity presented itself ... they offered me a University of London scholarship; I hadn't applied for it or anything, it was all very paternalistic. So I took up the scholarship, did a bit of tuition, got married, ... and before I'd got very far with my PhD I was offered a job, originally a one-year assistant lectureship ... '
(Interview, 1966 recruit, 1998)

It was common for lecturers to complete PhDs while in post, rather than before gaining a permanent job (or not to complete them at all after getting one) and, at this time, they even sometimes did this with MAs. Even among the professors or other heads of department, a number had no formal qualifications at all in sociology; of the 24 in post in 1972, four had no higher degrees, seven had their highest qualification at the MA level and, for the 11 with PhDs, at least three were in social anthropology and several others in miscellaneous fields.[10] BSA membership continued to rise, and by 1972 had reached 1,450. However, the rise cannot be explained solely by the expansion of university jobs, since there were then only 200 university teachers of sociology listed in the CUYB, and of them only 59% were members. (The declining proportion perhaps suggests weaker professional socialisation and cohesion, a plausible consequence of the rate and mode of expansion.)

'I remember sitting opposite John Goldthorpe at a BSA conference, and he said 'What did you do before you did sociology?', and I said 'Sociology', and he asked the same question again, he couldn't believe anyone had done sociology from the start that long ago.'
(Stacey, 1997)

The post-war graduate students who had been anxious about employment prospects found that such anxiety was now misplaced:[11] there were far more jobs for sociologists than there were appropriately trained candidates, creating a new problem. (The Chairman's report to the BSA's 1970 AGM mentioned that the EC was now 'called upon continuously to advise outside bodies on the nature of the subject to ensure that professional standards are maintained and that the content of the subject is not diluted ... '.) An Association of Teachers in Colleges and Departments of Education (ATCDE) representative reported that in the Teacher Training Colleges 'College organisation often demands that personnel without sociological qualifications teach ... ' (Reid, 1974).

But the expansion in posts did not continue. By the 1970s, there was a surplus of potential university teachers. At the height of the expansion, over 50% of the higher degree graduates of the previous year had entered the profession; in 1969–70 and 1970–1, this became less than 20%. The average number of applicants reported for each advertised junior post rose, from ten to 17 in 'social studies' (Williams et al., 1974: 190, 195). Williams and Blackstone (1983: 10) identify 1972 as an important turning point. For the first time since the Robbins report, a White Paper revised a forecast of student numbers downwards, and such revisions continued through the 1970s.

In 1965, a Social Science Research Council (SSRC) was set up by the government to provide funding for both the support of graduate students and the financing of research. Initially, a relatively high proportion of its resources went to students, in part to meet the demand for conversion courses. The total amount of money available for social science research increased considerably, and the expansion in teaching jobs was paralleled by an expansion in research; Smith (1975: 309) estimated that by 1973 at least 900 sociology graduates were employed in full-time research occupations (not all in universities). The increasing amounts of empirical research being carried out, especially in surveys, led to concern about the ethical issues which such work could raise, especially when done by inexperienced researchers. A BSA working party on ethics was set up in 1967, whose report was adopted as a 'Statement of Ethical Principles and their Application to Sociological Practice'. This was concerned with relationships not just with students, but also with research subjects, employers or sponsors, and research staff. A working party on research contracts was another response to such changes.

When a second conference for professional sociologists was proposed to the EC in 1960, on the teaching of sociology, the proposal was rejected. (This proposal was the response of Tropp and Joe Banks to an original suggestion that one should be held on 'the teaching of sociology and the training of social workers'.) In the early 1960s, a group of non-professorial university teachers began meeting informally; by 1964, this was so active that its secretary was co-opted to the BSA EC, and it soon became the Teachers' Section of the BSA. By 1966–7, its membership was 231 and, in 1970–1, it was 300; the (incomplete) available records of meeting attendance show numbers ranging from 23 to 62. Of the two meetings each year, one was in conventional research paper presentation format, and one was on a teaching issue. Teaching was a hot topic, and attendance was generally higher at the teaching-oriented meetings. Systematic data on the courses offered and their reading lists were collected from institutions to support discussion (Wakeford, 1963; Peel, 1967).

Membership of the section was, however, not confined to teachers, but was intended to be only for professional sociologists; it was designed to enable them to get away from the non-professional membership of the BSA still numerically dominant in the audience at meetings, and to sustain a conception of sociology as a serious discipline for which training was required. There was a system of 'gates' by which one could enter; holders of full-time university teaching posts in sociology were admitted automatically, holders of full-time university research posts in sociology were admitted if of equivalent status, and others could be admitted on such grounds as publications or standing in a cognate field. The definitions were not, thus, narrowly restrictive, though in practice university teachers were dominant.

In 1965, a *Register of Professional Sociologists*,[12] ' inspired... by the conviction that almost anyone in this country could pose as a sociologist because the BSA was not generally regarded as an organisation which only the properly qualified could join... ' (Banks, 1967: 6), was produced by the Teachers' Section. Those included, even when the count is confined to the ones holding university teaching jobs titled as in sociology or in departments called 'sociology', had very mixed qualifications in the field – many had degrees and other qualifications in quite other fields, though these included some, for example in social anthropology, which might be regarded as almost equally appropriate (see Table 3). The current jobs held included ones in social psychology, management, social administration and politics as well as a sprinkling of other titles.

Table 3 Highest qualification in sociology,[a] holders of jobs in sociology (%), Register

None	BA/BSc	MA	PhD	*N*
28	30	14	28	69

[a]Joint first degrees are counted. Where the field of a higher degree was not given, it is counted as in sociology if earlier degrees are.

The Teachers' Section also organised other activities. It 'from the first regarded its task as that of raising the quality of British sociology ... ' (Banks, 1967: 6), and its other activities were related to that task. In 1965, a summer school, with funding support from the Nuffield Foundation, was arranged; it was aimed at graduate students in small departments, and intended to compensate for the inadequacies of their research training and the narrow range of contacts they provided. In practice, it was found that there was considerable demand from people other than students, and those attending included teachers of sociology from universities and colleges of technology and junior research workers – but not the general-interest BSA membership. From 1967, the summer school was handed over to the BSA EC, and it has continued ever since, despite changing circumstances.[13]

One Teachers' Section meeting was held in a men's hall of residence. The only washing facilities were communal, and the only women's lavatory was down in the hall next to the porter's lodge. Obviously, nobody had thought of the problems this might cause for women present – of which I was the only one.[14]

Those involved in the Teachers' Section were also the prime movers in the establishment of *Sociology*, the BSA's first journal, whose first issue appeared in 1967. This move reflected dissatisfaction with the existing journals, the BJS and the SR, both departmentally based. The journal has continued and become very successful though, even at the start, it did not appear markedly different from the others. However, the editor (and departmental base) change every three years. The editor for many years attended the BSA EC and reported to it, though the EC did not intervene in non-financial matters; now the reporting is via the Publications Committee. There is also an appointed Editorial Board, which plays an important role in formulating policy and evaluating papers.

There was considerable activity on teaching matters, and not only at university level. In response to the widely felt needs, BSA set up a panel to advise on sociology curricula, whether in universities, technical colleges, colleges of education or schools; at the 1965 AGM, it was reported that 29 requests for advice had already been received, the majority from teacher training colleges.[15] In 1968, a subcommittee was set up to deal with the shortage of training for teachers of A-level social science. (At that stage, two of the national examining boards offered an A level in sociology, and there were plans for O levels.) In 1966, the BSA, in collaboration with the Association of Social Anthropologists,[16] organised a conference on 'The Teaching of Sociology in Colleges of Education'; about 130 attended. In 1968, an informal group of sociologists, social anthropologists and schoolteachers met to discuss the possibility of an alternative A-level syllabus to that provided by the Associated Examining Board, and this led to the creation of a formal joint committee with the Association of Social Anthropologists. A part-time research assistant was employed to collect material for the development of a proposal for a better syllabus, including historical, anthropological and sociological elements. The results were put to the Oxford and Cambridge Exam Board (EC 25 April and 26 September 1969, 27 February 1970). A Sociology Section was set up in the ATCDE in 1967 to discuss the teaching of sociology in teacher education, for which the BSA was seen as not sufficiently providing. This led in 1970 to the creation of another joint working party, to discuss ATCDE's desire to produce a handbook about sociology in colleges of education and BSA's concern about standards in the sector (EC 27 February 1970), though it is not clear that anything came of this. Discussions were also held with the Council for National Academic Awards (CNAA), the validating body for polytechnics, and with representatives of the Civil Service training college on their provision for sociology.

The weight of London, and the LSE in particular, on the executive has decreased over time as the constituency has changed, and the major drop came in this period. In the 1950s, the LSE provided a third of the members and other London people a further quarter; the London contingent was down to 43% in 1960–5, and 19% – at roughly which level it has remained since – for 1965–70. The London meetings gradually lapsed in the early 1960s, after a stage when it was tried holding them on Saturdays to make it easier for 'provincial' members to attend; their function was superseded by study groups.

The study groups in this period initially developed slowly, with new ones on Sociology of Language in 1960, Asia in 1962 and Sociology of Design in 1963. The lull in study group activity was followed by significant growth, reflecting first the preoccupation with setting up new departments and servicing the expansion, and then the much larger number of university sociologists once the expansion was under way. Theoretical work, and theoretical cleavages, became much more important than they had been before, and it was a new kind of theory; it was a time of intellectual ferment, which saw the emergence of Althusserian Marxism and ethnomethodology as important within British sociology.[17] A member of a slightly older generation described the situation as he saw it:

> the kind of criminology ... to do with where criminals lived or crimes took place, found itself confronted with criminal careers, Goffmanesque excursions, phenomenology, interactionist perspectives, which we didn't object to en bloc, but they began to build up as a kind of alternative world. So the first apostolic spring had been for empirical research, the second was denying it.
> (Interview)

The new study groups included Political Sociology, Political Economy, Sociology of Development, Military Sociology, Socialist Societies and Race Relations, as well as less politically relevant ones such as Uses of Mathematics and Computing in Sociology, Medical Sociology, and Sociology of Art. It does not seem at all surprising that the theme of the 1968 conference should have been 'Conflict' – though many of the papers actually given were not on the central theme, and the total effect sounds surprisingly tame from the printed programme. Other conference themes around this time were 'Race Relations' (1969), 'Social Control, Deviance and Dissent' (1971) and 'Development' (1972).

A selection of the papers from the 1969 conference was published as a book (Zubaida, 1970), and since then it has been conventional for this to be done every year as part of the task of the conference organisers.[18] BSA promotion and sponsorship of publications started in the late 1960s; a subcommittee was set up to deal with the issues involved in this. One of the first publications, *Comparability in Social Research* (Stacey, 1969), arose from a working party on the comparability of data; this was set up in response to concern about the proliferation of empirical work which lacked comparability in the definitions used, and so risked failing to be cumulative.

Not all the Association's activity followed directly from the continuing increase in sociological teaching and research; some responded to other circumstances. This was the period of student unrest, which caused enormous upheavals in universities throughout the country, and led to many divisions among staff. (For a sense of the tone of this, see Cockburn and Blackburn, 1969.) Sociology students were particularly likely to be involved (Blackstone *et al.*, 1970: 212–14), and sociology staff were perhaps unusually likely to be broadly sympathetic (though certainly not all were – see Martin, 1969). This contributed towards giving sociology a reputation which was not helpful to it in some political quarters, though it may have promoted its fashionability in others. BSA also had to deal with two associated *causes célèbres*, the Blackburn and the Atkinson 'affairs', concerned with staff appointments of people sympathetic to the student cause. The way in which the BSA responded to these caused some ill feeling, and several resignations from the Association. (The detail of these episode is given in Chapter 7.)

By 1974, it was evident that the many changes called for a review of the BSA's operation. It was agreed that, to cope with expanded activities, the EC should devolve work to a structure of subcommittees on programmes, publications, membership, research, teaching and finance, and that a development officer[19] and a part-time publications officer should be appointed. (It was assumed – wrongly, as it turned out – that the cost of the development officer would be largely covered by the extra subscriptions brought in.) The Teachers' Section would be closed; the reintroduction of two classes of membership, full and associate, was proposed but not implemented. (For more on this, see Chapter 8.)

The rise of the women

The year 1974 marked a crucial break within the BSA: the growing women's movement came to the forefront. The circumstances which had given rise to the Teachers' Section no longer held. Many of its initial leaders now had chairs in new departments of sociology, and large numbers of trained sociologists were being produced; study groups duplicated its research function, and the BSA EC had become very concerned with teaching matters. That owed much to the fact that the Young Turks had taken over the EC; by 1971, only one member of the older generation remained on it. But they hardly had time to enjoy their victory before coming under pressure from another group; as one of them said, 'The women took over when our generation had only just got in; they could at least have left us a few years in charge! I think several of my contemporaries felt that.' How did this come about?

Women had always been a majority among undergraduates in sociology, but fewer of them remained in the labour market and were interested in, or gained the qualifications preferred for, university work. By the earlier 1970s, women were 35% of those gaining higher degrees in sociology, 58 (15%) of the 384 holders of university teaching posts in sociology were women, and women took 21% of the new university jobs available, for which expansion meant that there was much less competition than there would soon be; the ratio of higher degrees to jobs went from 6.19 in 1972–5 to 75.4 in 1981–6 (Platt, 2000). Women were 23% of the BSA membership in 1970 (Collison and Webber, 1971: 524), and this had risen to 26% by 1973. Perhaps the absolute number is more important. It seems more plausible to explain the movement within the BSA by wider societal developments than by internal organisational or disciplinary factors; women may have suffered from discrimination, but it is not evident that this changed enough at this period to account for a significant new movement. These issues are discussed in more detail in Chapter 6.

The first conference on a gender-related issue was held in 1974 . The topic emerged more or less by accident when the one originally planned collapsed; it was 'Sexual Divisions and Society'. The organisers were active in the women's movement, and went to pains to draw in women, including some not previously active in the BSA. At the conference, a Women's Caucus was formed, and started to press for change within the BSA as well as to provide a supportive forum for its participants; the influence of parallel but slightly earlier US developments (Sewell, 1992) was obvious. Working parties were set up which led to the formation of an Equality of the Sexes subcommittee, represented on the EC since 1976, and gender equality became explicit BSA policy. Sheila Allen, one organiser of that conference, was unopposed for election as president of the Association in 1975; she was only the second woman president, but since then every third one has been female. There was sustained pressure for the raising of gender issues and means of improving the position of women, and many further developments followed from this, described in Chapter 6. The turn to sexual politics was also marked by the foundation of study groups (among many other new ones) on Sexual Divisions in Society (1975), Sexuality (1976), Gay Research (1976), Sociology of Reproduction (1976) and the short-lived Fatherhood Research (1980). (These were later joined by the Lesbian and Violence Against Women study groups.)

Some men were sympathetic to the women's movement's activities, but others objected that academic criteria were not being given sufficient attention, and saw the role within BSA of the movement as inappropriate politicisation of a learned society. One of those responsible for recruiting women to a committee reports that 'I got a lot of flak, flak from men – mainly from the older generation, professors of the subject senior to myself who felt that the BSA was selling out to sectional interests.' It is widely believed that a number of senior men resigned as a result, though it has proved hard to identify many in practice. Even men who were broadly sympathetic (and also some women) are shown by our interviews to have been somewhat unhappy about some of the more extreme manifestations of single-issue politics, if they did not feel it appropriate to express this openly.

Another spur to action was severe cuts to university funding. There had already been cutbacks under Labour in the 1970s, but further sharp cuts were made under the Thatcher government, starting in 1981 – a reduction of c.13% in 1981–4 – and these cuts fell more heavily on humanities and social sciences (Moore, 1987). A BSA *Cuts Bulletin* was for several years circulated to departments. Early retirements were actively encouraged, with a noticeable effect on the demography of the discipline, and the situation seemed threatening enough for the BSA to ask departments to refuse to accept transfers of students from any others closed as a result of cuts, and there was a move to urge that priority be given to the redundant in any new appointments. In the event, non-replacement rather than redundancy was the general pattern. In 1980, the EC noted that staff cutbacks were making it harder to find volunteers to organise BSA activities, so that more had to be done by paid employees, while the departments of potential editors of *Sociology* asked for larger contributions to the costs of running its office – hidden subsidies could no longer be relied upon. Sociology was out of political favour, and subject to many attacks. BSA devoted considerable effort to defence against cuts and attacks, and to public relations generally. When an attempt was made by Sir Keith Joseph, Secretary of State for Education and Science, to close down the SSRC, that was fought off – but at the price of changing its name to the Economic and Social Research Council (ESRC), to omit the word 'science'.[20] The Association of Learned Societies in the Social Sciences (ALSISS) was founded for combined action. (It is a measure of change since then that ALSISS has now become 'Academy' instead of 'Association', with selected academicians, and promotes social science in a much more consensual style.) In 1987, the daring move was made, on the recommendation of sociologist Ray Pahl, then a member of the UGC's social-science subcommittee, to request a UGC 'review' of sociology.[21] Such reviews for other disciplines had proposed significant cuts in the name of rationalisation. However, the review set out standards for satisfactory departments of sociology (University Grants Committee, 1989: 49–53), and this in some cases led to new appointments to meet those standards. The BSA's official representations to the review urged that the link between teaching and research should continue in all departments, and that attention should be given to regional needs and to the balance of age, gender and rank. It also, in one of the first signs of concern with this issue, argued that mainstream sociology departments should be maintained rather than sociology and sociologists being diffused across other disciplines' or cross-disciplinary departments.

In 1977, Julius Gould, a professor of sociology, published an attack on sociology (and other disciplines), accusing it of left-wing bias: *The Attack on Higher Education: Marxist and Radical Penetration*. This caused a public furore in the national press, encouraged by press releases. The EC issued a press statement taking exception to the use of names in the publication, and invited Gould to attend a meeting of its Professional Ethics Committee to discuss the issues. He did not, but instead resigned from the BSA. David Marsland in the 1980s also published a number of attacks from the right on British sociology. (See Chapter 7 for more detail on this.) Those were, however, very much minority stances, though others would have supported weaker versions of such positions on some issues. Those who took a leftist position were much more prominent.

In the broad sociological mainstream, there were divisions in relation to non-intellectual issues of BSA policy between those who took more 'ideological' stances and those who favoured a pragmatism which might involve cooperation with bodies and people which were not entirely congenial. It perhaps epitomised this division when the chair at an AGM remarked that the president's participation in many official committees had been shown to be excusable by the fact that she had made spirited criticism of their policy in her presidential address (Platt, 1988).

A number of other important developments took place over this period which were independent of the political issues. *Network*, a newsletter for members, was started in 1975, appearing three times a year. It rapidly became a forum for discussion on controversial issues as well as for announcements of meetings, professional gossip, BSA policy statements and organisational news. Other publication activities also expanded considerably; several book series designed to meet teaching needs at different levels were started. Various sets of guidelines were produced; some, like the *Guidelines for Applications for Research Funding* and on making book proposals to publishers, were designed to help individual members in their careers, and others, like the *Guidelines for Postgraduate Supervision* in 1978, were intended to outline good practice in relation to third parties. Regular meetings with representatives of the ESRC started; these representatives could be members of its staff and/or academic sociologists serving on its committees. Those meetings were held privately between the EC and the ESRC, but there also came to be institutionalised 'Meet the ESRC' sessions at every conference – at which the ESRC representatives, whether sociologists on its committees or members of its staff, were normally attacked. It was ESRC policy to liaise with and consult learned societies, but the BSA had ideological trouble in fitting into the presumed framework of speaking on behalf of the profession, which it tended to see as unacceptably elitist. Since, however, it also wanted the views of sociologists to be represented, it was anxious to take part, quite often making more egalitarian points than the ESRC could easily accept. One exchange, for instance, shows the chair of the ESRC sociology committee pointing out that the proportion of women on the committee was not out of line with the proportion of senior women in the discipline – to which the response was that the criterion of satisfactorily completed research could be used, in addition to the existing criteria, to bring in more women.

In the first half of the 1970s, a financial crisis built up as a result of high rates of inflation, which meant that the costs of routine activities rose enormously and, in 1975, short-term investments had to be sold to meet a deficit. In 1976, the controversial decision was made to meet the crisis by raising subscriptions for all full members, and also to introduce for the first time an income-related scale – which meant more than a trebling for the highest income group. A significant general salary rise soon afterwards made this less painful to those paying – and also put many members higher up the scale, making the return much greater than expected. In 1977, the treasurer proposed a strategy of improving services to members and diversifying sources of income, so that future rises would not be so great and create such ill feeling. The BSA took over the commercial management of *Sociology* from Oxford University Press and was soon making a good profit on it; it became possible to give it as a free membership benefit,[22] so that members received something of direct value in return for their subscriptions, and the possibility of a second journal began to be discussed.[23] A Book Club started in 1977, which offered sociological books at reduced prices to members, and this was sufficiently successful to be extended to include members of other learned societies and, although not originally intended to make a profit, became profitable; BSA books were available to members at reduced prices. Conferences were budgeted to make a profit. The result was a shift to more diverse sources of income, so that subscriptions covered a lower proportion of total expenditure. A period of high interest rates meant that investments did well, and a prudent reserve was built up.

From 1974 to 1985, there continued to be a rising trend of membership, but with some quite sharp annual fluctuations. The very large increase of 253 (80 of them students) in 1974 may be attributed in part to the Sexual Divisions conference; it seems equally plausible to assume that the unprecedented drop of 432 (340 of them full members) in 1976 was in response to the changed subscription structure. By the later 1970s, less than 40% of all university sociologists, though over 60% of professors, belonged – but total subscription income still rose. (For more detail on this, see Chapter 4.) By the end of the period, however, the total membership was 1,647; it was not until 1989 that the 1976 total of 1,792 was reached (and surpassed) again. Demography must have made some contribution to this, though it cannot account for everything; one effect of 'the cuts' was a 19% drop in the total number of university teachers of sociology, from 533 in 1981 to 430 in 1987.

By the end of this period, the BSA had a much wider range of activities and, at the same time as it incorporated some political themes of the times into its policies, had also adapted in a conscious and professional manner to changed circumstances.

Consolidation

Since the 1980s, there have been less dramatic, but equally consequential, external events to respond to. The rise of public pressure for the 'accountability' of universities, as manifested in the Research Assessment Exercise (RAE) and Teaching Quality Assessment, has created new areas of BSA activity, replacing 'cuts' as an area of concern. The Association has been consulted as part of the general consultation of learned societies in connection with these, has made representations about the form such exercises should take, and has nominated individual candidates for their panels. The Annual Report made to the 1999 AGM mentioned, for instance, that in 1998 the BSA had been consulted by the Higher Education Funding Council for England (HEFCE) on the next RAE and the new Institute for Learning and Teaching, and by the Quality Assurance Agency on quality management, and had nominated members for RAE panels and as academicians in the new ALSISS academy. It also supported 'SSP 2000', the UK Network for Teaching and Learning in Sociology and Social Policy, funded by HEFCE's Fund for the Development of Teaching and Learning, which has promoted and disseminated good practice. The latest such area in which BSA has played an active role is the production of the 'Benchmarks' for sociology, where discussion of drafts was conducted via the BSA website. The RAE made research more salient for members, and the importance of the ESRC for the funding of both research and special activities, such as the summer school, made its affairs a continuing preoccupation. Teaching as such had for some time no longer figured as a major problematic concern, in an established discipline with many experienced members. New developments have, thus, once again made teaching an active area, though now in response to external initiatives rather than to needs felt within the discipline.

There have been important organisational changes, some internally and some externally driven. At fairly regular intervals, internal operations have been reviewed, and attempts have been made to consider what the needs now are that the Association should meet, and to rationalise and economise by such strategies as avoiding the taking of decisions on minor matters in large meetings, and limiting the numbers of subcommittees. Treasurers have fulfilled their traditional role by declaring the need for urgent action to avoid impending financial crises, which fortunately have always been met. By 1989, a pattern where members' subscriptions provided only half the total income, while investments and profit-making activities such as conferences and publications provided the rest, was established.

The largest single change has been that associated with the move of the office, to Durham. The cost of maintaining a London base, and the increasing pressure from the LSE, made a move highly desirable; Anne Dix's retirement in 1992 provided the occasion for many tributes to her, and a review of the organisation and staffing of the office. It was moved to a cheaper location in a

Durham University science park, and the staffing structure was changed, placing a graduate administrator in charge with other staff in support roles. The larger staff has made more specialisation possible, including the creation of the role of conference organiser, and they took on additional tasks such as servicing the Heads of Departments (HoDs) organisation. However, with so much change and such a range of tasks, the office staff became overloaded, and the EC in 1999 concluded that they were too busy to develop or innovate, so that restructuring was again needed. It was remarked (24 September 1999) that 'the BSA has grown from a one-person, back-room voluntary group into a complex, professional organisation with a small professional staff within ten years and without anyone really noticing'; that perhaps exaggerated a little, but it is clear that it had elements of truth.

Legal and tax changes have also made it necessary for various practical matters to be reorganised. Changes to charity legislation which call for increased formal accountability meant that some practices needed to be tightened up, especially on the side of finance and auditing. Reports of the Association started to include the formal statement of the objects of the BSA as registered with the Charity Commission:

> *Advancement of education by the promotion and diffusion of knowledge of sociology by lectures, publications, the promotion of research and encouragement of contacts between workers in all the relevant fields of enquiry, and by undertaking such other activities as may be conducive to the attainment of these objects provided the same shall be legally charitable, but not otherwise.*

The agenda for the 1998 AGM reported that changes were needed to meet legal requirements and the responsibilities of an employer, as well as developing a more pro-active relationship with external bodies. In 1999, it emerged that there had been some accidental irregularities in relation to charities legislation which required emergency action, and that BSA Publications had not fulfilled all its legal obligations. A review of the Association's organisation and staffing structure was undertaken, which resulted in the decision at the 1999 AGM that BSA should change its legal status from that of an unincorporated association to a limited liability company, though one retaining its charitable status; this was completed at the 2000 AGM. That was necessary to ensure that individuals did not have to take the responsibility for entering into contracts personally on behalf of the association, to protect the legal trustees, and to allow members to pay their subscriptions electronically or by direct debit. Much that has been businesslike rather than ideological has been done. In 1997, for instance, the EC and office staff spent a weekend with a consultant to assist in clarifying goals and relating practices to them. It is hard to imagine that such decisions would have been politically conceivable much earlier. All these were important changes, but not ones that will make much obvious difference to the ordinary member's experience of the Association and its activities. What has made a difference is the development of the website to provide a range of information and services to members, including electronic conference registration and subscription payment as well as consultation on issues arising internally and externally.

Despite all this reorganisation, a full range of activities for members has continued and expanded. Some routine work has been the updating of earlier initiatives, revising the Guidelines, but this has also been extended to new groups, with Guidelines on Anti-Racist and Anti-Disablist Language and on the treatment of part-time and short-term contract staff. A subcommittee for Black Women has been set up, as well as a standing committee on Race and Ethnicity. Gender issues continue to be taken seriously, but the Women's Caucus has been less active and innovative; this could reasonably be seen as responding to a situation in which many of their original goals have been met, at least inside the BSA. (Some of its recent activity has been on issues not confined to women, such as the problems of those on short-term contracts.) The innovative electronic journal *Sociological Research Online* was started in 1996 by a consortium led by the BSA, and thrives. So do the longer-established *Sociology* and *Work, Employment and Society* but, in 1996, it was decided that the time had come again to have their publication in the hands of a specialist publisher, and a contract was signed with Cambridge University Press. In 2000, a widely felt need that was met by the creation, with BSA support, of SociologyPress, to publish the monographs that commercial publishers now rarely support. Study groups are very active, with at least two (Auto/Biography and Medical Sociology) publishing their own journals; in 1999, there were 23 groups – more than ever before. The annual conferences are large and successful, attracting 500 or more delegates and more than 200 papers, and have an established formula by which a range of other activities, including meetings of the HoDs group, take place there. 'Training-related activities' have become a regular feature of Association activity, both at conferences and as special events, and this is reflected in the creation in 2000 of a Professional Development Committee focusing on the needs of individual members.

In the early 1980s, membership had declined to about a third of the holders of university teaching posts, but now it has risen again to around a half. Total membership settled in the latter 1990s at around 2,400, of which 600–700 have been students. Excluding students and overseas members, 49% were women in 1998; 61% of the student members were women (Annual Report, 1998). Efforts have been made to recruit from other categories of potential member, such as researchers, and the general pattern of lack of competition for places on the EC has had the benefit that it has been possible for a policy of deliberate recruitment to it of members from underrepresented categories to be applied. The manner in which officers are appointed has been looked at by the EC several times. The AGM rejected a proposal from the EC that offices should be filled by nomination from and election by the membership (rather than by the EC's decision), to ensure that there were actually candidates for all the posts which need to be filled. There have been occasions when co-option to key posts has been necessary; the pressures of contemporary academic life have made it harder to find time to undertake such voluntary work. In consequence, some former officers have served again when otherwise they might have expected someone else to take their turn. The current system for filling offices, set up by the EC, is for nominations to be made from its members and, if there is more than one candidate, voted on. This certainly has greater formal propriety than the 1980s system, in which consultations by the president led to nominations which were automatically approved, though the outcome may well be little different from what it would have been if that had continued.

Over time, the Association has changed from a small one with a limited range of activities to a much larger one with a wide range of activities, some of them semi-independent. It has become a complex organisation with a professional staff, and has adapted to a situation where there are new external constraints and challenges and it can no longer rely on significant subsidies of either money or time. Sociology has become more diverse and fragmented as its size has increased, so different members may only participate in limited parts of BSA's activities. Anxiety has sometimes been expressed about whether 'mainstream' sociology still exists as it once did and, to the extent that this anxiety is justified, it is harder to maintain a general disciplinary organisation such as the BSA. But it still continues, and clearly remains a broad church which serves purposes for a variety of members, even though membership is not treated as a professional necessity. It has changed considerably, and many of the changes have responded to changes in the wider society rather than to sociology's intellectual development. Whether the overall pattern of change can be described as one of professionalisation is discussed in Chapter 10.

Notes

1   Apart from the one at Oxford, two of whose three members were undoubtedly in normal terms anthropologists!

2   These figures are drawn from the CUYB entries. It looks likely that not all heads of department were listed as such, and it is clear that some of those included were social workers rather than sociologists, so they account for some of those with apparently low qualifications.

3   For more about the Institute, see Platt (1971).

4   Whose Israel Sieff regularly appeared in the lists of the great and the good associated with bodies concerned with social policy matters, including PEP, of which he became Chairman in 1933 and later president.

5   At least one anthropologist (without the mixed anthropology/sociology identity sometimes held) was a member of nine of the 11 executives up to 1961–2, but after that this representation ceased.

6   In 1999, its formal status was, however, in the interests of constitutional uniformity, changed to that of a subcommittee.

7   Official statistics are not available for before 1965–6. For more details about sources and figures, see Platt (2000).

8   Until the 1960s, many of the universities which existed were formally only 'university colleges', and did not award their own degrees but 'external' degrees of London University; this was also usual in polytechnics until the later 1970s. For sociology, while that lasted it gave the LSE great power over the syllabuses and teaching at other institutions.

9   Williams *et al.* (1974: 101), in a study of a large representative sample of university teachers, plus analysis of 1968–71 vacancies and applications for them, found that for appointments to lectureships made in 1968–71, a much higher proportion of candidates with Firsts but no higher degree than candidates with PhDs were successful.

10   These figures can only be put in imprecise terms on some points, as the available sources do not always give a disciplinary field; however, it has been assumed that no BA before 1955 can have been in sociology unless from London, and that for those with first degrees and an MA from Oxbridge the latter is not an earned one.

11   For instance, by 1970, Asher Tropp and Joe Banks were both professors, at the Universities of Surrey and Leicester.

12   The *Register* did not include only Teachers' Section members, or all of those; it was the product of a questionnaire sent both to members holding teaching posts and to others whom it was thought appropriate to include.

13   For most of its history, it has been largely funded by a grant from the SSRC/ESRC.

14   This 'quotation' is from the author. The convention has been followed, where there are boxes with anecdotes from my experience of a kind equivalent to those from my interviews with other people, of leaving them without quotation marks or attribution, while quotations from other people have quotation marks and may or may not have an attribution. Any quotation without attribution is from one of the interviews.

15   But the BSA and university sociologists were not the only groups concerned about teaching needs. The Association for the Teaching of the Social Sciences (ATSS), representing O-level and A-level teachers of sociology and social studies, had been set up in 1964, and was concerned to promote school-level sociology and a sociological approach to 'social studies' in schools.

16   For more on the relation at this stage between sociologists and anthropologists, see Mills (2001).

17   For some material relevant to this, see Sklair (1981).

18   However, a set of 1964 conference papers had been published earlier under the auspices of SR: Halmos (1964).

19   She resigned in 1978, and was not replaced.

20   For practical convenience, SSRC/ESRC will generally be referred to subsequently as ESRC.

21   This of course covered only the institutions then known as 'universities', so it excluded the polytechnics where much sociology was taught. For an accessible account of its main features, see Westergaard and Pahl (1989).

22   This possibility, however, depended on a continuing hidden subsidy from the LSE to postage and packing costs.

23   *Work, Employment and Society* was created in 1987, and has been successful both intellectually and financially.

Chapter 4
The BSA and intellectual life

The BSA has played a significant role in the intellectual life of British sociology through its conferences and other meetings, study groups, journals and books.[1] In this chapter, the history of such activities and their organisation is outlined, and the ways in which those have reflected intellectual and social changes are discussed.

Conferences and meetings

In the earliest days of the Association, conferences were in principle held biennially, though this principle was not always followed in practice. Some plans collapsed. For instance, the 1959 conference was postponed to 1960, but did not take place then, and next it was hoped that a special conference with wide European representation might be held in 1961 to mark the tenth anniversary of the Association, but this idea had to be abandoned, largely on grounds of cost. It is clear that, in the 1950s and early 1960s, the EC regarded meetings under other auspices as sometimes making its own conferences redundant or not viable. (World Congresses of Sociology were held in 1956 and 1959, and had substantial British representation, and other meetings such as one in Edinburgh in 1959 on 'Darwinism and the Study of Society', not organised by the BSA, were mentioned in the executive.) But from 1964, the conferences became established as an annual event. However, before then there were several ad hoc meetings such as the ones in 1956 on the state of professional sociology, in 1959 on social mobility, and in 1960 on married women and employment, as well as the regular open meetings in London for members. Those meetings were gradually transformed into meetings of groups with specialised interests, which became the 'study groups' described below, although the two continued in parallel for some time. (General-purpose series of meetings after that were organised only by regional branches and the Teachers' Section. BSA Scotland has operated successfully ever since 1955, and holds meetings which have given special prominence to work on Scotland, though they have not been confined to that. A number of other branches existed at least for a few years in the 1970s, but they have not succeeded in maintaining themselves over the longer term and have left little central record of their activities.) In the 1950s there were, by modern standards, extremely frequent sociological meetings in London. In the year 1956–7, for instance, the report to the AGM lists eight general meetings (three with speakers from abroad), ten meetings of the Educational Sociology study group and 11 meetings of the Industrial Sociology study group; in 1959–60, there were two general meetings and two one-day conferences, the Theoretical and Comparative Sociology group managed to hold the extraordinary total of 17 speaker meetings and the Educational Sociology group held five. A number of these meetings had speakers from abroad. A shortage of main conferences thus certainly did not mean a shortage of opportunities for intellectual interchange, at least for those who could get to London and had appropriate interests.

The Teachers' Section, after its initial period of independence, was incorporated into the BSA in 1963, but continued to hold its own separate meetings until it closed in 1975. The early 1960s, when the section started, followed a bad period for general BSA conferences, and so its meetings may to some extent have provided a substitute for those. During the period in which their meetings ran in parallel with the main conferences, we can see from Table 4 that in many cases the Teachers' Section in effect piloted a topic in its substantive research meetings, which is not surprising given teachers' strong orientation to reporting on research in progress or recently completed. One of the strengths of the section was, of course, that it could choose its topics with no concern for attracting an audience other than that of professional sociologists, though members of other disciplines did sometimes attend its meetings; an officer reports that topics were chosen by 'the committee pushing on things they thought would represent a good attraction for a subsection of the sociological community ... we would try to generate names, and ring around.' He went on to make a comment with which others concurred:

My overall impression of those meetings was that they were very much more enjoyable and worthwhile than the annual conferences, because we would have 30 odd people there, all specifically interested in the topic ... and you got together people who were particularly interested and they used to go very well, and the social interaction was always enjoyable as well as the academic stimulation.

Table 4 Topics and attendance at non-teaching meetings of the Teachers' Section[a]

Year	Topic	Number attending
1963	Sociological considerations in rapidly developing countries	35
1964	Urban redevelopment, Participation and conflict in industry	41
	Action approach in industrial sociology, systematic models and social reality, social development and football	75
1965	Community study, urbanism, local studies	28
1966	Mathematics and sociology	58
1967	Political sociology	
1968	Sociology of religion	32
1969	Deviance, rebellion, revolution	
1970	British sociology in the 1970s	
	Social stratification	
1971	Family and industrialisation	40
1972	Aspects of urban sociology	
1973	Aspects of rural sociology	
1975	British sociology and professionalism	

[a]No information is available on the first few meetings, and attendance was not always mentioned in BSA AGM reports.

The paper on the section presented to the 1974 special meeting of the BSA points out that, in more than one case, its meetings led to the creation of a BSA study group for those with a special interest in that topic, and that this meant that its success made it 'in danger of doing itself out of a job'.

Main conferences were initially oriented to a wider constituency than sociologists, as they needed to be to have a potential audience of reasonable size, and the speakers were not only sociologists; some were drawn from other disciplines, and from outside academia. Conference titles are listed in Table 5. The 1964 conference topic is perhaps the first to be based on theoretical ideas developed by sociologists, rather than recognised as an issue in the wider society. We can track some of the movements within sociology through the conference titles. Conflict, race and power are themes with an obvious relation to the radicalism of the late 1960s and early 1970s; the 1971 title marks the return of what had been criminology to the sociological mainstream associated with the National Deviancy Conference,[2] while 'development' comes to the fore to replace the earlier 'modernisation'. The growth and impact of the women's and gay liberation movements are shown in the 1974 title and subsequent ones raising issues of gender and sexuality.[3] Later themes such as the life cycle, science, the body and time relate to areas of emerging strength and specialisation, while the two on health indicate the continuing importance of medical sociology.

Table 5 Conferences

Date	Title	Location	Number attending[a]
1953	Social Policy and the Social Sciences	London	
1955	Political Behaviour ...	London	
1957	Sociology in Retrospect and Prospect	London	243
1962	Problems of the Affluent Society	Brighton	
1964	The Development of Industrial Societies	Nottingham	112
1965	Organisations in Contemporary Society	London	180
1966	Urbanism in Contemporary Britain	Leicester	118
1967	Leisure in Industrial Society	London	
1968	Conflict	Reading	
1969	Sociology of Race and Racialism	London	223 [b]
1970	Sociology of Education	Durham	322 [b]
1971	Social Control, Deviance and Dissent	London	
1972	Sociology and Development	York	300 +
1973	Social Stratification	Surrey	343
1974	Sexual Divisions and Society	Aberdeen	203
1975	Advanced Industrial Societies	Kent	407
1976	Sociology, Health and Illness	Manchester	450
1977	Power and the State	Sheffield	474
1978	Culture	Sussex	503
1979	Law and Society	Warwick	522

(continued overleaf)

Table 5 Conferences (continued)

Date	Title	Location	Number attending[a]
1980	... British Sociology 1950–80	Lancaster	338 [b]
1981	The Sociology of Inequality	Aberystwyth	288 [b]
1982	Gender and Society	Manchester	400 +
1983	... The Periphery of Industrial Society	Cardiff	231
1984	Work, Employment and Unemployment	Bradford	436 [b]
1985	War, Violence and Social Change	Hull	
1986	Sociology of the Life Cycle	Loughborough	
1987	Science Technology and Society	Leeds	
1988	Sociology and History	Edinburgh	
1989	Sociology in Action	Plymouth	
1990	Social Divisions and Social Change	Surrey	412
1991	Health and Society	Manchester	
1992	A New Europe?	Kent	
1993	Research Imaginations	Essex	
1994	Sexualities in Social Context	U of Central Lancs.	545
1995	Contested Cities	Leicester	538
1996	... Ethnicity, Nationalism and Globalization	Reading	380
1997	Power and Resistance	York	470
1998	Making Sense of the Body	Edinburgh	508
1999	For Sociology	Glasgow	361
2000	Making Time/Marking Time	York	435

[a]Where no figure is given, no data on attendance have been found.
[b]These figures have been counted from the published lists of delegates. Since those are produced before the conference starts, they omit late registrants and so underestimate the totals. Other figures are taken from reports made by the organisers or kept in the office, and those have been preferred where available.

The extent to which the title chosen conveys the actual content of the conference has, however, diminished as the number of papers given has become larger, and the drift has been towards titles of a broad nature which do not limit contributions to any particular specialism. Recently, it has also become customary to have an 'open' stream for which papers on any topic can be offered, though the old tradition of connecting the work one is doing with a theme which one would not otherwise relate to it in order to make a paper look relevant remains active. For some time the topics were formulated by the EC, and an organiser prepared to take the task on was then sought. More recently, the system has developed where the membership is invited to make proposals, which are voted on at the AGM, and there has been a conference team of four or five people. It used to be seen as inappropriate for those proposing a topic necessarily to be responsible for the organising work or to arrange it at their own institution, and conference teams were composed of members from a number of different institutions with only one member from the institution where it would be held. More recently, it has become usual for the proposers to put forward an organising team as well as a topic, to use their own institution, and to have only one outside member.

At first, meetings were normally held in London, usually at Queen Elizabeth College. The first one to be outside London was held in Brighton, in connection with the foundation of the new University of Sussex – but not at the university, which by 1962 did not yet have appropriate buildings, though a visit to the campus site was included in the programme. There was then a period when London and other venues alternated until, in the early 1970s, the pattern of meeting at a different university outside London each year was established; the first polytechnic to host the conference was Plymouth in 1989. It looks as though attendance was likely to be lower when the location was geographically more peripheral. Not every campus can provide the facilities needed, which accounts for some of the repetition of venues; the idea of having a permanent site, or rotating among a limited number, has been mooted to overcome the practical problems of dealing with a different site each year – but that would make it impossible to find local organisers for every year.

One feature of the conferences which is worth mentioning is the presence of delegates from abroad. There have been many foreign plenary speakers over the years, often of the utmost distinction. There have also been many foreign delegates and non-plenary speakers; before the period of globalisation, the 1975 conference stands out by having on its non-plenary programme Crozier, Erikson, Himmelstrand, Korpi, Therborn, Touraine and Willener (four Swedes and three French) giving seven of the 48 papers. The conferences have, thus, offered an important opportunity for interaction with wider sociological worlds. But which worlds? All but one of the plenary speakers have been from either Western Europe or North America, though the balance between the two has shifted over the years, in what to me is a surprising direction: in the 1950s and 1960s, the great majority were from Europe, while in each subsequent decade the clear majority has been from North America. Perhaps this owes something not to intellectual change, but to changes in the basis of conference finance which have made more money available for travel expenses, plus the falling cost of transatlantic travel.

The whole conventional format of the conference has changed, in ways which reflect other changes within the Association. One important change has been the gradually increasing provision of sessions other than those at which research papers are presented. It is now automatic that the Women's Caucus, the Post-Graduate Forum and the HoDs will meet, and that there will be a 'meet the ESRC' session. There have also sometimes been training activities: sessions in which experts update participants on the latest developments, workshops on the use of computer programs such as Nu*dist, guidance on how to use the official 'benchmarks' in curriculum design. Journal editors have spoken about the running of their journals and how to write for them successfully, and there have been sessions on the job market for postgraduates and on how to write research proposals. Tours of sociologically interesting local places may be arranged, there have been exhibitions of art or computer software, films, and occasionally an associated conference for sixth-formers. In addition, the organisers have experimented with the format of research sessions: there have been a variety of round tables, workshops, panels, 'meet the author' sessions etc., though no general direction of change except towards greater diversity is evident here.

Some other changes can be summarised numerically. Until 1968, the conferences always lasted from the evening of one day until the lunchtime of the second day after that – not quite two full days of sessions; from 1969, the usual pattern became to have an additional day, settling down in the 1980s to almost always taking place from a Monday afternoon until lunchtime on the Thursday, making three full days of meetings. Table 6 shows what this involved in terms of papers, though what happened was not just that more papers could be fitted into a longer total time but that more were offered simultaneously. Row 1 shows the expansion in the number of sessions on offer, and rows 2, 3 and 4 show how the number of papers given increased to make what originally offered a rather uniform experience to delegates much more diverse.

If we look more closely at the 1970s, the extent to which the 1974 conference was a watershed, initiating major change, is evident: under each heading, 1974 made a noticeable change from 1970–3, which carried forward at a similar level into the later 1970s and beyond. This represents the democratisation of the conference, though some would have a less favourable term for it. The old pattern was essentially one where the paper-givers, plenary or not, were invited speakers, while in the new pattern that developed there has been a general invitation to submit proposals and the great majority, if not all, of them are accepted; the organisers' task is not so much to choose between them as to organise them into reasonably coherent sessions. (The organiser of the 1975 conference remarked in his report that 'no offer of a paper was refused ... Of the papers offered, there were a number which I did not feel would be appropriate for the meeting. However, because of the "democratic" norms of the Association I felt they should be included' [Box C7, LSE].) Even estimated attendance figures are not available for every conference but, where they are, Table 7 shows how the pattern has changed. Initially the number of papers represented only a small proportion of those attending; this rose a little in the 1970s, averaged around a third of those present in the early 1980s, and became around half in the 1990s. This has shifted the balance of paper-givers towards more junior members of the discipline, and they now include many graduate students and rather few of the most senior members. It is generally recognised that, whether or not one is altogether happy that so many papers should be given, it is hard to get funding to attend unless one is offering a paper, and so to enable the maximum number of people to do so is an important support to the financial viability of the conference.

It has become conventional to have 'streams' of related interest running through the conference. (Under this system, each paper, inevitably, is likely to have a relatively small and specialised audience.) The streams show a tendency to similarity between conferences, indicating some of the assumptions made about how to organise knowledge and what is politically necessary for an acceptable proposal. Before 1971, the stream titles were defined by substantive topics, often ones related to current issues of state policy. From the early 1970s, the titles generally become more theoretical and specifically sociological; after 1974, gender, feminism and sex roles figure regularly.

Table 6 Changes in conference pattern

	1950s	1960s	1970s	1970–3	1974	1975–9	1980s	1990s
1 Average number of separate paper sessions	8	11	55	27	65	75	101	90
2 Average number of non-plenary papers	11	12	54	30	62	70	117	183
3 Average number of sessions per time slot	1.8	1.9	4.5	2.6	5.0	5.1	7.2	6.6
4 Proportion of sessions plenary (%)	39	28	5	12	3	4	4	4

Table 7 Ratio of non-plenary papers to attendance[a]

Year[b]	Non-plenary papers	Attendance	Ratio (%)
1957	14	243	6
1965	17	180	9
1966	12	118	10
1969	22	223	10
1970	15	322	5
1972	30	300 +	10
1973	45	343	13
1974	62	203	31
1975	43	407	11
1976	63	450	14
1977	87	474	18
1978	57	503	11
1979	102	522	20
1980	95	338	28
1981	97	288	34
1982	106	400 +	27
1983	123	231	53
1984	132	436	30
1990	192	412	47
1994	218	600 +	36
1995	276	600 –	46
1996	203	362	56
1997	296	c.500	59
1998	272	496	55

[a]Note that although this is close to the proportion of the attendance giving papers it is not quite the same, since some papers have multiple authors.
[b]Only those years for which data are available are listed here.

Conferences contribute to the intellectual life of the discipline after they are over, too. Since the 1969 conference, each has published a selection of the papers, edited by the organisers, as one or more books. It has not always been easy to find a publisher, given their reluctance over collective edited works, but the tradition has been maintained and some of the resulting books have become important sources. The idea of having an open conference with no central theme has been mooted on a number of occasions, and one argument against this has been the lesser likelihood that it would provide a group of sufficiently related good papers to make a viable book.

Study groups

'Study groups' bring together members who share an interest in a particular area of research, and their main activity is the holding of meetings at which research papers are presented.[4] The first were founded in 1955, and more soon emerged. The history of the general pattern of study group development has to be treated with a broad brush, as the records are not always complete; it is evident that some convenors were much more conscientious than others in sending reports to the BSA office. Some groups have been relatively transient, many have had their ups and downs in activity, and it is not always clear when they have really continued to exist. Others, however, have had long records of successful activity, and even operate almost as independent societies.

The first study groups were on Industrial Sociology and Urban Sociology. Sociology of Education was added, and then ones for Theoretical and Comparative Sociology in 1957,[5] Sociology of Language (which shortly became Sociology of Communication) in 1960, Asia in 1962 and Sociology of Design in 1963. It appears that these study groups flourished for a few years and then declined; Urban Sociology lapsed when the convenor, Ruth Glass, was ill and then was abroad for a time. By the 1966 AGM, the honorary general secretary could, however, report the foundation of two new groups, on Theoretical Sociology (meeting at the new university of Essex, opened in 1964) and on Social Policy, to add to the three surviving ones (Design, Educational, Industrial). There were no more formations until the late 1960s, when a burst of fresh study group activity began. This may be assumed to reflect, first, the preoccupation of many teachers in the earlier 1960s with setting up new departments and servicing the huge student expansion, and then the much larger number of university sociologists once the expansion was under way. A fairly typical issue of the News and Notes newsletter from the early 1970s advertises single meetings or programmes of meetings for eight groups, gives contact details for a further nine, and has one notice of interest in forming a new group.

Table 8 summarises the numerical pattern of development of study group activity, showing how the number of different groups not only increased very strikingly in absolute number in the 1970s, but also increased in ratio to the number of members available to take part in them. It does not, of course, follow that the number of active participants in each group followed the same curve, and it seems likely that many of those were not BSA members, which would help to explain why so many groups could be supported simultaneously with what seems such a small potential base. It is noticeable that some of the groups founded in the 1970s did not last very long (see Table A4 in the Appendix); the drop in membership no doubt contributed to this, but so did the atmosphere of fleeting and competing intellectual fashions, and the many political divisions of the period.

We may note also that the changing study group topics tell us something about intellectual movements in British sociology. Their messages should be interpreted cautiously, because any study group depends on having at least one person prepared to do its organisational work, and may collapse if that person is unable to continue; similarly, a group with a relatively small constituency may last for a number of years on the basis of the enthusiasm and commitment of just one or two people who organise interesting meetings. If we look at which groups were founded, and continued active, at which period, three tendencies are noticeable. The first is a trend towards increasing specialisation and 'sociologisation'. The groups founded in the 1950s and 1960s have broad remits, defined by substantive topics of a common-sense nature such as 'education'. After that, some of the topics become technical (Computers in Survey Analysis, Ethnography), more theoretical titles begin to appear (Political Economy, Deviance, Urban Poverty and the Labour Process), and there are some more narrowly defined topics (Class Formation and the Third World, Violence Against Women, Figurational Sociology and Max Weber alongside Theory). The second trend is the influence of changing intellectual fashion: Education and Industrial Sociology were what one did in the 1950s, Revolution and Deviance came later and, in the 1990s, there are lifestyle topics such as Food and Consumption. (It is puzzling that there has never been a group for social stratification, despite the salience of the theme in British sociological work.) The recently founded Auto/Biography group has been successful enough

Table 8 Number of study groups, related to membership

Years[a]	(A) No. of study groups	(B) No. of members	Average of (B)/(A)
1955–6	3	470–498	161
1961–2	6	547–625	98
1965–6	8	–797	
1971–2	22	1,414–1,384	64
1975–6	31	1,721–1,792	57
1981–2	29	1,364–1,331	46
1985–6	29	1,647–1,568	55
1991–2	24	[2,000+][b]	83
1995–6	24	2,600–2,586	108
2000–1	22	c.2,600	118

[a]Years have been taken at five-year intervals to simplify the presentation of trends – and to overcome the problem of occasional missing data.
[b]This figure has been treated as 2,000, so clearly the figure in the last column should be larger – by an unknown amount.

to be able to found its own journal. The third trend, a subtype of the second, is the continuing importance from the mid-1970s of areas to do with gender and sexuality: Sexual Divisions, Human Reproduction, Lesbian Studies, HIV and AIDS.

It is possible that we would learn more about the processes of group formation by relating BSA study groups to ISA 'research committees'. If a movement of thought is international, similarities in the BSA pattern could be explained by those wider factors, while marked discrepancies suggest British idiosyncrasies. Parallel groups were formed in the two associations at very similar periods in Industrial, Urban and Political Sociology, Deviance, Race Relations, Sexual Divisions[6] and the Sociology of Science. However, since some British sociologists were also actively involved in the ISA, such similarities do not necessarily indicate *independent* responses to the same trends. One might also be tempted to turn the explanation the other way round: perhaps the BSA did not have a Stratification group because the very active ISA one catered for all the needs of those interested? (And it was organised by David Glass, who was among the LSE staff who became disaffected from the BSA.) This is a tempting line of thought to explore, but to take it seriously would require more detailed research on both sets of groups.[7]

All study groups but the most short-lived and unsuccessful will have made a contribution to discussion and the creation of networks, but some have done much more than that. An example of one that made a major contribution is the one on Leisure and Recreation, which apparently took a field where a critical and theoretical approach had been rare and with a series of workshops, and publications which were much reprinted and cited, was at the leading edge of significant intellectual change internationally.

The Medical Sociology group has been particularly successful. Forty-nine people attended its initial meeting in 1969; its own annual conferences were initiated; by 1973, the first newsletter was produced, and went to 450 people; and 1974 saw the publication of the second Register of Medical Sociology (the eighth appeared in 1998); by 1977, the conference was large enough to have ten streams, and by 1992 it had 420 participants (Pope and Ziebland, 1993); by the early 1980s, a number of regional groups had emerged. It seems to have been especially important to its members because many of them were working in medical contexts in isolation from other sociologists. It is an interesting case in its relation to the centre. A tension between 'sociology' and 'medicine' seems to have been felt from the beginning. In the second newsletter, Phil Strong suggested that 'we seem to be dropping the less "respectable" members, the non-sociologists, while gaining others who define "positivism", "interactionism" or "Marxism" rather than "medicine" as the core of their professional being' (Strong, 1973–4) while, in the third, Paul Atkinson suggested that 'In the past, much of the soul-searching has been concerned with our standing with medicine … At last year's conference, I got the impression that there was greater emphasis on the sociological component of our title; but there is a long way to go, and we still seem to be a bit short on theorising' (Atkinson, 1974). Later in the year, an editorial showed a somewhat pragmatic approach to the BSA:

> *Every year the approach of the annual meeting makes one of the few occasions when membership of the BSA has any real significance for members of the Medical Sociology Group. Then it has concessionary value – as it does for subscriptions to various journals – but does it have much more than this? ...*
> (Johnson, 1974)

At least in its earlier years, people who were researchers rather than university teachers are said to have been dominant and, in addition to sociologists, medical professionals of various kinds attended its meetings (as well as groups of anthropologists and social historians when they were not numerous enough to support their own meetings). One early participant says that relations with the BSA were strained through the 1970s, especially over the BSA's efforts to encourage BSA membership by having a big member/non-member price differential, which was seen as likely to drive out participants important to the vitality of the meetings. In addition, career researchers felt that the BSA was much more responsive to the situation of teachers than to theirs, and ignored the institutional environment in which they worked: 'Researchers tend on the whole to be more pragmatic, because they need to be ... The BSA seemed to do a lot of posturing which threatened the business of making a living' (Dingwall, 1997).

In its report for 1973–4, the Social Psychology Group described problems similar to some of those of the Medical Sociology Group:

> *we have considerable problems with our membership in that it is so diverse in its interests and contains many who are only marginally involved in sociology ... we have decided to ... go back to having ... meetings on different sociological themes. This unfortunately is not going to meet the needs of the pure psychologists who are members of the group, but we feel that as a sociology group we should focus on sociological issues rather than trying to tailor our activities to the interests of psychologists.*

It seems likely that these tensions account for the relatively short life of the group, which had no institutional base for a constituency like that of medicine; one may presume, too, that the psychologist members had an easy alternative home in the Social Psychology Section of the BPS.[8]

Sometimes the course of a group's development was affected by political vicissitudes. The 'Race' group was founded in 1970 as Race Relations, but after that start its activity lapsed. John Rex played a role in reviving it, but the running was in the hands of another person who came to take the radical line associated with a group from the Institute of Race Relations, and who at its first meeting said that Rex should not be allowed to speak (Rex, 1997). An undated memo in the records, probably from the late 1970s, from the convenor, said that 'The steering committee is determined that the group's future meetings will endeavour to make sociology that is geared to exposing and explaining the operation of white institutional racism, and if possible contributing to black development.' There is no record in *Network* of what was done under this programme; the failure to advertise meetings there suggests that in the event it was not very active, which is confirmed by the AGM report for 1980 that it had not managed to hold any meetings that year. Shortly afterwards another report mentioned moves to revive it and, by 1983, it was again meeting, with another convenor and speakers on some topics of a conventional sociological kind. But in the later 1980s its concerns appear to have been very much focused on combating racism; for instance, the annual report for 1988 advertises a forthcoming workshop 'to take participants through some of the key stages in tackling racism in their organisations'. The 1987 report concludes that

> *The group is most successful when it draws on a variety of groups interested in race relations such as teachers in schools of higher education, and race relations workers. Where possible, future activities will seek to maintain the association.*

This shows how it has been possible for study groups to bring in wider constituencies, though it is questionable how far the associated activities were always distinctively sociological.

Another case where extra-sociological interests of a rather different character have been involved is the study group on Religion. In its first version, it had an inaugural meeting in June 1967, organised by John Peart-Binns of the Church of England's Advisory Council for the Church's Ministry;[9] he resigned from the BSA in 1968 on leaving London, and the group appears to have become inactive. It tried to start up again in 1971, but the plan was rejected because, as proposed, it was not predominantly BSA. A fresh inaugural meeting was held in 1975, at the initiative of an academic sociologist of religion. It has become a very successful and active group, which publishes a *Register* of members and research and holds its own residential conferences; a number of books have come from its conference papers. It has been active in contacts with Eastern Europe, and scholars from there have regularly attended its meetings. The group's annual report for 1986 mentions that, of its membership of a little over 100, only 40 were also members of the BSA, and roughly that proportion appears to have been maintained subsequently. The group's conferences have been sufficiently independent of the central BSA to have been timed to clash with its annual conference in at least one year (though on other occasions it has organised meetings at the main conference). However, the officers have normally been university sociologists, and its meetings have consistently been on sociological topics, though also attended by many from other fields – including, at one on charismatic religion, charismatics themselves. A report from it in *Network* in March 1997 states that 'The Group intends to maintain its links with the BSA, and its wide membership ... '; this suggests a semi-detached relationship in which the Group defines its identity as independent of the BSA, while it has nonetheless faithfully maintained that relationship for many years.

There are, of course, also other study groups which have had identities much more narrowly associated with mainstream academic sociology. An example of a not very successful group is the one on the Sociology of Sociology and Social Research. This ran for a number of years, and had regular meetings with some interesting papers, but it corresponded to no recognised sociological specialism, and the number of people with sufficient interest to attend regularly was not enough to justify its continuance. In contrast to this, the Theory group in its various incarnations has always had a substantial constituency and, despite a number of organisational lacunae, has held meetings over the years which could be seen as tracking the course of development of aspects of sociology in Britain. In its first incarnation as 'Theoretical and Comparative' it showed a markedly cross-disciplinary approach, with papers in the 1950s on 'Mechanics of small groups' and 'The concept of system in the context of physics, biology and social studies'; it is not clear whether this broad approach reflected the shortage of sociologists at the time, or what they found interesting and relevant; cybernetics and organisation theory figure quite largely. In addition to such papers, however, there were others by such continuing luminaries as Norbert Elias, Zygmunt Bauman, Ernest Gellner and Talcott Parsons. It faded in the early 1960s, and when it was revived in 1965–6 the opening papers were of what is now a more conventional character: Percy Cohen on 'The status and use of sociological theory', Gianfranco Poggi on 'Dominant and recessive themes in sociological analysis' and Martin Albrow on 'The concept of rationality in social theory'. Information on the next period is scant, but the annual report to the 1987 AGM claimed regular meetings for ten years, with a 'general policy to keep both one eye on current debates within the discipline (i.e. "what is in the air" in theory) and another on the longer-term tradition of sociology and sociological theory in particular'. In 1986, the group's largest meeting ever, with 126 participants, was held on Feminist Theory, and there was another on postmodernism; the following year, there were meetings on the body and on globalisation. International contacts were strong and, in 1985, a meeting on 'Contemporary Sociology in Germany' had a number of German speakers. In the later 1980s, it looks as though the Weber study group took over the theoretical banner, though a book of papers from a conference came out (Lassman, 1988), but the Theory group was revived once again in 1991, and in recent years has held meetings on Risk Theory, Cultural Politics and Citizenship, and Social Theory. By 2000, the group had a website and an e-mail discussion list.

An area of controversy has been the relationship of the groups to the central BSA, which has regarded them as what they formally are – subgroups within the Association, which provide appropriate activities for its members. One way in which this has been shown is in the expectation that study groups should hold meetings at the annual conference, whatever else they do at other times. In the first conferences, the study groups had a role as part of the main programme, but the practice developed of having a slot in which they could meet which was aside from the main programme. They have frequently met at the conference, though the policy that all should do so at every conference was not successful, because attendance was poor when the theme of a conference did not appeal to that group's constituency. A number of study groups have been organised jointly with other bodies, outside the BSA. Political Sociology was joint with the PSA, Sociology of Development and Urban Poverty and the Labour Process were joint with the Development Studies Association, and Sports and Games/Leisure and Recreation with the Leisure Studies Association; there may have been others. Other study groups too have had many members who would not identify primarily as sociologists. Such groups inevitably pull outwards from the central BSA, intellectually and sometimes also organisationally; this can be regarded either as an undermining of the discipline, or as creditable outreach and interdisciplinarity. (One participant in the Medical Sociology group remarked that 'We have a lot of discussion of what counts as medical sociology rather than social medicine.')

The question of how to treat people interested in a study group who are not members of the BSA has caused problems from time to time. Some of these are members of other disciplines, or practitioners rather than academics, and as such they have been reluctant to take full BSA membership. (Some study groups have made a membership charge to non-members of the BSA, but not all have done so.) But should the BSA support and subsidise the interests of non-members? From an organisational point of view, clearly it should not, but some study group convenors have taken another view, either on ideological grounds or because of the character of their constituency. For the ideological side, a letter was sent to a meeting of study group convenors, held in April 1976, which expressed hostility to the 'elitist' proposal to charge BSA non-members for admission to study groups, and also suggested that

> It is rather sordid to raise the matter of funds at an academic meeting, and somewhat embarrassing. Perhaps all group convenors should be fitted out with a bus conductor's punch and a small ticket machine ...
> (Schlesinger, 1976)

That was a relatively extreme view, though its political tone fitted the temper of the times. Many convenors would probably not have regarded it as unreasonable that study group participants should in one way or another pay for what they received but, if they were lawyers, physical educationists or nurses, they might well have shared interests with some BSA members but not wish to join themselves because they had parallel affiliations elsewhere. The organisational problem this creates is a continuing one, shared for instance by the ISA in relation to its 'research committees'.

Journals

The first journal of the BSA was *Sociology*, which started publication in 1967. It was felt by the Teachers' Section that in the BJS and the SR 'there was not enough controversial material, discussions and criticisms, and the journals were not doing all they could to stimulate communication among sociologists' (EC minutes, 21 February1964), and so a delegation had met Donald MacRae, then editor of BJS, who proposed offering up to four pages per issue to the BSA for news items.[10] The BSA EC was not pleased that this initiative had been taken by the Teachers' Section, but followed it up with further discussions, initially about modes of association with BJS. MacRae proposed that the Association should have up to four pages, and the subscription should be combined with its membership. This was, however, rejected; the EC felt that it would only be acceptable if the journal were the official one of the BSA, which appointed the editor and had a majority on the editorial board. At this point, serious development of proposals for the BSA's own journal started.

Was the imputation that the other journals were uncritical justified? Not wholly. If we look at their 1966 issues, before *Sociology* could have affected them, it is amusing to find one article attacking the person who had put to the EC the Teachers' Section view that there was not enough criticism (Dunning and Hopper, 1966) with a reply from him, and another by him, in which he attacked the ideas of others (Goldthorpe, 1966). Extending the analysis to 1967 and 1968, we find in SR several articles with titles including such phrases as 'a critique' (Coulson et al., 1967) and 'myth' (Fenton, 1968), which their content justifies, as well as a review which says that 'It is scarcely possible, in a short review, to demonstrate the distortion which Stark's assertive generalisations create ... ' (Wilson, 1967), and some similarly critical articles, with several rejoinders, in BJS. This does not seem a picture of a situation lacking in critical interchange, even if more might have been better.

How far were the original ideas for the new journal implemented in practice? In 1967, and for some years from then, both BJS and SR had a standard content of nothing but conventional articles, book reviews and lists of books received; *Sociology* too naturally provided all of these. To start with it also had a 'News and Notes' section, which lasted only from 1967 to 1972; this relied mainly on the submission of information from departments, and the news was generally about the departments rather than the BSA's activities, so in that sense it was not specifically a BSA journal. (BJS had had a few 'Current Notes' when it started – at the period when the BSA was entirely run from the LSE, and BJS was to some extent treated as if it were a BSA journal – but these had gone by 1960.) There were some systematically critical articles (e.g. Brown, 1967; Giddens, 1968) and, from the second issue on, rejoinders and critical notes begin to appear, perhaps in greater quantity than in the other journals – but the difference does not seem very great, and I would hesitate to conclude that there was in practice a clear difference between *Sociology* and the other journals in their type of content, though there may have been in its style or quality. (Michael Banton, the first editor, says now that he would have been happy to publish critical comments on articles if they had been submitted.)

The absence of very marked differences is less surprising given the first editor's report that 'I decided not to write an editorial for the first number, because the only thing I could have said would be "we will publish the best stuff we can get"'. Thirty years later, he did not recall having received from the EC any advice about the kind of journal they hoped for (Banton, 1997). However, he emphasised that 'I was clear that it should be the journal of the association. I did enquire in university departments about who wanted to review, and I think the reviewing was distributed without any favouritism.' There were only just enough submissions to sustain three numbers per year, which helps to explain why several articles on mathematical sociology were published at a time when they found acceptance elsewhere difficult. There was, thus, only limited scope for any editor to give the journal a distinctive character. It was, though, a national rather than a departmental journal.

In 1973, Peter Worsley wrote an 'open letter' to the EC in which he expressed dissatisfaction with the intellectual state of the journal, arguing that so far it has been run 'on Adam Smith lines ... i.e. it takes the best of what people put on to the market', while to be effective it should 'grapple with and represent the major contending theoretical styles in the discipline'. What should be sought is 'an orientation to encouraging and looking for work which is both of high quality and theoretically informed, and good as research, too ... '; the implication is perhaps that there has been too much empirical research which does not show those qualities, while it is explicitly regretted that Marxism, ethnomethodology, symbolic interactionism and the ideas of the National Deviancy Symposium have not been represented. The foundation of *Economy and Society*[11] is seen as an implicit criticism of *Sociology* (Worsley, 1973). Is this fair comment? Maybe. But journal editors are always to some extent at the mercy of their potential contributors. There have been repeated attempts by editors to invite a wider range of contributions, and to deny any prejudice against particular types of work:

> *Sociology hopes to express the diversity as well as the development* [of British sociology] *and ... will be happy to consider for publication not only reports of finished research but also more speculative contributions to debate and controversy in all areas of sociological inquiry.*
> (September 1976)

> *Our only policy on selection is that the papers selected should be good of their kind. We hope to reflect all the diversity of current sociology, and an effort is made to choose referees sympathetic to the style of work of each paper. We would like to encourage the submission of work in all fields or styles, whether or not they have typically been represented in our past issues.*
> (November 1986)

In 1978, the gesture was made of making the first issue a special one devoted to papers from 'a single tradition in the discipline', that of ethnomethodological studies of practical reasoning and natural language use, implicitly to demonstrate such openness; it was pointed out that the special issue had not been conceived in advance but planned on the basis of papers independently submitted. (But perhaps some readers would see a hint of what critics had accused the journal of in the comment that the empirical studies reported were 'a constructive and promising sequel to the earlier, more programmatic approaches ... '). Morgan and Stanley (1993: 18–21) – after covering some of the significant debates in British sociology which have been carried out mainly in the pages of *Sociology* – point out four which have *not*, and three of those, on race, health and postmodernism, have more specialist journals which have taken the lead there. They add that one reason for the absence of postmodernism may be the (ill-founded) perception that *Sociology* is mainly concerned with 'empirically-grounded discussions'. There has clearly been a belief in the British sociological community, well founded or not, that *Sociology* is committed to positivistic empirical work, and any such belief inevitably works as a self-fulfilling prophecy.

'Departmental' is not actually a very good description of the other two journals at the time when *Sociology* was founded, despite the fact that BJS was the LSE's journal, while SR, which originated as the Institute of Sociology's journal, was now run from Keele. The BJS editorial board for years included anthropologists, and its contract specified that it could publish articles on social psychology, social philosophy, social administration and social history too; this represented the Ginsberg conception of sociology. The SR board represented

Keele rather than Keele sociology, which is not very surprising when we recall how few sociologists there were at Keele then. (In the 1950s, it had been edited by an economist; in 1967, its editor was sociologist W. M. Williams of Swansea.) Its composition, however, could also be seen as reflecting the old Institute of Sociology conception of the field, and the recurring presence of geographers seems still related to Geddes' long-ago interests.

Another feature of the editorial boards is perhaps equally significant in its symbolism: BJS's was clearly the old guard, the senior members of the LSE staff, while *Sociology*'s was, although relatively senior, a younger generation – and (initially) picked by the editor to represent not an institution, but major areas of specialisation in the discipline. Both BJS and SR have moved over time to become more exclusively sociological, and to include significant representation from other institutions, so that their boards in the 1990s look more as though their members have been recruited for their expertise.

A further point on which one might anticipate some difference between the BSA's journal and others was conformity to its policy on gender issues, so we review some points where those could arise. By February 1980, the guidelines for contributors to the journal drew attention to the BSA's policy of opposition to sexism, and the code of practice on how to avoid it. It might be expected that there would have been a higher proportion of articles by women in *Sociology* than in the other comparable journals – and there was, but apparently only for a brief period. Table 9 shows that in 1977, when the BSA had just started its serious emphasis on feminist concerns, there was a drop in the proportion of women among the other journals' authors, in parallel with a marked increase in *Sociology*; it seems plausible to suggest that women chose to submit their papers there instead of elsewhere. Soon, however, there was no clear difference, and, indeed, *Sociology* appears to do slightly worse than the others. It is not surprising that the climate in the BSA should influence other journals too.[12]

Table 9 Proportion of women authors (%)

	BJS	SR	BJS+SR	*Sociology*
1967[a]	16	26	23	11
1972	13	22	16	17
1977	15	9	11	39
1982	15	15	15	14
1987	16	23	19	28
1992	21	50	35	31
1997	32	46	39	27

[a]All tabular data on Sociology are taken at five-year intervals, starting in the year of its first issue.
The count here is of authors, not papers. Short 'comments', 'replies', obituaries and review articles have been omitted, but longer similar items which look more like conventional articles are included. It should be noted that a fair sprinkling of the authors are not British.

The BSA policy of gender egalitarianism has been explicitly applied to editorial boards, and Table 10 shows how this started to take effect in the later 1970s. For the other journals too, the proportion of women has risen since then, but the rise started earlier for *Sociology* and the figures have remained higher. Since 1982, the proportion of men on the editorial board has been somewhat less than their proportion of BSA members; this would, of course, be an automatic arithmetical consequence of aiming for gender equality on the board when the numbers in the membership are not even, though the actual split has in the latest years favoured women rather than merely giving them equality. Conversely, journals whose boards are departmental or institutional are more likely, when there is a higher proportion of men in the relevant group of staff, to be forced by the arithmetical constraints of the situation to have more men whatever their gender policy may be.

Editorial teams are recruited now always for a period of three years, and are based in one institution, which is expected to provide some support. (In the 1998 Annual Report, concern was expressed at the increasing difficulty of getting such institutional support as teaching release or the use of dedicated equipment.) The teams have consisted of one or two editors, one or two book review editors, and an editorial assistant to run the office. The editors are appointed by the EC. Initially, this appears to have been done by simply approaching individuals who seemed suitable, in an intermediate period having a search committee chaired by the chair of the Editorial Board. More recently, the procedure has become more open; bids for the editorship are invited, and the choice made from among the bids by a search committee. It is now conventional for there to be joint male and female editors.[13] (For a list of editors' names and institutions, see Table A2 in the Appendix.) Their institutional bases have reflected the general patterns of change in higher education: initially, not very large or well-established departments, then more established ones at old universities; from the 1980s, an alternation of old and first-generation new universities; in the 1990s, the first second-generation new universities (former polytechnics).

Sociology has increased markedly in size over its life-span, as Table 11 shows. It had three issues per year until 1980, when the number became four; there has also been the very occasional special issue. The numbers of articles

Table 10 Gender composition of editorial boards: proportion female (%)

	BJS	SR	*Sociology*
1967[a]	11	–	8
1972	11	–	–
1977	10	17	33
1982	–	18	41
1987	–	42	50
1992	31	39	56
1997	29	27	58

[a]*In earlier issues of BJS and Sociology, a distinction was made between 'editorial board' members and 'editorial advisers'; the two are combined here.*

have risen correspondingly; the proportion contributed by *Sociology* to the total number of articles in British general journals has risen to c.40% in the 1990s. Since 1984, the financial situation has allowed it to be given as a free benefit to full members and, since 1985, it has permitted reproduction of its articles for teaching purposes without charge, so that it has made an additional contribution to the diffusion of knowledge. It celebrated its 25th anniversary with a book showing how it had contributed to significant debates in British sociology over the years (Morgan and Stanley, 1993). It is now very much an established journal: in 2000, it ranked eighth among sociology journals in the world listed by the *Social Sciences Citation Index* (SSCI) for its citation 'impact', well ahead of both BJS (36th) and SR (20th).

Twenty years after *Sociology* started, the Association started its second journal,[14] *Work, Employment and Society* (WES), in 1987. This was the product of lengthy discussions about the appropriate topic area for a second journal and its financial viability; the eventual topic area is one which was both of considerable interest with new developments in it, and where there is a constituency beyond academic sociologists. Its editorial manifesto declared that it would be concerned with 'work' broadly defined, and not confined to the social relations of employment; feminist work has shown the need for this. It would welcome contributors from outside sociology, with other disciplinary affiliations; the need to assert a distinct disciplinary identity for sociology is no longer as great as when *Sociology* was founded. It also encouraged a comparative focus, and planned a regular feature on current societal trends in its field. WES rapidly became successful. By the end of 1990, only about 20% of the papers submitted were being accepted; by 2000, its impact factor ranking by the SSCI was 26th among world sociology journals. A particularly notable feature is that it has held several WES conferences, of which the first was in 1989; their success indicates that there is a real intellectual community in which the journal plays a meaningful role. In 1996, it became available free to members as an alternative to *Sociology*.

More recently still, a third journal of a different kind has been started: *Sociological Research Online* came on line in 1996. For this, the BSA formed a consortium with the universities of Surrey and Stirling and Sage Publications, which made a successful bid to the JISC/eLib [Electronic Libraries] project for funding to support its setting up. It is an electronic journal, which takes full advantage of the opportunities that the technology offers. Papers are submitted

Table 11 Number of pages in Sociology

Year	Average number per year
1967–9	392
1970–4	491
1975–9	581
1980–4	644
1985–9	677
1990–4	821
1995–9	855

and refereed by e-mail, and can be published almost as soon as they are accepted, because the medium has no costs for extra 'pages'; the latter feature, combined with an emphasis on swift refereeing, makes it very popular with authors. It maintains a website which offers more than just the text of the journal; its 'Pinboard' provides notices of events, the opportunity to submit queries and requests for advice, reports on conferences attended, letters to the editor, and a World Wide Web directory. Its editorial manifesto says that it 'publishes high quality applied sociology, focussing on theoretical, empirical and methodological discussions which engage with current political, cultural and intellectual topics and debates'. Its 'applied sociology' is considerably more wide ranging that what often goes under that title. A special feature has been 'rapid response' features on issues in the news, addressed by a number of invited contributors; these have included, for example, ones on genocide, terror, violence and war in relation to events in Kosovo, on the genetic modification of food, and on land reform in South Africa. This too has had a considerable success. In 1998, it won the Charlesworth Group Award for Electronic Journals, and it has successfully bridged the transition period from the first three years – when the subsidy enabled it to be available free – to the need to charge for access.

Books

The BSA has been responsible for books as well as journals, and not only those based on conference papers. In 1972, a series called 'Studies in Sociology', edited by Anthony Giddens, started; the aim was to produce short books on 'major problems and issues' which made 'original contributions to areas of current debate or controversy'. The first was by Giddens on *Politics and Sociology in the Thought of Max Weber* (1972), and the second by Michael Mulkay on *The Social Process of Innovation* (1972). This series continued for a number of years, and included some volumes, such as Barry Hindess' *The Use of Official Statistics in Sociology* (1973), Steven Lukes' *Power* (1974) and Michael Mann's *Consciousness and Action among the Western Working Class* (1973), which had a very considerable impact. Other books of a different kind were produced around the same period: Margaret Stacey's collection *Comparability in Social Research* (1969), and Betty Gittus' collection *Key Variables in Social Research* (1972). These stemmed from a BSA Working Party on the Comparability of Data, set up to meet the perceived need, at a time of proliferation of empirical work, to encourage theoretical relevance and greater definitional uniformity so that research could be more genuinely cumulative. These were followed up later, to update and extend discussion, by Bob Burgess' *Key Variables in Social Investigation* (1986). A third kind of publication was aimed at other aspects of the professional role: a register of postgraduate theses in progress, a sourcebook on *Sociology Without Sexism*, the report on Joe Banks and David Webb's work on sociology graduates ('Ideas or People … ', 1977). More recently, there is the new series 'Sociology for a Changing World': this has included such books as Heidensohn's *Crime and Society* (1989), Webster's *Science, Technology and Society* (1992) and Solomos and Back's *Racism and Society* (1996), with the general remit of focusing on key recent changes and reviewing major developments in contemporary sociology, using comparative material to set debates in an international perspective. One book aimed at sixth-formers was published (Burgess, 1989); this was intended to promote sociology by giving a taste of the richness and excitement of sociological research to supplement the usual textbook approach. The Association also gave financial support to the production of a handbook edited by Chris Middleton on *Teaching Sociology*, this time aimed at teaching in higher education. Not all the ideas for books or series were successful, however; one plan, for the publication of theses, fell through when the publisher reneged. That was perhaps an instance where the BSA view of what would be professionally desirable did not chime with publishers' views of what would be commercially successful; other worthy ideas were also floated which did not result in eventual production. Nonetheless, it is clear that the books which have appeared have not merely been well received in themselves, but have often met disciplinary needs in a timely way.

Most recently, the BSA has taken an important step to combat the trend among commercial publishers to be interested only in textbooks. It has supported the establishment of SociologyPress, a non-profit enterprise whose aim is to publish monographs and edited collections in sociology which are chosen on intellectual rather than commercial criteria. It is hoped that it may in time publish for and sell to the international as well as the British sociological community. At the time of writing, the first books have appeared, but it is too soon to evaluate its success. However, it certainly offers a solution to the widely felt problem of the lack of book outlets for work not aimed mainly at students.

We have shown how the BSA has played a variety of roles in the intellectual life of British sociology, attempting to make provision at levels ranging from the A-level student or first-year undergraduate upwards. It has influenced developments both by taking direct action itself, and by affecting the general climate of opinion. It has reflected intellectual trends in its meetings and publications, and has also helped to diffuse and form them. As well as responding to requests and proposals from members, the Association has taken responsibility for the diagnosis of collective needs and has attempted to meet them. The manner in which these things have been done has taken the colouring of the general styles, intellectual and political, of the consecutive periods and, here as elsewhere, we can trace the influence of wider trends in the profession such as expansion beyond London, and the impact of the women's movement.

Notes

1   Summer schools are not dealt with in this chapter because they have been intended as a training activity, and have not purported to present new intellectual contributions. However, each has had a theme and, in a number of cases, they have brought together young people who have entered the profession and for whom the intellectual networks formed at a summer school have been of continuing importance.

2   For a sort of manifesto for this important group, see Cohen (1971).

3   See Chapter 6 for much more on this. Allen and Leonard (1996) provide a useful discussion of the ways in which the agenda has changed from the first to the latest of these conferences.

4   The 'study group' format has occasionally been used as a way of incorporating a group as part of the BSA which is not in the usual sense a study group; this device has been used for the Women's Caucus and also for some regional or occupationally specialised groupings. These groups are not dealt with in this section.

5   Almost all the speakers at the first meetings of this very active group, convened by S. Andreski, were of foreign origin, which perhaps says something about the intellectual situation of British sociology at the time.

6   There is some specific evidence that British women were inspired by discussions, especially with US feminists, at the 1970 World Congress.

7   Another possibility would be that, since 1973, there has been a national Research Seminar on Social Stratification, initially funded by the SSRC, and this has met the needs of workers in that field while remaining independent of the BSA.

8   This was founded in 1940 – and, curiously by modern standards, Morris Ginsberg was its first chairman.

9   The group on Sport had a somewhat similar start. The suggestion to set it up came from the Senior Inspector of Physical Education of the Inner London Education Authority, who was a member of the analogous ISA research committee.

10   He also mentioned that the great majority of papers submitted to it came from the USA or India, and speculated that the reason for receiving so few submissions from British sociologists ('especially from outlying areas'!) was that people were under the impression that they would not be accepted.

11   Its first issue had appeared in 1972. Its editorial manifesto declared that 'All the social sciences are in a state of crisis', seen as arising from the dominance of empiricist conceptions, and committed the journal to work on 'theoretically grounded research problems relating to whole societies.' The editorial group was one of young sociologists on the left.

12   It should be noted that, although the proportion of women looks low, it does not compare unfavourably with the proportion of women in university sociology – and in 1977 in *Sociology* much exceeded that. Of course 'university' women are not and have never been the only women active in sociological work and writing, and there may have been a somewhat higher proportion of women in other fields which in principle are part of the relevant base with which to compare these figures. However, the relatively low representation of women cannot reasonably be interpreted as an indicator of discrimination against them in journal processes.

13   This pattern was initiated by me (JP), rather than originating as a policy decision; I asked to recruit a colleague (who happened to be male) to supplement my intellectual range, and was allowed a deputy. A male/female team was very much in tune with general BSA policy and, since then, the post has been fully joint, with any division of labour to be agreed between the two holders, although a single editor remains formally acceptable.

14   Meanwhile the newsletter *Network* had been started and, although not in the conventional sense a journal, it has at times carried extensive book reviews as well as other discussion of intellectual issues of the day.

Chapter 5
Membership and activists

This chapter is about the BSA membership: who joins, and how this has changed over time. Plainly, membership is not regarded as a professional necessity, even on a less formal basis that that of associations such as the BPS, where it is required for certification to practise, so some description and explanation is called for. After an account of the general membership, we go on to consider those members who play an active role, in particular the members of the executive.

How many members?

There is continual fluctuation in the number of current members. The best available figures for the review of trends are those presented in annual reports, though we do not know how those were compiled or whether that has been done on a consistent basis, and these have been used in Table 12; they usually refer to the end of the previous calendar year. However, we can see that practice in details of reporting has changed over the years; gaps in the figures represent the absence of the information required in the relevant report. We distinguish here only between student members and other members. Membership categories have changed in various ways over time, some of them mentioned in Chapter 2.

Some of the variations over time reflect changes in numbers in the discipline, while some probably reflect the popularity of particular conference topics and locations. The large rise in membership in the 1960s and the first half of the 1970s follows the growth of university staff numbers though, interestingly, the marked drop in numbers in the 1980s was not followed by a corresponding drop in membership. The growth in student membership in a very broad sense follows the enormous growth in numbers of graduate students in the 1970s and early 1980s (Platt, 2000), but it does not correspond closely to the detailed changes, so it is clear that other factors were also involved. By no means all members have, however, been sociologists, at least in any narrow sense of the word; the number of non-student members has always been considerably greater than the numbers of teachers of sociology at British universities, the only list of professional sociologists with which we can compare them.[1] (However, there has regularly been a noticeable contingent of members from academic sociology overseas, although their proportion has not been high enough to make a major difference to the figures.) In the early period, when the office compiled occupational data on members, this showed that, by October 1951, more than half held jobs outside universities or social research, the largest contingent coming from 'social services and public administration'; the 1960 list, not quantitatively analysed, conveys a similar impression. The largest single rise in membership was in the year of the Sexual Divisions conference, perhaps reflecting the significance then of the women's movement outside as well as inside specifically sociological circles. Disciplinary composition of the membership from universities was also broad, but has probably become narrower over time. Data presented in the Annual Report to the 1999 AGM show that, by 1998, the overwhelming majority of members were from universities: 55% from 'old' universities, 24% from 'new' universities, and 6% from universities overseas; the 6% in other specified forms of employment came from health, government, voluntary organisations, research institutes, freelance work, schools and further education.

Table 12 BSA membership as reported to AGMs

Year of AGM	Full members	Student members	Total members	Year of AGM	Full members	Student members	Total members
1952			400	1977	1,087	273	1,360
1953			408	1978	1,075	329	1,404
1954			432	1979	1,083	412	1,495
1955	458	12	470	1980			1,525
1956	478	20	498	1981			1,364
1957	498	52	550	1982	1,079	252	1,331
1958	495	50	545	1983	1,134	266	1,400
1959			522	1984	1,411	83	1,494
1960	504	31	535	1985	1,551	89	1,647[a]
1961	516	31	547	1986			1,568
1962	536	89	625	1987			1,545
1963	577	83	660	1988			1,723
1964	604	92	696	1989			1,869
1965		127		1990			1,900
1966	695	102	797	1991			
1,967	702	98	800	1992			[2,000+]
1968	867	134	1,001	1993			[2,000+]
1969	978	165	1,143	1994			c.2,300
1970			1,184	1995			2,600
1971	1,228	186	1,414	1996			2,586
1972	1,209	169	1,384[a]	1997			2,513
1973	1,273	177	1,450	1998			2,216 [b]
1974	1,326	142	1,468	1999			2,411
1975	1,499	222	1,721	2000			2,379
1976	1,445	347	1,792				

[a]The attentive reader will have noted that the figures for 1972 and 1985 do not add up correctly; they are, however, those given in the written reports to the AGMs – and the discrepancy is small.
[b]No figures were actually given in this year's report, probably because a change in the subcommittee structure dealing with membership meant that the responsibility was in transition when it was compiled; the figure given here is the one provided for 1997 in the 1999 report.

We need to bear in mind, though, that even constant numbers can be consistent with changing social characteristics of the membership. Table 13 looks at this from the point of view of membership among those listed in the CUYB. Professors have consistently had a higher rate of membership than their juniors over the whole period,[2] for whatever reasons.

The large drop in membership in 1976 followed the raising of subscriptions and the introduction of an income-related scale. It is widely believed that the drop was particularly marked among the most senior members, for whom the new scale more than trebled their subscription rate. Indeed 85% of professors of sociology were members in 1973,[3] while the proportion had dropped to 61% in 1976 and remained close to that level in the 1980s. But there was a comparable sharp drop in membership among non-professors over the same period, which suggests that we should look at the matter in more detail. Table 14 compares the membership of individuals before and after the rise, among those listed in the CUYB at both dates.[4] We see that it is indeed true that a relatively high proportion of professors who were members in 1973 had ceased to be members in 1977 – but so had quite high proportions of their colleagues at lower levels, with more than half of those who had left by 1977 coming from the lowest-paid group, the lecturers, which suggests that factors specific to the members whose subscriptions had been raised the most were not the only ones

Table 13 Rates of BSA membership among sociologists listed in the CUYB (%)

Year	Professors	Others	All
1960	90	60	64
1964	100	70	73
1972	85	56	60
1976	61	34	37
1981	63	33	36
1987	59	40	42
1997	65	47	50

Table 14 BSA membership among 1972 and 1976 CUYB sociologists, 1973 and 1977

Year	Rank[a] Professors	Readers and senior lecturers	Lecturers and assistant lecturers	All groups
% Membership 1973 and 1977	53	46	25	34
% Membership neither year	8	27	39	31
% Membership 1973 but not 1977	34	24	28	28
% Membership 1977 but not 1973	6	3	7	7
N	53	59	175	287

[a]Where the person's rank changed between 1972 and 1976, the rank used here is the one in 1976, since that is presumed to be the one relevant to the 1976 decision.

that were relevant. However, it is understandable that more public impact was made by the withdrawal of a relatively small number of the more prominent members of the discipline, even if more than 60% of those in senior posts did not change their membership status.

Not all of those who resigned did so on financial grounds. It is noted that five of those who left were on the staff at the LSE, where there had been tremendous political divisions in this period over many matters connected with student unrest, including the Blackburn 'affair'. One of the LSE professors says that he resigned under the impression that the LSE had in consequence been blacklisted by the BSA – which it had not; there is probably an understandable confusion here with the Atkinson 'affair'. But he may well have been correct in perceiving disagreement between the politics dominant in the BSA and his own position. The personal reasons of others at the LSE are not known, but could also have been connected with the events of the time. But of the eight non-professors present at the LSE at both dates who were members in 1972, four were no longer members in 1976, so again perhaps rank was not crucial. The proportion of members in the LSE department fell from 76% in 1972 to 35% in 1976. (One of its former junior members remarked 'when we found the BSA was a little out of control, we just got in a huff and considered ourselves above it ... Insofar as anyone at the LSE had a feeling for it, it was that there should be one great centre and they would be it, with the Polys round their feet; they never came to terms with places like Essex.') Another of the professorial resignations was that of Julius Gould, and that was in direct response to the BSA's summons before its Ethics Committee. (On these events, see Chapter 7.)

Some informative comments were made in interviews[5] about the reasons for ceasing to belong, or to participate actively, around this period.

Two of the early professors mentioned reasons to do with the general expansion:

> *I felt a commitment to the BSA, and I would have continued going to conferences and the like if I'd had the opportunity, but things got hectic ... I went to a few BSA annual conferences, but they weren't the same as the Teachers' Section, they got big, there weren't so many of my friends there, it was not so enjoyable.*

> *Once people are established and have got chairs, they stop coming to the BSA. When you're young you want to meet people, to make personal connections with people who might get you a job ... Turned off by women, some might have been, but most men of my generation stopped going once they got chairs and didn't need the slave market etc – and they were preoccupied with their own departments. Jesus Christ, the initial explosion of sociology was horrendous ...*

On the other hand, reasons of a more ideological character were also mentioned, from varying standpoints, and these shade over into more intellectual reasons:

the older generation's distaste for the student rebellion tone of the '60s even when they were on the Left ... I suppose that disenchantment with the late 1960s radicalism spread into the sentiments of the senior generation of sociologists. The withdrawal of many of the senior generation from the BSA had something to do with that; they saw radicalism as not easily compatible with a proper academic neutrality.

It's the taking it over by what are essentially political interest groups, feminist, Marxist or whatever, which is wrong.

One of the second generation of professors thought that senior people were intimidated by the 'professionalism' favoured by the younger generation:

I can't imagine the GMC or the Law Society leaving it to junior chaps from say Scunthorpe helped out say by someone from Crewe to run it. There's no reason why the BSA should be like those bodies, but that was what they said they wanted it to be.

A younger person who had been active in the BSA, but gave it up, says that this was because it was not concerned with promoting high standards, unlike the Royal Economic Society, a properly elitist learned society.

However, a member of a younger cohort made the obvious riposte to some of the political objections:

What they said was that it was all becoming too political, it was no longer a serious academic thing, all about politics ... – I guess that was a lot of old blokes not wanting to share their power.

Taking a right-wing political stance has not necessarily led to withdrawal. A continuing member, clearly on the right politically, remarked that

It seems to me that the BSA has been the major vehicle for a social struggle between two groups (only loosely left and right) – those who seek for social knowledge a mission to change the world (and who failing would make our discipline a heretical cult on the margins of society), and those, including me, who seek a mission merely of understanding ... (if we fail, sociology becomes mere research technics).

We are in no position to evaluate the accuracy of the alternative views and interpretations – and see no reason to believe that incompatible explanations may not each have been true for some of those involved, or even both part of the truth for some persons. However, it seems clear that there was a shift in the temper of the times with which some were unhappy and, with whatever justice, associated with the BSA.

But there is a considerable flow of members in and out, even when there is not some major event such as the move to income-related subscriptions, or political turmoil. Some of this is probably due to pure carelessness. (An annual routine on the EC has been the circulation of a list of those who had not renewed their subscriptions, so that EC members could chase up those whom they knew. It was also frequently reported that people failed to change their payments when rates changed.) Some is due to people joining only for individual conferences, perhaps especially likely to be done by students, members of other disciplines and overseas visitors – that is, those who are more marginal in relation to the continuing discipline in Britain. Among mainstream professional sociologists, some have been faithful long-term members, some have left for specific reasons, some have joined late, and others have never been really involved. It is, therefore, worth looking at the continuity of membership over a longer time span. Among those on the CUYB lists, people who appear there for at least three consecutive dates have been classified as BSA members 'always', 'sometimes' or 'never'.[6] Exactly a quarter of them had been members 'always', and 49% 'sometimes'. In the 'sometimes' category are many individuals who were members in 1972 but not in 1976 and have never rejoined; this was a cohort loss which, given the size of the cohort and the extent to which its members have remained in the discipline (on which see Platt, 2000), goes a long way to account for the relatively low total membership through to the 1990s. However, the sample covered also shows a number of longstanding university teachers who had joined for the first time by 1997, so the upturn has not been produced only by the entry of new members of the discipline. It is probably safe to assume that those who remain members for relatively long periods are the mainstay of associational activity.

In contrast to some of the comments cited above, it is appropriate also to look at some of what was said by those interviewees explaining what BSA membership meant to them, and why they joined and did not resign:

- *... when I became a university lecturer in 1972 I just joined because that seemed the sort of thing you ought to do.*

- *... more or less out of a sense of it was there and that was what I did for a living, an automatic thing like joining a trade union.*

- *... she felt as department chairman that it was improper to say you should belong, but one was left under no illusion that one should ...*

- *I didn't ever consciously join the BSA, I had gone to* [university] *to work with* [sociologist active in BSA] *and he said 'I've given your name to Anne Dix' and that's how I came to join!*

- *A lot of people in* [university] *were active in BSA, it was the sort of thing you do because other people do.*

- *It's hard to be a sociologist without belonging to the BSA, even though a lot of people succeed in doing that ... If people say to me what do you do and I say I'm a sociologist, one of the ways I can prove it is that I'm a member of the BSA; I just feel that I belong to its collective.*

- *What you noticed about the conferences in London was that generally just I would turn up, and* [two other London people] *– but they'd all come from the Outer Hebrides, it was important to them to meet their fellows.*

It will be noted that these remarks are far from politically ideological in tone, although some of those giving them have been politically active both within the BSA and outside it; the overwhelming impression is one of a sense of belonging to a social unit where membership of the BSA is simply appropriate, and that not joining would be more of a gesture than joining. Obviously, that view was not universally shared.

Who has belonged to the BSA?

So far we have been mainly concerned with the total number of members and its determinants, but we need also to look more closely at the social characteristics of those who have been members, and how those compare with the characteristics of non-members. Our ability to deal with this is limited by the uneven quantity and quality of the available data, discussed in the Note on Sources, but they allow some points of interest to be brought out.

Gender has been an important issue within the BSA, so the sex ratios of BSA membership over time, and how those relate to the sex ratios in the wider discipline, are of significance. Table 15 shows the sex ratios among BSA members. (The membership lists pose some problems for counting gender, though they are the best source we have.) We see from it that the proportions of men and women among members had until recently remained perhaps surprisingly constant. But the 1997 figures show men clearly in the minority for the first time. The last column allows comparison with the gender ratio of university sociology, and shows that the BSA's non-student membership has always had a higher proportion of women than there have been among university sociologists. This could reflect the significance of women among those who are not university sociologists, or it could reflect the greater propensity of the women among those to join. Table 16 suggests that the former factor made a larger contribution in the earlier period, though the latter became more important later. Initially, a higher proportion of the men in university sociology than of the women belonged but, after the 1960s, the tendency was for a slightly higher proportion of the women to join. A great turn-around took place between 1964 and 1972, with women's membership proportion rising while men's fell. Perhaps this was at least in part due to the declining proportion of women listed in joint departments who were not 'really' sociologists and so gave a misleading impression of the real base, in which women were equally or more likely than men to join? However, between 1972 and 1976, women's participation fell in parallel with that of men while, after 1976, it recovered somewhat faster. By 1997, though, the participation rate of women was again well ahead of that of men – though this apparent shift may be primarily due to the inclusion in the CUYB for the first time of the staff of the former polytechnics rather than to any actual change in members. Some caution is needed in interpreting these figures as being about gender dynamics, when the apparent changes may owe as much in reality to questions of definition.

An interesting possibility to explore would be the role of social influence in the department in determining rates of membership, which would give a truly sociological explanation. Unfortunately, many departments have been too small for much of the time for a departmental 'rate' to have much meaning. However, some figures have been compiled for the larger departments; Table 17 shows the results for those which had at least eight members of staff listed.

Table 15 Sex of BSA membership

| Year | % BSA membership male | | % University sociologists male | |
	Students	Non-students	All members	CUYB list
1956	71	63	63	85
1960	59	65	64	79
1966	57	73	71	75
1973			74	84
1977	55	71/71[a]	67/68[a]	81
1982	41	65	61	81
1988			62	79
1997			46	71

[a]The first figure given above treats all those with initials only in the Register [see Notes on Sources] on whom there is not independent information as of unknown sex and excludes them; the second figure includes them and assumes that only 70% of those remaining unidentified were men. (If all the unidentified were men, there would be 82% male.)

Table 16 Among sociologists listed in the CUYB, the proportions of men and of women who were BSA members

Year	Men (%)	Women (%)
1960	70	33
1964	82	43
1972	59	64
1976	37	35
1981	34	43
1987	41	44
1997	49	58

Table 17 Proportion of departments with at least eight sociologists where at least half of those listed were BSA members

Year	Yes	N
1960	[2]	3
1964	[5]	5
1972	74%	19
1976	31%	29
1981	18%	34
1987	32%	31
1997	61%	38

The pronounced curve shown here broadly follows the pattern of individual membership (shown in Table 12), perhaps implying that the department as such did not add as much to individual motives as one might have anticipated. Some departments have certainly had much higher membership rates than others, but it is not very evident why this should be so.[7] But there have been some notable differences between departments in more active participation, discussed below.

'The whole idea of the democratisation of the BSA as opposed to a meeting of top scholars, which was what Ginsberg had in mind – if you do that and the subject's expanding it's bound to happen that all sorts of people will come forward that you've never heard of. In those days it was very much people known to one another, and now it's so much larger it's bound to be different.'
(Banks, 1996)

BSA membership might reasonably be regarded as an indicator of the social integration of the discipline. In that sense, it is not surprising that its more senior (and presumably on average older) members have had higher rates of BSA membership, or that at the period when there was rapid and large expansion, with the recruitment of many young people with little background in sociology to teach it, the general membership rates should have fallen. The exceptionally high membership rates in the earliest period both reflect and help to account for the extent to which, when the community was a very small one, everyone tended to know everyone else. ('It was a club almost, a network.') Some colleagues have suggested that this also relates to what turned out to be a temporary phase in which there was a high level of intellectual consensus on the proper content of sociology, especially associated with those active in the Teachers' Section, which was rapidly broken up by the new movements of the later 1960s and the 1970s. Some, however, offered intellectual developments as a reason for declining interest in the BSA. I asked one interviewee why he had become less active in the BSA, and the response was:

> When Economy and Society *took off from 1972 there was the whole meetings and activities around that, which drew me and some other people away from mainstream sociology, and then I started working much more in area studies ... work which has a more interdisciplinary focus ... and so I became more active in professional associations to do with that.*

Other people have moved their main activity into specialist associations in such areas as criminology or health. The 1970s saw so many different potential reasons for a drop in membership that one cannot pick out any one of them as the key; the 1980s saw not only a more stable profession but also the evident need to rally to its defence against 'the cuts', while the 1990s were less dramatic and more pragmatic.

The activists

Members can play an active role within the BSA in a wide range of ways: organising a study group; being a departmental representative;[8] editing *Network*; belonging to an editorial board or editing a journal; directing or tutoring on a summer school; putting motions to the AGM; taking part in a conference organisation team; undertaking research on behalf of the BSA; being a member of the EC etc. It is clear that those who get drawn into one kind of activity are more likely to get drawn into another, whether because they become known to those who are searching for promising recruits or because the initial activity makes BSA matters more salient to them. It is not practicable to compile material on all modes of BSA activity, so we concentrate here on membership of the EC,[9] and consider how people have been recruited to it and what their characteristics have been.

At some stages there were contested elections though, in more recent times, these have become rare, and occasionally the number of members has been made up by co-option when not enough candidates were nominated. Perhaps the contested elections were not always very real; a 1950s member of the EC remarked that 'it was manoeuvred, you were told to vote for a few people'. The later 1960s and early 1970s were a period of real contests; in 1969, for instance, 315 voters chose among three candidates for president and 15 candidates for EC membership.[10] A leading EC member at that period said 'there was always some kind of competition; we endeavoured, we would ring round to get more candidates. You didn't need to do much arm-twisting.' For some time now, any arm-twisting has been less effective, and there have seldom been contested elections; in effect, though not constitutionally, the EC has often nominated its own successors. The only group outside the EC which is known to have actively put forward candidates for it is the Women's Caucus; the level of activity there has varied from year to year, but it does something to account for the proportion of women, and in particular of active feminists (see Chapter 6). However, the head of at least one polytechnic department encouraged its members to involve themselves in BSA activity as part of a general campaign to make themselves better known on the national scene, despite an unhelpful geographical location, and it has made a valuable contribution to the BSA's affairs: 'I always felt I had an obligation to link my faculty and university to people and organisations. As a sociologist ... it was easiest to start in sociology with something like the BSA' – and so he did. There may have been more such cases. Personal networks have also inevitably figured in the identification of potential members, though this should not be seen as corrupt; indeed, it has probably made an important contribution to the recruitment of younger members, and members from outside higher education, who would not otherwise have become involved.

Elections have never directly chosen the working officers, who are appointed by the EC itself from among those elected; those chosen have normally served a period as an ordinary member of the EC and become known as useful committee members, and for a long time there has been the practice of appointing people as assistant officers with the expectation that they will succeed to the main office after this period of induction. A few instances are known where relatively senior people were invited to stand for ordinary EC membership on the understanding that they would be nominated for offices to which they were thought well suited (because of their administrative records) in the following year. The post of treasurer has sometimes been hard to fill, so active recruitment and even direct co-option have been necessary. In the 1980s, one of the few specific duties of the president (presumed not to be a potential candidate) was to identify candidates for office, making informal consultations among the current EC members, so that the formal election at the EC meeting after the new year's EC elections required little time and no voting. More recently, this system, which seemed quite effective but was hardly consistent with democratic theory, has been discarded and replaced by one where nominations are made and voted on within the EC.

Who has taken part?

The pattern of participation has certainly changed over time, as the tables below demonstrate. The first executives had a distinctive pattern, consisting almost entirely of professors, numbers of whom did not hold appointments in sociology (Table 18). The presence of a handful of members of other academic disciplines to represent the wider social-scientific community continued through the 1950s; in the early 1960s, there was still the occasional anthropologist or social administrator, but then this representation died away.

Membership was in due course relatively proletarianised, showing a steady decline in the proportion of professors from the 1950s to the earlier 1980s; this may have owed as much to decisions by the more senior as it did to a revolutionary take-over:

Table 18 EC membership (presidents omitted) by rank (%)

	Professor	Reader/senior lecturer[a]	Professor	Other[b]	N
1951–5	73	6	8	12	64
1956–60	43	19	25	10	65
1961–5	42	19	25	0	65
1966–70	31	24	36	4	70
1971–5	31	35	19	11	70
1976–80	20	33	41	0	70
1981–5	11	44	36	3	70
1986–90	26	49	19	3	70
1991–5	29	46	17	9	70
1996–2000	46	26	19	9	69

[a]Included here are people occupying senior positions not clearly professorial, such as director of a research unit.
Polytechnic ranks have been treated as equivalent to university ones, though they were not used in quite the same way.
[b]This includes everyone outside academic life.

In the period 1980–4 when I was on it a lot of us were junior, there were very few senior people around, if you were lucky one or two professors, most of us were lecturers; I remember one senior person once commented on this, and [junior colleague] and I were very irritated ... why weren't those senior people around, and of course one reason was that there was not a large number of professors who were members of the BSA, or active members.

However, even when the proportion of lecturers had gone up markedly, those with senior posts have remained in the majority and, since the later 1980s, the proportion of professors has risen again.

Table 19 shows a marked discontinuity in average ages between the 1960s and the 1970s, which reflects neither the emergence of Teachers' Section members to centre stage (which happened earlier) nor the withdrawal of the professoriate or the rise in the proportion of women (which happened later). Perhaps it owes something to the youth emphasis of the student movement starting in the late 1960s, although youthful revolutionaries are not themselves evident among the EC members of the period, combined with the general youth of their newest teachers at this time of maximum expansion.

Gender changes do, however, clearly owe something to the other revolution of the times: an important shift followed the ground-breaking Sexual Divisions conference, the setting up of the Women's Caucus and the start of explicit equal-opportunities policies in the Association. But there was another striking rise in the proportion of women in the middle 1980s, for which no such easy explanation is evident.

Comparison of Table 20 with the data in Table 15 on the gender of non-student members of the Association reveals a striking pattern: until 1975, the EC was more masculine than the general non-student membership; in the second half of the 1970s and the early 1980s, women were represented on the EC in proportion to their prominence in the general membership – and then they became in their turn markedly over-represented, until the drop in the male proportion of the general membership brought the figures back into line.

In a break in the proceedings of an EC meeting in the later '80s, a group of women found themselves together in the cloakroom, and as we washed our hands and combed our hair we chatted about the business in progress. One remarked how pleasing a reversal of tradition it was that a group of *women* should be sewing things up privately in the toilets.

Another important shift in the social character of the EC has been the increasing prominence of people employed in the (former) polytechnics. Table 21 shows the rising numbers of terms served by polytechnic/former-polytechnic teachers, who in the early 1990s indeed became a majority of the EC's members. All the working offices have been held by members of this group, though none has yet acted as president.

It is helpful in understanding patterns of participation to think of it not just in terms of snapshots of individual characteristics at different times, but of BSA careers. The earliest BSA careers, at the stage when the Association was

Table 19 Average age of EC members (at 5-year intervals)

Year	Age
1951	51
1956	47
1961	47
1966	46
1971	40
1976	40
1981	41
1986	41
1991	48
1996	50

[a]Age was calculated by subtracting year of birth from the starting date of the term of EC membership, so it is not precisely accurate.

Table 20 Sex of EC members

Year	% Male
1951–5	91
1956–60	90
1961–5	86
1966–70	87
1971–5	83
1976–80	67
1981–5	63
1986–90	44
1991–5	43
1996–2000	47

Table 21 EC membership-years from (former) polytechnics

Years	EC membership-years
1951–5	0
1956–60	0
1961–5	0
1966–70	4
1971–5	8
1976–80	12
1981–5	8
1986–90	18
1991–5	33
1996–2000	19

preoccupied with its legitimation and institutionalisation, appear to have relied largely on seniority and imputed representative status in the academic community generally. Very soon, however, younger people who took a special interest in the BSA as such started to emerge and to find ways to become involved, and more specifically BSA-related career patterns developed; the increasing diversification of BSA activities helped in this. A full BSA activist career could not more recently be described only in terms of EC membership, though; it might start with study group membership and conference attendance, go on to editorial board membership or tutoring at a summer school, and take in some subcommittee service before finally culminating in joining the EC. There has been a penumbra of ex officio memberships of the EC, or invitations to its meetings to report or as an observer, which means that many people have some experience of it before joining the elected membership, and this familiarisation and establishment of contacts assists an easy transition to full membership. The substructure has been sufficiently elaborated for it to have been possible to make a career mainly concerned, for example, with publications, or with gender issues intellectual and political. A hypothetical typology of BSA careers might include Dr Intellectual, who gives papers when the conference is directly relevant to his research, runs a study group and belongs to an editorial board, but never bothers to vote or takes on purely administrative tasks, counterposed to Dr Politico, who attends the conference regularly mainly to go to the AGM (the mark of the true BSA hack) and organise her mates to support her motions there, holds committee positions sought with a view to promoting external agendas (maybe feminist), always votes in elections, and presses for BSA interventions on issues of academic freedom or the politics of national and international academic life. (Mr Passive, of course, drops in and out of membership depending on the accident of conference topic and whether he remembers to renew his subscription, and does nothing besides attending the conference occasionally, while Ms Sue Peractive gives papers regularly, acts as departmental representative, has organised a conference and tutored in a summer school, has belonged to several subcommittees and writes regularly for *Network*.)

Some people have had only short EC careers, while others have followed the pattern of working their way up from rank and file member and going through the offices. A conventional sequence would be member/secretary or treasurer/chairperson, and 11 of the chairpersons have followed this pattern; another ten substituted the vice-chair for secretary/treasurer in the sequence. Until 1968, presidents were drawn from the most senior members of the current executive; since then they have normally come in from outside the current EC, but have had longstanding previous membership of it, or have participated in BSA activities in other ways.[11] Of the 18 presidents, seven had previously been chairperson, two had been vice-chair, two secretary, one treasurer and one just an EC member; a further three had edited a BSA journal. The remaining two (Bottomore and Hall) had played other prominent roles in the sociological community and were longstanding BSA members. Seventeen were professors by the time they became president.

How have people become drawn into the sphere of the EC? The interviews with activists can throw some further light on this. Some careerism may have been involved, but was certainly not necessarily present, although BSA work may have come to play a role in the shaping of their wider occupational careers. Repeatedly, people explained how they became involved by saying that someone who was already active got in touch and asked them to stand and, rather than mentioning any personal motives, they suggested why that might have been. The reasons proposed ranged from 'the word had got round that I had some ability to manage an operation' to 'I was suing the university [for sex discrimination] about not getting promoted ... and that somehow made me visible' [and potentially an appropriate member of the Equality of the Sexes (EoS) Committee]. The latter case led in due course to the main EC. Another less direct mode of recruitment was shown in the case of someone who first got involved through the Scottish branch, where the system of departmental representation led to him drawing the short straw to act as his department's representative because he was its youngest member.

One of the few people to mention a personal motive without anyone else taking the initiative was a woman from the polytechnic world, who became drawn in at a later career stage:

> I suppose I became more and more interested in the wider political world in which sociology operated ... as I occupied more and more senior positions ... It was only about the '80s, having been quite a visible figure in CNAA circles, I thought I should be more involved in the BSA. I did it through the Equality of the Sexes committee. At their first conference on women and research they were proselytising for people to become more involved in the committee, and I thought, why not?

Becoming an officer might be assumed to be more actively intentional, but it does not always seem to have been so; one secretary from the 1970s remarked:

> They can never find anyone, it was like the Army, you 'volunteer'! I recall that at my grammar school, a teacher said to me we need a bassoonist, and you're it ...

Another, who took on the office at an early career stage, said:

> I got on the EC, and I became secretary simply because there was no-one else who would do that! ... I remember making an outburst on the executive that there should be senior members of the profession who would do this job ...

He has made a career in academia which has included heavy administrative responsibilities in both university and trade union, and perhaps that accidental start may have helped to set him on that route. Two treasurers accounted for their assumption of the role by the fact that they had 'a bit of business experience' and 'I've never minded figures, they're not threatening or intimidating to me, it's never been a problem to me'. A vice-chairman suggested that his immediate accession to that rank was 'because all the business meetings took place in London, and most other members were a long way away; when representative functions were performed it tended to be in London, so they wanted somebody in London'.

The people who became committee members and officers often say that they took pleasure in that sort of activity and found it interesting, but the picture given by their accounts of their experience is, thus, one where in practice the system relied heavily on talent-spotting rather than on candidates putting themselves forward and, although some of them will have won an election, on something resembling informal co-option as a mode of recruitment. I did not interview defeated candidates, and it is possible that their stories would be different.

What has the role of departments been in contributing members to the EC? There is no doubt that departments have varied very considerably in their involvement. Departments which have had at least three different people on the EC for a number of years (consecutively or with only one-year breaks) are shown in Table 22.

There is nothing surprising in finding that, initially, the largest departments and a smaller one in London figure, then that the first 'new' universities appear and in the most recent period the polytechnics/former polytechnics, but the pattern does not simply follow that of changes in higher education. (In the earliest period there was much more continuity of membership, which means that the same individuals made a very large contribution of years. Some individuals have moved department several times and taken their BSA activism with them; those cases suggest that personal character may have been at least equally important.) An obvious hypothesis would be that those departments

Table 22 Departments with at least three different (near-)consecutive EC members

Year	Location
1951–64	Bedford
1951–70	Liverpool
1951–70	LSE[a]
1953–68	Birmingham
1965–77	Manchester
1966–74	Leicester
1967–76	Durham
1970–85	Bradford
1973–81	Glasgow
1974–85	Lancaster
1976–86	Warwick
1985–93	Cardiff
1986–95	Plymouth
1989–97	South Bank
1994–2001	Surrey

[a]Not all of these years strictly belong to the departments of sociology; numbers of LSE members came from the departments of anthropology or social studies, and four of the Lancaster years were served by Janet Finch, whose post was in the department of social administration.

with a higher density of BSA membership were the more prominent on the EC; we can explore this using the data on those with at least eight members. Tables 23 and 24 show what we find once the 1960s, when there were so few such departments that their numerical dominance made their prominence almost inevitable, are over.

Only from the later 1980s does it look, from the two tables taken together, as though the departments with higher proportions of BSA members were really more likely to have any EC members. (Some large differences are made to the figures in Table 24 by single departments – nine member-years from Lancaster for 1980–2, and five for 1975–7 – which makes them less meaningful.) The overall impression is, thus, that there were some departmental differences greater than could be accounted for by size alone, but that the factors on which we have material do not throw a lot of light on why that should be so. Another plausible hypothesis could be in terms of networks: the first recruit in a department may occur at random from the point of view of departmental character, but once present is likely to draw in colleagues who seem useful and interested, so that the departmental contribution lasts until those colleagues have served their time.

Departmental ethnographies would probably be needed to understand fully the processes involved. However, for the LSE we do have a level of knowledge approaching what that would provide. For the first ten years, about a third of the EC's membership came from the LSE (not always from the sociology department), and about half of all members of the LSE sociology staff in 1955

Table 23 In departments of at least eight, the number providing at least one EC member/year[a]

Year	<50% BSA members	50%+ BSA members
1972	3 (of 5)	4 (of 14)
1976	7 (of 20)	3 (of 9)
1981	8 (of 28)	2 (of 5)
1987	3 (of 21)	7 (of 10)
1997	3 (of 15)	10 (of 23)

Table 24 In departments of at least eight, the average number of EC member-years provided[a]

Year	<50% BSA members	50%+ BSA members
1972	1.6	0.57
1976	0.79	1.0
1981	0.75	2.0
1987	0.29	1.5
1997	0.40	0.96

[a]Member-years are counted for the years before and after the date given (which is a year for which CUYB data have been compiled) as well as for that year.

and 1960 had been on the EC. This was due not simply to the LSE's special role, but at that period there was an extreme concentration of BSA members in London and, in addition, transport time and costs meant that it was common for the London members to be given key policy roles because it was so much easier for them to meet. As the LSE's relative prominence sank, there was some resentment of new departments coming to prominence, as well as the conflicts of the period of student unrest described above. The result was that the LSE representation faded away through the 1960s and, although it has remained quite a large department, its only appearance after that until the present day has been for three person-years in the late 1970s.

Another way of characterising departments would be in terms of their academic status. Simpson and Simpson (1994) argue that the participation in office of 'top' departments is an important indicator of associational character, and see the decline of this over time, which they chart for the ASA, as showing a move away from a scholarly society dominated by a disciplinary elite to a professional association of organised subgroups. In Britain, there was not the kind of public ranking of departments widely accepted in the USA until the Research Assessment Exercise and its immediate predecessors started, so it is only from then that we can generate relevant data. When that is done, it is immediately evident that departments from the research elite were far from dominant in BSA offices in the period covered.[12]

The size and character of the total membership have been determined by the fluctuating tides of academic demography, intersecting with gender factors and with particular historical events, some of which have been internal to the BSA and some of which have involved BSA reactions to external developments. The meaning of what it is to be a sociologist has changed over time, but identification as a sociologist – whatever one's departmental location – must also have encouraged membership, while membership must surely also have encouraged such identification. But there has always been a flow of movement in and out of the Association, as some people join for short-term motives or feel only a weak disciplinary tie. This has meant that the Association cannot absolutely count on the level of commitment it needs to work effectively, and so has always felt the need to make efforts to attract and maintain membership; see Chapter 8 for some of the ways in which this has been discussed. The Association has provided many different modes of participation, and these have been open to a wide range of members. In particular, the EC has been more representative of the whole range of the membership than has that of some other associations, despite – or perhaps because of? – the frequent lack of competitive elections. In so far as this has indicated a situation in which the discipline's intellectual elite, or elite by rank, participate relatively little, some people have seen that as weakening the Association. However, the extent to which such a situation has held has often been exaggerated, and others would see that price as one worth paying for greater openness and democracy.

Notes

1   Despite several efforts to distinguish between professional sociologists and others, these never came to anything, and membership has always been extremely open, though the sponsorship of an existing member has been asked for. A routine item of EC business has been the approval of applications for membership, but it is unlikely that for most of the time this was more than a formality. However, in my own experience there were two bases for actual discussion of applications, when the applicant was not obviously a sociologist or with a sociological sponsor: the first was a speculation that they were seeking to use BSA membership as some kind of certification or claim to prestige, and the second that they might be right-wing spies seeking to discredit sociology. (The latter obviously relates to the period when there were politicised public attacks on sociology.) Since there have been no formal qualifications required for admission to the BSA, to base a claim to status on it could only be done to audiences who are unaware of this, and it would seem a little odd to join in order to 'spy' when so much of the activity (conferences, publications) has been open to non-members. In the nature of the cases, specific evidence was not available on such points and, in the event, it was almost unheard of for an application actually to be rejected.

2   This 'finding' may owe something to the often clearer disciplinary identification given for professors; especially in the earliest period, the necessity of counting as sociologists some departmental members who almost certainly really had primary affiliations with social work or other disciplines must to some extent have led to a distorted impression.

3   But a subcommittee in 1972 already diagnosed the situation as one where there was 'an alienation of these "tribal elders" who in other professional bodies would be involved in such activities as membership of SSRC and CNAA committees as the appropriate representatives of the body of the practitioners of the discipline, considered as a corporate entity' [EC 15 December 1972, Doc. B. item 11].

4   In principle it would be methodologically appropriate to compare these data with a 'normal' rate of turnover at such an interval, but the levels of change and general turmoil around that time were such that history moved too fast for the concept of normality to seem applicable.

5   Although those interviewed are not at all a cross-section of ordinary members, they represent positions which some members have taken – and are often reporting on earlier career stages when they were 'ordinary' members. But it would make no sense to quantify any aspect of these data, and the material should be read merely as examples.

6   'Sometimes' cannot be misleading, since it remains true whatever happened on the dates on which there is no information; but 'always' and 'never' can mislead because the data cover only times at intervals of several years, and it would be possible for individuals to drop into or out of the association within that interval without it showing in the data. The lack of a membership register for 1992 created a problem. The working assumption was made that, if someone was a member before and after, then they could be deemed to have been a member in 1992; if, however, 1992 was the third date in a sequence of only three that was so ambiguous that the cases were not counted.

7   It is perhaps worth mentioning that only five of the 11 departments with eight or more members ranked 2, 3a or 3b in the 1996 Research Assessment Exercise had a membership rate in 1997 of 50% or more, while the figure for the 22 of them ranked 4, 5 or 5* was 73%. That would, however, support two different lines of interpretation about the direction of causation: BSA participation improves your research by keeping you in touch, etc. – or strong departments are more inclined to participate, have more research to report on at conferences, etc. On the other hand, one informant remarked of Leicester in the 1980s that: 'There was the assumption that the department was above that kind of thing, it had so long been a centre of sociology.'

8   The system of departmental representatives was started in 1975, as part of the new
     Development Officer's proposals for increasing membership and improving the
     distribution of information about BSA activities.

9   Within the EC, we also concentrate on the members who are in principle elected. That
     is, the sometimes considerable periphery of ex officio members and invited observers
     (journal editors, EoS Committee representatives, *Network* editor, BSA Scotland
     representative, summer school organisers, conference team representatives …) is
     ignored.

10   That was the most 'political' period in the history of British sociology. It is interesting
     that, despite developments in its larger society, the American Sociological Association
     seems to have maintained the tradition of politicised contests into the 1990s; Lipset
     (1994: 215) points out that this made it more politicised than other comparable social-
     science associations.

11   This means that they do not normally have the problems which can arise when
     presidents are elected on general honorific grounds without previous active experience –
     on which see Faris (1981: 51).

12   The rank data used came from the UGC research rankings of 1986 ('outstanding'), and
     the UGC Research Assessment Exercise rankings of 1992 and 1996 (5 or 5*), and the EC
     members from the years 1985–6, 1986–7 and 1987–8, 1991–2, 1992–3 and 1993–4, and
     1995–6, 1996–7 and 1997–8 respectively. (Three years were used, rather than just one,
     to give a larger number of cases.) Of the person-years of officership covered, the top
     rankings accounted for two, none and two of the 15 in each period. If the categorisation
     made by the 1989 UGC Review as a department with a 'distinctive research training
     tradition' is used, that category – which does not overlap as much as one might have
     expected with the top RAE grades – gives four person-years for the 15 officerships for
     1987–8, 1988–9 and 1989–90.

     A limitation of these data is that, except for the last period, the then polytechnics were
     not covered in the rankings; those would, however, have been unlikely to be ranked in
     the top research category. In addition, some university departments do not appear in the
     sociology listings, probably usually because they were joint departments which had been
     submitted under another head.

Chapter 6

'For women only'?[1]

The women's movement has played a sufficiently important role in the BSA's affairs to justify a chapter focused on gender issues. The chapter title quotes the message which for a number of years appeared at the head of each issue of the *Women's Caucus Newsletter* (WCN);[2] this raises one of the themes on which there have been controversy and changing positions over the years. Other chapters have mentioned gender aspects of their topics. This chapter is not merely about gender differences within the BSA, but about gender politics and its influence, especially as represented by the Women's Caucus. Relevant aspects of the wider women's movement will be referred to briefly as a very important context for developments within the BSA, but no attempt will be made here to give any general historical account of it; that task is left to others.

The origin of the Women's Caucus

Although there was no active feminist movement within sociology at an earlier stage, at least some of the women trying to make academic careers had reason to become sensitive to feminist issues:

> When I started in sociology as a career [in the early 1950s] *there was an awful lot of hostility to women, really a lot.* [A male colleague] *took me on one side and said 'You'll be much happier if you give up the idea of a career and stay at home and have a family'; in those days, I wasn't going to do any such thing, but I didn't punch him on the nose ... I didn't want to be a battleaxe in those days – now I'd like to be! It was still half in and half out in those days; it was accepted that women just had to fit in, and must not raise gender issues.*

The Caucus was founded in 1974, at the Sexual Divisions and Society conference. It seems possible that if that conference topic had not been initiated, more or less accidentally as far as deliberate policy-making by the BSA was concerned, the Caucus or an equivalent group specific to the BSA might only have emerged later, or even not at all. The conference topic originally planned had been 'Europe', relating to Britain's 1973 entry into the Common Market, with Margaret Archer as the organiser. But it was felt that the topic required a number of speakers from Europe, and the BSA could not afford their expenses and did not succeed in getting funding from elsewhere. This theme was, therefore, abandoned, and the EC's discussion of alternative themes resulted in the choice of the family, on which there had not been any previous conference. Sheila Allen, another EC member, was asked to organise this, and agreed on condition that she could recruit help and do it her way. She recruited Diana Barker [now Diana Leonard], who was then secretary of the Family study group, and their joint work eventually resulted in the metamorphosis of the topic into Sexual

Divisions, a title reflecting ideas becoming current in the women's liberation movement in which they were both involved.

They made a special effort to increase the numbers of women present and giving papers, which was not easy given their minority status in academia at the time, and in order to achieve this they had advertised in the feminist press, and had tried to draw in women from related disciplines and from outside academia, while keeping the conference sociological in character. These efforts had some success, and obviously made it likely that a larger proportion of the attendance than usual would be feminists. However, an analysis of the delegate list[3] suggests that the differences were not as striking as has sometimes been suggested. Women were only 46% of those listed.[4] Only 11 of the total names came from Britain outside higher education and other categories of normal attender.[5] Of that 11, two can be identified as men and three as women. That suggests a maximum of nine women who might have been feminists from outside academia and social research. But it was certainly true that a much higher proportion than usual of those who gave papers were women; excluding plenary sessions, they were 59% at the 1974 conference, as compared with 17% for 1973 and 7% for 1975; that, as well as the topics of the papers, must have contributed to the special atmosphere of this conference.

The formation of the Caucus appears to have been a spontaneous response among women attending the conference, though one may wonder whether a few activists might not have come with the idea already in mind of organising something. It was not a move which came completely out of the blue, although there had been no earlier public feminist activity within the BSA. The women's liberation movement was by then in full swing internationally, and in Britain a first Women's Liberation conference had been held at Ruskin College Oxford in 1970. The shared demands stated as a result of this were for equal pay for equal work, equal opportunities and education, free contraception and abortion on demand, and free 24-hour child care (Bouchier, 1983: 94). (In 1974, two more demands were added, for legal and financial independence for all women and an end to discrimination against lesbians, and in 1978 one for freedom from the threat of violence or sexual aggression.) These demands were not the property of any central organising body and did not bind anyone, but they suggest main areas of concern. The developing movement contained many different strands, and some cleavages and conflicts.

A Women's Caucus had been operating in the American Sociological Association since 1969;[6] 'caucus' was an American concept. As one of those involved in the BSA remarked, 'We didn't know any other word really; I mean you couldn't call it a cell'.[7] Some women members of the BSA were active in the wider women's liberation movement, and a few had discussed these matters with American women at the ISA World Congress of Sociology in Bulgaria in 1970. (Others among the older members had had career experience[8] and grievances that had led them to formulate views which then were not yet called 'feminist', though soon they would be.) But it would be a little misleading to see the founding of the BSA Caucus as arising simply from a movement among women in sociology. The women present and involved in the first foundation of the Caucus were not only academic sociologists; a few were from outside academia, and some from other disciplines. (It is not possible to distinguish those from other disciplines on the attendance list, which gives only name and institution. One of those present at the early meetings suggests that the level of hostility to the BSA was in part due to the presence of women who were not really engaged with sociology, and so did not think first in terms of working within it.) The meeting at which the Caucus was founded was called by a few women who simply put up a notice inviting all women present at the conference to a meeting; a large proportion are said to have taken up the invitation. At the founding meeting, two motions were also drafted for the AGM, and both were passed. The first set up a subcommittee to enquire into the position of women in the sociology profession,[9] while the second set up another subcommittee to enquire into the coverage of social relations associated with sex and gender within sociology and social policy courses in British higher education. The formation of the Caucus was announced formally to the BSA after the conference; the first issue of *Network*, in January 1975, reported that the Caucus had already established regional groups and produced four issues of a newsletter, and that a meeting at the 1975 conference would discuss 'possible formalisation of the group structure and future activities'. A related BSA study group on Sexual Divisions and Society had also been formed. These activities were effectively part of the wider movement and some of the more academic developments within it. A Women's Research and Resources Centre was set up in London in 1975, and academic journals were beginning to appear; women sociologists were involved in these activities (and many others) as well as those inside the BSA.

The Working Party on the Position of Women in the Profession had six members, three women and three men, only Keith Kelsall being a current member of the EC. (At least one more woman had been invited to join, but appears not to have done so.) The Working Party on Social Relations associated with Sex and Gender in Sociology and Social Policy courses in British HE had five members, three women[10] and two men, again with only one current member of the EC. (But by the 1975 EC, the working party members were more heavily represented; Sheila Allen became president, Margaret Stacey vice-chair, and Hilary Rose a member.) Both working parties were set up for one year in the first instance.

The Working Party on the Position of Women in the Profession put forward recommendations to the 1975 AGM, which were referred to the EC for 'urgent consideration'. Bitter arguments at the AGM over the need to consider women's problems at all were reported (Elston, 1976: 3). The recommendations were that:

(i) *'The BSA should ask sociologists to eliminate all enquiries, both overt and covert, relating to the applicant's personal life, particularly marital status and child care, when interviewing potential students or staff.*

(ii) *Sociology department heads should be asked to review their staffing position and if they find a sex imbalance, they should consider how this came about. Particularly, they are asked to review their appointing and promotion policies.*

> *(iii)   The BSA should encourage systematic research into the position of women in general and in the profession in particular.*
>
> *(iv)   The EC should seek appropriate machinery to ensure that close attention continues to be paid to research, and action taken to eliminate the present inequalities between men and women sociologists.'*

The EC agreed to accept the recommendations, and to circulate the report to the membership. In addition, the president would sign a letter in the name of the Working Party, drawing attention to the recommendations, which would be sent to heads of departments (who were not necessarily members). It is evident that the nature of the recommendations, which address the profession at large rather than the BSA's own activity, was such that there was little or no more direct action that it could take.

The Working Party on Social Relations Associated with Sex and Gender in Sociology and Social Policy courses in British Higher Education reported in 1975 on data it had collected on exam questions at 15 universities. This concluded that the topic of sexual divisions was very much under-represented, and that, where there were related questions, they were on a narrow front, and usually really about women rather than sexual divisions. The questions which did appear were unevenly distributed across papers, and often absent from very relevant contexts. Another, broader report was supposed to have been produced for 1976, but I have been unable to trace a copy or summary of it. (See below for a 1985 attempt to address similar issues about the curriculum.)

At the 1976 AGM, both Working Parties recommended that they be dissolved, and that an EC subcommittee should be established with the remit:

> *(a)   to investigate and to advise the BSA on policies which contribute towards equality of access to and equal treatment of women sociologists within the profession*
>
> *(b)   to investigate and to advise the BSA on making recommendations for teaching and research in sociology which contribute positively towards the position of women in sociology*
>
> *(c)   to investigate in conjunction with the Professional Ethics Committee complaints alleging discrimination against women and allied matters.*

This recommendation was approved, and the EoS was set up. The EC had also accepted the recommendation that the subcommittee should have members at least half of whom should be women, and that it should have at least two members in common with the Professional Ethics Committee.[11] Its first members were five women – two nominated by the Caucus as regional representatives – and three men. (Over time, its size has increased, but its membership since 1977 has been overwhelmingly female, usually with only one male member at a time.) For most of its history, membership has in principle been by election by the BSA membership; in practice, here as in other BSA subcommittees, it has often been problematic to find enough candidates, so the election process has played little real role in its composition.

The mandate they set themselves at their first meeting was defined as 'to investigate and advise the BSA on policies which contribute towards the equality of access to, and equal treatment of, women sociologists within the profession; to advise the BSA on making recommendations for non-sexist teaching and research in sociology and which contribute positively towards the position of women in society; to investigate, in conjunction with the Professional Ethics Committee complaints alleging discrimination against women and allied matters'. Discrimination against women as a group is taken as well established, but 'We will also deal with the cases of discrimination against individual men, should it ever become a problem' (David and Sharma, 1977). In practice, it has always been concerned with the position of women.

The relationship between the Women's Caucus and the EoS has been such that, despite their formally different statuses in relation to the BSA, they cannot really be discussed separately. The Women's Caucus was for a long time very much concerned to keep at a certain distance from the BSA as an organisation, in order to maintain its independence and a distinctly feminist and exclusively female character – while at the same time demanding recognition and representation on the EoS, and requesting financial support for its activities. A report on the Caucus at the 1976 conference mentions, as a 'thorny issue' raised not for the first time, that of whether Caucus membership should be open only to BSA members. The conclusion was that all women sociologists should be strongly recommended to join the BSA – which implies that it remained open to non-members.[12] The Caucus was given study group status in 1982, so that it could have access to BSA funding on the same basis as study groups. However, the general rule is that study groups are open to all BSA members, so the fact that it was allowed to maintain its policy of admitting women only created an exception. The EoS, on the other hand, has always been a formal subcommittee of the BSA EC, of which its chairperson has been an ex officio member.

The Caucus has not had formal membership, and often operated in a decentralised way, sometimes with regional branches, so firm central lists of who has belonged and what their characteristics were have not been kept, and cannot now be made – if they ever could have been. (In so far as lists were kept, those were regarded as confidential, and guarded closely, because of the perceived potential career risks of being identified as a Caucus member.) Similarly, it has been a matter of feminist principle to operate non-hierarchically, so that official leaders cannot be identified, although named individuals have from time to time become prominent by taking on organisational tasks; some key activities have been carried out by collectives. Minutes have not been kept, though volunteers have sometimes written accounts of its discussions for either the WCN or *Network*. The practice of holding meetings at conferences has meant that attendance has been influenced by the conference topic, making continuity somewhat problematic, and this has been almost as bad in the written documentation. Between the 1970s and the 2000s, there have been many fluctuations in the Caucus' affairs and activities. Regional groups have come and gone, and the WCN has had an interrupted history; one of the problems in establishing continuity has been the heavy reliance on groups of graduate students, who cannot personally own the collective memory, to produce it.[13] As early as 1981, it was suggested at the conference meeting of the Caucus that it had lost its edge through meeting only there (WCN, May 1981), and after that there are recurring complaints of poor attendance and lack of contributions for the WCN. The 1993 issue of the WCN, also mentioned that the Sexual Divisions study group, had been dormant for long enough for the mailing list to be lost. These fluctuations in activity are typical of many voluntary organisations, reflecting the difficulty of maintaining a scattered network without any central office or officers. It is not surprising that the EoS, with a formal structure and back-up from the BSA office, has shown more continuity of activity, even if the character of that has changed.

Organisational features such as these make it hard to document some of the things about its operation which one would like to deal with. However, the EoS has been a relatively conventional committee with membership and minutes, so we can document that more confidently, and it has been one of the main mechanisms through which the Caucus has worked within the BSA. A report from Caucus meetings at the 1976 conference states that 'we decided to use this new committee as our coordinating centre'; volunteers agreed to stand for membership and, if elected, to take responsibility for maintaining contact between the EC and the Caucus and between the regions within the Caucus. What, then, were the activities in which these closely connected groups engaged?

Feminist activity within the BSA

The Caucus has always acted within the BSA on issues which it sees as especially relevant to women, even if not formally about them. Thus one of its earliest activities was to attend the 1974 meeting on reorganisation of the BSA (see Chapter 8 for more on this), and to support a motion there which was seen as having the effect of preventing it being harder for women to be full members of the Association than for men.[14] Similarly, the Caucus supported the 1975 motion for the introduction of income-related subscriptions, on the assumption that women were more likely to be in the lowest income groups. However, the WCN (1982: 6) reported that few women had attended the 1982 AGM (despite their reported strong representation at a conference with a gender theme), and that a new subscription structure seen as unfavourable to women had been passed; it was suggested that, in future, a Caucus discussion should be held before the AGM about the issues coming up. Another matter that was taken up was the financial difficulty of the unwaged and low-paid in getting funding for sociological activities. In response to this concern, felt to be one which affected women more than men because of their more precarious employment position, a 'Support Fund' was set up in 1983, for a trial period of three years, to help maintain participation by those in such positions; this was seen as especially necessary in view of the effects of the cuts. It was administered by the EoS (Annual Report 1983). The Support Fund has in fact continued ever since, and a majority of its users have been women, many of them graduate students (probably not the main group originally envisaged); its prime uses have been for conference attendance, and minor research-related expenses. As an expression of the same concern, a questionnaire was circulated by the EoS on members' availability for part-time work (Annual Report 1989); the resulting Directory was lodged in the BSA office for reference.[15] In the 1990s, somewhat different issues came to the forefront of concern. A very successful conference on 'Writing and Publishing' was held (Annual Report 1997) which led to the production of a booklet of hints and guidance. The issue of part-time and contract work was taken up again, and a workshop on contract research and fixed term contracts was organised at the annual conference (Annual Report 1999). Guidelines on Authorship have been developed, which recommend appropriate ways to attribute authorship of publications in the light of the different kinds of contribution which may have been made to the work; a draft was published in *Network* 78 (2001).

Of course there was also action on many issues that were overtly concerned with women as such. Among other very early activities were the production of a pamphlet in 1975 on 'Equality of Women in the Sociology Profession', the creation of the Sexual Divisions study group, and the proposal of a BSA policy on sex equality. This was put forward by the EoS, and approved by the 1978 AGM. It stated that:

> *It is the policy of the BSA actively to promote the equality of the sexes. To this end all members who are involved in appointing committees or personnel to run, teach, or talk at seminars, conferences, summer schools and the like, are asked to ensure as far as they are able that women and men are equally represented on all such bodies and in all capacities.*

It will be noted that the policy applies in principle both to the BSA's internal affairs and to the activities of its members outside it. The difficulty of using the mechanisms of the BSA to affect events outside its control is a recurring one. (Queries about the theory of this could be raised, too: one man generally sympathetic to feminism rhetorically asked 'were the feminists trying to improve the quality of sociology, or to change the world? I'm all in favour of changing the world, but I'm not convinced that the BSA is a good vehicle for doing that, or that the BSA is even the best place to start'.) Below, we review the extent to which this policy has been effectively implemented internally, and what the consequences have been. Externally, a questionnaire was sent to departments employing sociologists about their representation of women in different categories of staff, and heads of department were asked to comment on a document on non-sexist institutional policies, although few did (Annual Report 1979). Following up the policy, the EoS and the Caucus over the years made representations about the need for more women speakers at conferences and tutors at summer schools, encouraged more women to offer conference papers, put up candidates for the EC and its subcommittees – and urged Caucus members to vote for them. Possible cases of sex discrimination were investigated, and sometimes over the years support was given to women taking legal action against their institutions or pursuing personal cases in other ways. Discussions were initiated with the academic trade unions AUT (Association of University Teachers) and ASTMS (Association of Scientific, Technical and Managerial Staffs); clearly some of these matters could raise questions about which bodies were the appropriate ones to deal with them.

The organiser of the 1975 conference asked me, at a rather late stage, if I would like to give a paper on the convergence thesis, on which I had given a conference paper some years before, from the women's angle. (I replied that I was not aware that there was a women's angle on that, and if there was I didn't think I had it, and did not offer a paper.)

It was clear that novel political necessities had driven him to scrape around for anyone who might count as meeting them and could fit plausibly into the conference as planned. (In the event, female speakers were outnumbered 11:1.)

A number of activities were concerned with employment prospects. An application was made to the Equal Opportunities Commission for a grant to study the impact of the university cuts on equality of employment chances, but this was not successful (Annual Report 1982). In 1982–3, the EoS then, in response to a request from the Caucus, attempted an overview of the current position of women in sociology. This was done by writing to 200 women on the Sexual Divisions study group and Women's Caucus mailing lists. Sixty-five replies were received, 26 from tenured lecturers and only five from the unemployed; a suspicion was voiced, however, that 'many women are in such marginal positions that they are not visible within the BSA' (Annual Report 1983). [The concern within the BSA with unemployed sociologists at this period was by no means confined to women. This presumably reflects the sudden drop in university job chances for those who previously, in the time of expansion which had now suddenly ended, would have seen entering university teaching as a normal transition (Platt, 2000).] The responses showed that these women still felt marginal, feared future unemployment and felt they had to do better than men to be recognised, and that feminists were overworked because of student demand not met by new appointments (EoS Committe, 1983). Much later, a workshop on 'Women in sociology: paths and hurdles to success' was organised at the 1997 annual conference, with prominent woman speakers talking about their own careers. In the early 1990s, work was done on systematic advice to women on how to present an effective curriculum vitae when applying for jobs.

In the late 1970s, issues to do with child care were prominent in the EoS. It urged that higher education institutions make provision for maternity/paternity leave and for child care for their teachers, and asked BSA members to campaign for this locally and in trade unions (David, 1977); the issue of workplace nursery provision became especially salient at the period of financial cuts in universities. As a result of the EoS representations, conference child care was funded by the BSA for the first time in 1977, and there has normally been some crèche provision ever since. Another general feminist issue soon actively raised was that of sexual harassment, as a manifestation of inequality between the sexes. The EoS (30 January 1981) noted that although it wanted to raise the issue it would be wise, in view of the then current TV version of Malcolm Bradbury's *History Man* (1975) to proceed carefully to prevent the attraction of unfavourable publicity for sociology; however, an article about it was published in *Network* (Gamarnikow, 1982). The WCN (1982: 5) reported that the overall response on the issue had been disappointing, although it was felt that this might be due to the novelty of the idea rather than to the absence of harassment. However, EC Guidelines on dealing with sexual harassment at work were produced, and the Annual Report for 1987 was able to say that a statement on sexual harassment had been endorsed, and that the Guidelines were being revised. By the late 1980s, a new focus of interest became the position of black and ethnic minority women, and several activities were organised specifically for them; eventually, this initiative led to the formation of a continuing black women's group.

There was also much feminist action in relation to sociology's intellectual content, in both teaching and research.[16] Table 25 lists some of the main public activities related to gender issues which were organised by the Caucus, the EoS or the BSA as a whole. It will be noted that some of these were for women only (but none for men only), while some of the later ones, even if organised by the EoS, did not have specifically feminine themes.

Table 25 *Caucus/EoS/BSA events and publications on topics related to gender issues (Activities confined to women appear in italics)*

Year	Events and publications
1974	Annual Conference theme: 'Sexual Divisions and Society'
1977	'Sociology without sexism' bibliography produced
1978	Summer school: 'Feminism and sociology'
1980	Guidelines on non-sexist language
1982	Theory study group conference on 'Gender and Social Theory'
1982	Annual Conference theme: 'Gender and Society'
1985	Survey of gender teaching in sociology
	Women and Sociological Research Workshop
1986	Theory study group conference on 'Feminist Theory'
1987	*Women and Sociological Research Workshop*
1988	Theory study group conference on 'Men, Masculinity and Social Theory'
	Women and Sociological Research workshop
1989	*Violence Against Women study group founded*
1990	*Women and Sociological Research workshop*
1994	Annual Conference theme: 'Sexualities in Social Context'
	*Lesbian Studies study group founded**
1997	Writing and Publishing day conference
1999	Writing and Publishing day conference
1999	Workshop at Annual Conference on doing and managing contract research
2001	Authorship Guidelines

[a]Unlike the Violence Against Women group, this does not formally declare that it is open to women only, but it is evident that in practice it is only intended for them. An article on it in Network for March 1997: says that 'these meetings provide a forum for lesbians in academia (staff and students, past and present) to not only meet each other and discuss our work but also to share the trials and tribulations of (being a lesbian in) academic life!'

One of the earliest initiatives was for Caucus members to agree to raise the need to have more papers relevant to sexual divisions in BSA study groups they attended (WCN, 1975: 4). In 1981, data were collected on the content of sociological theory courses, intended to provide a basis for a workshop at the 1982 annual conference, whose theme was 'Gender and Society'.[17] This reflected the feeling that (male) theorists were giving insufficient attention to feminist theory, or to the need to revise 'general' theory to take women into account. Also in 1982, the Theory study group held a conference on 'Gender and Social Theory', but this gave rise to considerable dissatisfaction and controversy – see below. It was probably in response to that that in 1983 the BSA allocated money for a women-only conference on the relationship between feminism and sociological theory, but this does not appear ever to have taken place; it vanishes from the paper record. In 1986, however, the Theory study group held a conference on 'Feminist Theory', organised – because of this and of the dissatisfaction with the predominance in the group of male participants and speakers – by Sue Clegg of the Caucus (WCN, 1986: 22). This attracted a much larger than usual attendance, of 100 women and 26 men. That was followed in 1988 by another Theory group conference on gender issues, this time on 'Men, Masculinity and Social Theory'; this also attracted a large audience, though with a different sex ratio – 45 women and 56 men (WCN, March 1983: 10). It would be interesting to know the extent of the overlap between the audiences at these conferences and others held by the Theory group, but data on that are not available, so it is not clear how far the usual attenders had been persuaded to extend the range of topics in which they were interested.

In 1988, the possibility of a second BSA journal was under discussion, and a gender focus was mooted. The Women's Caucus response to this was somewhat ambivalent, because 'while there is a clear need for more journal space to be devoted to the work of feminist sociologists, a journal in the area of gender studies might inadvertently serve to marginalise this work still further' (Annual Report 1989). If, however, the discussion continued, it felt that the Caucus should be involved. For 1990, the 1991 Annual Report shows that the Caucus expressed concern at the lack of 'a specific stream on gender' at recent conferences,[18] and it was felt to be time for another annual conference focusing on gender issues; the theme 'Sexualities in Social Context' was put forward, and this became the title of the 1994 conference. A series of workshops funded by the BSA on 'Women and Sociological Research', aimed at younger researchers, was held, starting in 1985; much of their content appears to have been directed at women, but not specific to those doing feminist research. These were very well received; the 1990 one had more than 120 participants, with 100 turned away because of pressure on accommodation (Annual Report 1990). Several booklets drawing on these workshops were produced (see, for example, EoS, 1994). In the 1990s, there were workshops on 'Writing and Publishing', and the first of these also led to the production of a booklet (Boyne et al., 1999).

In 1978, *Sociology without Sexism*, 'a sourcebook of non-sexist teaching materials', was published. Guidelines on non-sexist language to be used in *Sociology* were mentioned in its Notes for Contributors from 1980, and by the 1985 Annual Report they had been revised for teaching application and were being distributed. At much the same period, the EoS carried out a survey of teaching on gender. The sample used was not an optimal one for representative purposes as, in the effort to maximise response, 'To improve our chance of obtaining motivated respondents ... [those approached to report on departments] ... were mainly women and generally sociologists with some commitment to equality issues' (McNeil, 1985), drawn from BSA departmental representatives and other female members. Those surveyed reported little general departmental policy on gender issues, and much sense of isolation as feminists. However, McNeil pointed out that the liberal ideology of faculty autonomy, which meant that discussion and assessment of colleagues' courses was discouraged, also meant that feminists were allowed to do their own thing. (A full report on the survey is published in EoS Committee, 1986.)

Controversial issues

Two connected episodes of the early 1980s gave rise to significant controversy among feminists, throwing some light on ideological positions held at that time. The first episode was David Bouchier's writing of a book on the history of the British feminist movement. Many feminists took strong exception to the whole enterprise; he mentions in the book that he was subject to attack, on the ground that academic interest in feminism on the part of men is a form of exploitation, before he had written a word of it (Bouchier, 1983: 170) so, clearly, this was a critique of general principle. He is referred to as notorious in the WCN of October 1982, so it is evident that knowledge of his work in progress had already been diffused. There was anger that he still continued to analyse feminism and the Women's Liberation Movement without full access to documents or feminist political practice; that access was being denied to him, so consequent shortcomings of his work cannot be treated as due merely to his incompetence or lack of effort. The January 1983 WCN reports a meeting at which there was discussion of how to attack Bouchier's work. It was felt there that the central issue was the unwillingness of the women's groups to be studied by Bouchier, and argued that, since the BSA accepted the autonomy of the Women's Movement, for him to do so contravened BSA principles. It was proposed, therefore, to report him to the BSA's Ethics Committee. However, the next WCN reveals that the letter reporting him had not been sent because those responsible for drafting it had found the task impossible, though why that was so is not explained. When the book was out, *Network* (29: 6–7) published a symposium criticising Bouchier both for writing his book at all, and for doing it in ways that feminists did not like; it was seen as '*on* feminism and not *for* feminism'. It is assumed that only someone personally involved could have the correct understanding, and that he did not have the necessary access and rapport. This critique seems more like a rejection of the acceptability of any book by a man on the topic, given that in the book he makes several statements that show considerable sympathy with both the methodological argument and the feminist movement:

> the internal dynamics of groups or the experiences and consciousness
> of women ... are no man's business, and many works are suggested in
> the Further Reading at the end of the book which will give the enquirer a
> different, more intimate and more committed interpretation of the
> meaning of feminism. (Bouchier, 1983: 6)

> The fact, too, that ideas are more personal than political actions, and are
> often developed out of the personal experiences of women, means that
> a man's view of feminist theory must be a view of the surface. Beneath
> that surface are debates and subtleties accessible only to participants.
> (Bouchier, 1983: 89–90)

He justifies his enterprise, however, by arguing that what he did was 'a study of
the *public face* of feminism as a social movement' (Bouchier, 1983: 6), and so
not open to the criticism that he has attempted to deal with issues to which he
could not have access. Not every committed feminist took the same line on
appropriate ways to treat his work, even if she shared the diagnosis of the
problem. One who shared the feeling that a man and an outsider was bound to
give an inaccurate picture nonetheless defended his right to carry out the research,
and maintained that the aim should be to defeat him by argument.

The second episode is the Theory study group's 1982 conference on 'Gender
and Social Theory', at which Bouchier was one of the speakers. The October
1982 issue of the WCN started by criticising it on the ground that the expense
of attendance effectively excluded feminists, and suggested that the absence of
a fares pool, cheap alternative accommodation or a crèche made it difficult for
feminists, especially if unemployed, to attend, and thus made it easy for feminism
to be 'appendaged'. In the next issue, there was a long reply from a feminist
who had played a key organisational role in the conference. She apologised for
some of those organisational features, where she had followed the normal
practice of the Theory study group; however, she pointed out that a whip-
round for the unwaged had been taken among the waged, although few of
them had had their own costs covered by their institutions, and that this had
been sufficient for the travel costs of those who had complained. She added
that she thought more would have been contributed if many people had not felt
that the points in a letter circulated by them at the meeting had been made in an
unpleasantly aggressive manner, and that she shared their unhappiness about
that. Moreover, she thought that two of those who signed the letter had expressed
such anger at Bouchier's work that it made rational discussion of his research
impossible, and that others found this intimidating; she reported that several
women later spoke to her privately about experiences of intimidation by
feminists, and deplores behaviour which gave rise to such complaints. Since
those she criticises did not reply, we can only speculate what they might have
said, but may presume that they regarded their anger and its mode of expression
as justified and appropriate.

The question of what role there was for men in the women's movement, or
in gender studies, was thus a contested one, which also arose in a number of
other contexts. It is reported that some men wanted to attend the Women's
Caucus meeting at the 1975 conference; it is not clear whether this was because
they were fully sympathetic, or wanted to make a point against separatist
activities. At any rate, they were not allowed to take part. One man made a

humorous remark about this in a conference report (Taylor, 1976), and received a non-humorous reply from the Women's Caucus Northern Regional group, pointing out that the Caucus was not an official BSA body, and so was not bound by its policy of open meetings:

> as ours is in essence a political struggle, we think it important that
> members of this disadvantaged minority should work together, without
> outsiders, however sympathetic, be they men or non–sociologists, to
> share common experiences, define our objectives, forge our policies,
> and consolidate our achievements.
> (Network 6: 10, 1976)

Another man, in general very sympathetic to feminism, expressed an ambivalence which was probably more widely shared:

> I had difficulty with certain aspects, maybe because I didn't understand
> well enough. There seemed to be a thread running through the debate
> in the BSA which said we must have private meetings and debates, and
> I think I, with one or two other men, felt that was all very well but why
> didn't they engage back with us? For those women we the men were the
> problem, so tell us about it, let's have it out, what were the issues

Some feminists have taken this argument into specifically intellectual territory, but not all of them have done so. Michèle Barrett mounted *Network*'s metaphorical Soapbox in 1986 to argue that feminist political organisation should be defended, but that feminist arguments would not really be heard as long as intellectual separatism was maintained. The idea of feminist methodology for her:

> is based on a complete relativism – men have their truth and we have
> ours – which I would reject ... In practice the epithet 'feminist' has been
> hijacked for a subjectivist position within sociology that some of us
> rejected back in the '70s along with Garfinkel et al ... As an academic
> strategy ... it requires no change from men ... It simply sets up an
> alternative channel of work for women, and principally about women.
> (Barrett, 1986: 20)

The question of whether the intellectual need was for a focus of study on women also had some disagreements, though these are less salient in the sources; Jalna Hanmer suggested, after the 1982 conference, that most work there had still been on women but maybe 'the next advance may be problematising men as a field of study so that gender divisions in sociology means men and women' (Hanmer, 1982: 1); she did not suggest whether this should be done by men, women or both.

The opposite position to Barrett's was reported as collectively taken in the same year in a discussion on violence against women, where 'the pressures from male tutors/supervisors to engage with these male theories [like discourse theory] were seen as undesirably transforming such matters as male sexual violence into 'purely "academic" concerns' and so defusing feminist anger and alienating academic women from others who found such language inaccessible, as well as putting pressure on them ' to take time and energy from our own concerns to get to grips with their mystifying and difficult languages' (WCN, 1986: 2). This seems a line of argument hard to reconcile with a commitment to the academic life.

Another area of divergent views, in this case exemplified more in our sources as a divergence between pro-feminist men and feminist women, has been that of what men should do. Hearn and Morgan suggested that Women's Studies belonged entirely to women, but that

> the Critique of Men is by both women and men ... men's critique of men, ourselves, is to be developed in the light of feminism ... the underlying task ... is to change men, ourselves and other men. This is premised on the assumption that we learn to understand the world by trying to change it and not by trying to detach ourselves from it ...

Men should not risk disadvantaging women by applying for jobs in Women's Studies or for related research grants (Hearn and Morgan, 1989). Some women, however, saw even the idea of 'men's studies' as a reassertion of men's dominant position which would take jobs away from women and narrow the political agenda; anti-sexist work was acceptable, but not any strategy which would marginalise radical analyses as 'just another set of "variables"' (Canaan and Griffin, 1989).

In the 1990s, such strong political and intellectual separatism has become less marked within the BSA, and Equality of the Sexes activities have become less clearly aimed at women only. In 1997, the day conference on Writing and Publishing was advertised in the WCN as for 'sociologists at various stages of their academic careers' [WCN, 1997] with no reference to gender; that fits with the fact that the WCN had by then, by a transition process not flagged in publications, come to be a leaflet inserted in *Network* and circulated to all BSA members, not just women who had actively affiliated themselves with the Caucus. In the same spirit, that issue, looking for new recruits for the EoS, urges that 'we would like to encourage men to join us, since we aim to promote equality for both sexes and would like to point out that the EoS is not just a forum for women, but for women and men' (Bhopal, 1997).

Outcomes

There can be little doubt that the women's movement has made a very considerable difference to the BSA, both directly and indirectly, despite its organisational difficulties, shortage of resources and lapses of continuity. We can recapitulate here some of the points which have been reported in more detail in other chapters:

- *Sociology* is now normally edited jointly by a man and a woman, and women have become the majority among authors of its articles.

- Two annual conferences since the 1974 one have had a gender theme, and those which did not have almost invariably had a gender stream, whatever the theme topic.

- Female plenary speakers have become much commoner at conferences, and the proportion of women non-plenary speakers has risen (with variations by conference topic) until at half of the conferences from 1991 to 2000 they were in the majority.

- Several study groups have been founded which deal with gender and women's issues.

- Women have become the majority of executive members, and the sexes have, while not alternating mechanically, been very evenly represented among the officers. (Much the same applies to summer school directors.)

Examination of the characteristics of the women who have been members of the EC suggests a strong direct Caucus influence. In the absence of a Caucus membership list, the only way in which women who have associated themselves with it can be identified from the available records is by a mention of their names in connection with some activity; this must provide only a minimum estimate, especially given the scarcity of records. However, using this measure we can see that at least eight of the ten women who served on the EC from 1974 to 1979, 18 of the 27 who served in the 1980s, and 17 of the 31 who served in the 1990s, had been associated with the Caucus.[19] It is not clear whether we should interpret this as showing that the relatively small group of Caucus members was extremely active and successful, or that the relatively large number of Caucus members meant that a high proportion of women sociologists interested in the BSA were bound to be drawn from among them. The former interpretation is supported by the deliberate nomination of Caucus candidates in some elections, but that is only documented as having happened in a few cases, though there were more cases where quite a lot of effort was made to encourage women to stand.

Less open to summary in facts and figures are possible changes in styles of participation, or of intellectual work. One Caucus activist wrote of the 1977 conference that 'For the first time that I can remember personal experience was a valid topic for discussion following some of the papers – surely an entirely healthy antidote to the competitive, male, more-theoretical-than-thou ethos which has been in evidence at other conferences' (Woodward, 1977: 10).[20] Have such changes occurred more generally? It is possible, given the pervasive cultural influence of feminist ideas on such matters, though we cannot measure this. (This was the period when autobiographical essays by sociologists, such as those in Bell and Newby (1977),[21] became quite a common genre, and 'reflexivity' entered our general methodological vocabulary.)

However, we might still need to be a little cautious about interpreting all these changes as due to pressures from the women's movement. The last two items listed might be to some extent accounted for by the changing gender composition of the discipline, and the increasing proportion of women among BSA members. But it is arguable that those factors have themselves been influenced by the women's movement, in which case that is not really an alternative line of explanation. Equally, we might be cautious about assuming that these outcomes have been produced specifically by the Caucus as such, as distinct from individual women who have been active both within it and outside it. The lack of structure and formal organisation of the Caucus makes the level of influence achieved more impressive.

There may have been a cohort effect in some of the changes that have taken place within the women's movement's concerns as they have been expressed within the BSA. Margaret Stacey suggested this in a 1993 interview about her own experience:

> The WLM was composed of a bunch of women around a certain age, all of whom were acting together, who felt a great sense of solidarity and sisterhood, and to start with they were quite sure that there had never been any feminism before ... as soon as they all began to turn 40 they began to get worried about grey hair or wrinkles or something, and now they're all worked up about the menopause ... Wait another 15 years, and they'll all start talking about how dreadfully badly old women are treated in our society ...
> (Stacey, 1993: 9)

In several of the autobiographical essays by women sociologists in Britain and the USA mentioned above, they stress the importance of the changing historical contexts in which their experiences have evolved. It is not known precisely how many women of what statuses have been involved in the Caucus at different periods, but many of those initially active were rather young at the time, and twenty years later had senior positions (some in Women's Studies). Their personal needs will no longer be quite the same, they are probably much busier (a number of resignations from the EoS were due to other work commitments), and the torch has been taken up by younger women who start their careers in a new situation in part created by the activity of their predecessors.

In its beginning, the Caucus performed an important political, mobilising and consciousness-raising role. Over time, this seems to have become diluted as times changed; many policy issues were won, the larger number of women became more prominent in the discipline, and the EoS was thoroughly institutionalised in the BSA's structures. In the 1998 Annual Report, it is stated that the EoS 'is an activity based rather than policy forming committee'. It is surely because action has been quite effective that it has now become less salient and less aggressive in tone. When women are over-represented in some of the BSA's main activities, it hardly makes sense to treat them as an oppressed minority, and the apparent assumption in some of the earlier feminist statements that women need special sheltered environments because they are shy, lack self-confidence and have difficulty with technical and theoretical language seems somewhat insulting. (Or simply applicable to the youngest members of the discipline rather than to their seniors of either sex. The high representation of graduate students in the Caucus may do something to account for the emphasis it has shown on lack of familiarity with the BSA, and on the need for support to those lacking in self-confidence at early career stages.). By the 1990s, statements about the purpose of the Caucus emphasised socialisation into the BSA, and particularly its annual conference. The 1998 WCN, for instance, said that the WC meetings at the conference facilitate

> the introduction of women to conference and the BSA within a supportive,
> interactionist 'womanist' culture. This has often proved to be a
> counterpoint to mainstream events at conference which are more formal
> and hierarchical. Many women remember Caucus as a friendly place
> where, as new members or first time conference goers, they could meet
> other women and obtain information about the conference to 'get their
> bearings' so they could feel more confident in engaging in the conference
> agenda ...

This sounds as much or more like a body whose function is to help new
participants as one for women as such. When concern has switched to the
induction of younger members, and to racial issues, it is reasonable to wonder
why young men too are not entitled to supportive activities. It sounds as though
the EoS, despite its name, is no longer really a committee focusing wholly on
gender issues. The Caucus has become a meeting held at the conference which
is organised by the EoS, without any independent organisation of its own: 'there
is no mechanism for establishing contact with the Caucus participants after the
conference' (WCN, 2001: 1) This is a notable shift from a founding conception
in which the Caucus insisted on its independence from the BSA, and used the
EoS as its mode of intervention in BSA affairs.

The functions of the Caucus in its earliest days were well described by
Mary Ann Elston (1976: 3) as being 'to break down the isolation of many
women in sociology in Britain; to unite them in the political struggle for changes
in work conditions for women both in and outside sociology and against sexist
ideology and practice in sociology and society'. She saw a potential conflict
between

> a view of the caucus role as a pressure group operating within the BSA
> and as relating primarily to the feminist movement beyond the narrow
> confines of professional sociology. It is not that these are necessarily
> opposed views but rather that we should recognise that we should be
> doing both ...

The refusal to recognise a barrier between academic life and struggle outside
sociology, and between politics and intellectual life, was not at all specific to
the women's movement at that time, which is not surprising given that many of
the women involved belonged to a left-wing milieu whose house journal was
the *New Left Review* and where such ideas were current. In the previous issue
of *Network*, for instance, a piece by Paul Corrigan had been published which
diagnosed 'a crisis in the class nature of our intellectual work', and urged
sociologists to 'link our "objectivity" with a different set of constraints; until
we begin to see a way of clearly linking our research to class interests' and
become organic intellectuals for the working class (Corrigan, 1976).

The relationship of the Caucus to the BSA as an organisation has been an
interesting one. The BSA has acted in an extremely inclusive way, creating special
arrangements to allow it both to maintain its independence and not to be
regarded as part of the Association, *and* to have formal representation and
public legitimacy within it. The constitutional devices of treating it as a study
group, but without the usual conditions of a study group, and of creating the

EoS on which it was represented, were used to make this possible and, on a number of occasions, money was given for all-women activities, although no other activity open only to one section of the membership, and equally open to non-members, was supported. This BSA stance could be seen as one of inconsistency, capitulation to entryism, or organisational impropriety – but it could also be seen as morally right and/or as effective practical politics, or what used to be known in the 1960s as 'repressive tolerance'. Whichever interpretation one chooses, a challenge has been absorbed and institutionalised.

Notes

1   Bev Barstow, whose thesis is on the history of the Women's Caucus, is joint author of this chapter.

2   For this reason, any material below which draws on the newsletters from the period 1981–5 does not use direct quotations or mention the names of authors. This was agreed, through consultation by the current Women's Caucus convenor, as an appropriate way to deal with this.

3   The official delegate list is the only available source of numbers for the complete attendance. However, such lists are normally compiled a little before the conference starts, on the basis of registrations so far, and so do not include late registrants; in this case, the list even omits some of the speakers, so it is clearly incomplete – but it is the best source we have. It did not give gender, so that had to be discovered from other sources; in 82 cases, no source was found. Those not identified have been excluded from the gender count; there are certainly enough of them for full information on them potentially to change the picture given above.

4   Students accounted for 7% of that; there was a much lower proportion of students among the men. A number of the women students became prominent in the Caucus, and in some cases also in sociology more generally.

5   These included people working in government or other social research units, a journalist, and publishers' and funding-body representatives.

6   For material on developments in America, see Chamberlain (1988), Riley (1988), Berger (1990) and Sewell (1992). Riley and Berger provide edited collections of autobiographical accounts, several of them by women who reflect on the significance of gender in their careers.

7   Younger readers may not recognise the reference here to Communist Party organisation.

8   For two accounts of this, see O. Banks et al. (1980) and Stacey (1993).

9   It is probably not purely coincidental that there had already been an American Sociological Association Ad Hoc Committee on the Status of Women in the Profession, whose report (Hughes et al., 1973) had been published in 1973; Sheila Allen mentioned that she and others were familiar with it.

10   One of these women had, however, made a recent gender transition.

11   This provision lapsed fairly soon when the Professional Ethics Committee ceased to exist.

12   The oddity of regarding it as acceptable to belong to a Caucus of an association without being a member of the association has parallels in the objection at the same period, described in Chapter 4, to charging non-members of BSA for attendance at study group meetings.

13   It had regular issues until 1977, then there seems to have been a gap, after which it restarted in 1981, numbering its first issue 1, and only in the second issue apologised for the assumption that there had never been a newsletter before; it then ran for several years, but with a gap in 1987–9, and in November 1991 says that it is back after a break of two years; by 1993, it is again said to be some time since the last issue, and there then seems to have been a gap until 1997, when it restarted as one issue per year with *Network*.

14   However, the WCN claim that they made a large difference on this issue seems unconvincing, at least quantitatively, given that only 29 votes were recorded, and that, on the key issue, those who did not abstain were divided 13–11. Thus even if 'about 20' women were present and voting, they cannot all have voted the same way! Perhaps more of the women were present for the lunchtime Caucus meeting than for the official business, and of course it is perfectly possible that a quite small group was large enough to turn the balance.

15   In 1982, some members of the EC had spoken at a commercial conference for school students; it was agreed that the names of those known to be unemployed should be given in response to any future requests for names of suitable speakers (EC 7 May 1982). It is not known if any further requests were received in response to which this policy was followed. It does not seem very probable that commercial organisations would have responded favourably.

16   For a useful overview of developments in feminist thinking and their impact on British sociology, see Maynard (1990).

17   The workshops which eventually appeared in the conference programme did not, however, include this; the nearest topic was one on 'The situation of women post-graduates doing feminist research'.

18   A rather puzzling complaint, given that there were such streams clearly labelled in 1986, 1987, 1988 and 1989 and that, although the 1990 conference did not have 'streams' quite as clearly identified in all its documentation as some of those had had, there were 15 'thematic sessions' listed with gender-related titles, a number of them organised by or with papers from prominent Caucus members. (*Network* 46: 10, 1990).

19   Despite the youthful bias of the Caucus, the women from it who came onto the EC did not noticeably reduce the average age of members. In the 1970s, indeed, they tended to raise it; the discipline as a whole was young then, and the men were young too.

20   However, I remember at the 1974 conference sitting in one session next to a keen feminist to whom I whispered that I had a personal experience relevant to the discussion, though it was not appropriate to mention. She urged me to speak up, so I reported how when I had told my mother that I was giving a paper at the conference her response was to ask me what I would wear! A male colleague still remembered this more than 25 years later – and what I wore, which would please my mother.

21   These unselfconsciously did not include any by women, an editorial decision which would very soon seem unacceptable. They were shortly counterbalanced by Roberts 1981.

Chapter 7
Affairs of the head: conflict and defence

From the later 1960s, the BSA was heavily involved in a range of overlapping issues. These concerned the university and wider politics of the time, the employment situation of individual sociologists, academic freedom and its limits, and the public relations of sociology; they reflected a range of conflicts, and often required defensive action. This chapter focuses mainly on some particular cases which were of importance historically, raising broader questions about the functions of the Association and illustrating the circumstances with which it had to deal.

The BSA EC has shown a continuing concern with issues of academic freedom and related matters abroad as well as at home, often ones arising from political conflicts of various kinds. For example, the secretary's report to the 1975 AGM displayed a range of such activity:

> We have this year ... enquired into and given advice on the problems of two members at Kingston Polytechnic in relation to the publication of sponsored research, attempted (unsuccessfully) to persuade the General Teaching Council for Scotland to recognise a graduate member as qualified to teach relevant subjects in Scottish secondary schools,[1] blacklisted Simon Fraser University, Canada, in line with a similar action taken by the Canadian Sociology and Anthropology Association, investigated suspected disqualification of candidates without British degrees for a teaching post at Manchester Polytechnic, urged the Home Secretary to grant political asylum to two leading Hungarian sociologists and made representations to the Prime Minister of Malaysia about the imprisonment of two distinguished sociologists without trial ...

(Several more items relating to British problems were also mentioned.) In 1977, the EC minutes for 3 September have an item headed 'Refugee and imprisoned sociologists', which lists cases in Argentina ('there should be standard procedure for such cases'), Czechoslovakia and Malaysia.

Many of the British issues dealt with under such headings look as much like matters for a trade union as for a learned society, since they directly involved employment relationships. However, the difficult of drawing a clear line between the two is shown in many particular cases – for example, complaints about the ownership of and credit for research data, or the appointment procedures at a polytechnic where the complainant suggested that 'the procedure as a whole had been ambiguous and that political criteria had been overtly introduced into the process of assessment of candidates'. The possible role of political criteria in academic life became a hot topic, as the cases reviewed below show.

It seems plausible to suggest that some of the employment-related cases dealt with arose as part of the gradual institutionalisation of procedures in novel situations and types of institution, especially where those in managerial roles came from backgrounds alien to the culture of new groups such as sociologists, and rapid expansion was taking place; it would not be surprising in such circumstances if there were considerable initial friction and misunderstanding. One might also ask, however, to what extent the frequency of complaints was due to the frequency of good grounds for complaint, and to what extent to the propensity of sociologists to be hostile to establishments. That is a good question – but unfortunately the data do not enable us to attempt to answer it.

However, there were certainly some cases where sociology students and staff behaved, in the period of 'student unrest' that started in 1966, in ways which would not previously have been regarded as acceptable in academic life and, although they were far from the only people in universities to do so, it is probably true that sociologists were among the groups more heavily involved. (Sociology appealed to the radicals of that iconoclastic era, and the age structure of sociology staff made them closer to students than was typical of other disciplines, and so more open to the influences which led to the development of the student movement.[2]) But even if that were not true, the public perception among more conservative groups within the universities, and in the press, was that it was, and this had unfavourable consequences for the image of sociology. Michael Posner, the Chairman of SSRC from 1979 to 1984, once remarked that when he received complaints about SSRC-funded research it was always called 'sociological', although it usually was not by sociologists. (Malcolm Bradbury's satirical novel *The History Man* (1975), whose 'hero' was an opportunistic radical sociologist who slept with his students, may have affected this image as much as it traded on it; at any rate, it certainly caused some anxiety among sociologists.) The BSA thus had general reason to be concerned about the image of sociology, and there was frequent discussion in the EC about public relations.

There were three 'affairs' involving individuals and political issues of the time which gave rise to strong controversy both within and outside the sociological community, and where the BSA was involved: the Blackburn affair, the Atkinson affair and the Gould affair. These merit particular attention both for those reasons, and because each of them raised issues about the sphere of action of the BSA as well as about norms of appropriate behaviour for academic sociologists; they are examined in turn below. Given that the general situation in which they occurred was of considerable importance in explaining how such cases arose, and that changes since then have made the events of that period seem very distant, some illustrative material about ideas and movements of the time is also included in boxes.

The Blackburn affair

This took place against the background of significant unrest at the LSE. That started in 1966 with a protest (on grounds arising from his role in Rhodesia) against the proposed appointment of Dr Walter Adams as the next Director of the School; as one part of this, a meeting was called to discuss direct action to prevent it. Two student leaders were suspended for disobeying an instruction from the current Director in connection with that, in response to which there was a student strike and sit-in.[3] Various other episodes of turbulence followed, including an attempt to invite large numbers of non-students taking part in a demonstration against the Vietnam War to spend the night (when the building was normally locked) in the School. In 1969, gates were installed at several points in the building to block unauthorised access. Militant students objected to this, and in somewhat chaotic circumstances they set about destroying the gates. Legal and disciplinary action was taken against some participants, two American students involved were deported, and the School was closed for several weeks. When it reopened, 'Lectures were boycotted, lecturers were verbally and at times physically attacked; the reinstated gates were damaged; metal glue was used to block doors all over the School; stink and smoke bombs were dropped into meetings ... ' (Dahrendorf, 1995: 470) – and so on. (One member of LSE staff interviewed reported that 'There were more and more *insane* things happening, like people taking down the numbers of the floors at the LSE because that was a form of categorisation; I was put on trial for being on their premises!') All this naturally received lurid and extensive press coverage.

'The first concern of a revolutionary student movement will be direct confrontation with authority, whether in the colleges or on the barricades. But the preparation and development of such a movement has always entailed a searching critique of the dominant ideas about politics and society – in this way practice and theory reinforce one another ... the student who takes up sociology, economics or political science finds he or she has to reject the conformist ideas and technocratic skills which his teachers seek to instil.'
(Blackburn, 1969: 163)

Robin Blackburn, an assistant lecturer in sociology at the LSE of leftist sympathies, was dismissed in 1969 in connection with the gates episode. ('Good cause' dismissals have been almost unheard of in academia.) The facts of the episode were in some public dispute at the time, but Blackburn did not personally take part in the destruction of the gates, though he spoke immediately afterwards in support of it. The formal charge taken to have been established against him was that he had 'given support and approval to the conduct of students in forcibly removing the gates', both at a meeting that evening and on television some days later. Blackburn was not a member of the BSA and did not ask for its support, so it responded to this as a general freedom of speech issue rather than a personal case. A letter was sent to the Governors of the LSE which urged that since the case 'centred on an area of freedom of speech not widely considered hitherto' there should be 'careful re-consideration because a dangerous precedent might be set which might have serious consequences for academic freedom'. A detailed reply was received which explained the procedure followed, and concluded by expressing concern about the disruption of lectures and stating that

> *violence, incitement to violence, or support and approval for violence expressed at times and in circumstances which make it tantamount to a direct encouragement for its repetition are inconsistent with the obligations of a member of the academic staff.[4]*

This reply was deemed by the BSA EC not to have met the points raised, but no further action was proposed unless fresh developments warranted it; it was agreed that under some circumstances the Association might wish to blacklist sociology posts at the LSE. What those circumstances were was not specified in the minutes, but presumably they did not occur, since the blacklisting did not take place. (Although at least one member of the LSE staff resigned from the BSA under the impression that it had.) An unsuccessful appeal was made by Blackburn against the verdict of dismissal for misconduct.[5]

As part of its general response to the events of the time, the BSA in June 1969 also issued a defensive press release[6] about the role of sociology students in episodes of unrest [EC 26 September1969, item 20(ii)]. This pointed out that many sociology students had chosen the subject for vocational reasons, aiming at socially valuable careers in fields where there was a demand for their skills. It went on to say that the sole purpose of sociology teaching was not vocational, and that the comparative study of social systems 'will obviously raise issues which those who simply wish to see the status quo perpetuated will find disturbing', but that this will help to prevent social ossification. However, the huge increase in demand for sociology means that many students are taught with extremely unfavourable staff/student ratios; recent statements by militant students show 'a turning away from critical discussion and towards political dogmatism' which can perhaps be attributed to the lack of personal attention which such a situation has made inevitable. Sociologists have a special contribution to make to the understanding of the student unrest as well as to the skills needed by government, industry and planning – so the answer is to improve their staff/student ratios, rather than to permit an educational backlash against them. How successful this politically careful attempt to turn attacks on sociology into support for more of it was is not known; however, the agenda for the September EC reports favourable comments from a number of vice-chancellors to whom it had been sent. (The fact that one vice-chancellor had called in his professor of sociology to explain it to him could, though, suggest that it had been pitched at too high an intellectual level.)

Revolutionary Socialist Students' Federation manifesto:

'RSSF commits itself to the revolutionary overthrow of capitalism and imperialism, and its replacement by workers' power ... RSSF believes that the institutions of higher education are a comparatively weak link in British capitalism, and that the ruling class's field of action can be severely restricted by correctly waged struggles for student control and for universities of revolutionary criticism ... RSSF will build red bases in our colleges and universities by fighting for the following Action Programme:

- All power to the general assembly of students, staff and workers – one man[7] one vote on the campus
- Abolition of all exams and grading ...
- An end to bourgeois ideology – masquerading as education – in courses and lectures ... '

[The RSSF was only one group among the numbers of students taking part in various forms of 'unrest'.]

'The youth culture which reflects the uncertainty about values and status in contemporary society, finds its fullest expression in organised recreational activity – in the entertainment industry. Student unrest is merely the most recent, but, because of the willingness of student leaders to seek ideological legitimation, and to stimulate more direct action ... in some ways the most dangerous manifestation of the generational struggle ... demands for freedom from conventional, customary, moral and – eventually – legal restraints were disseminated and endorsed by pop entertainers and pop journalists ... as part of that sensationalism on which mass appeal and mass circulation now depends ... That the young have been most affected by the new entertainment values arises because it is always the least socialised members of a society (those with least informed taste, and least understanding of social values) who are most vulnerable to sensationalism and the appeal to primitive appetites ... Students are no longer a class apart from youth in general; the universities have lost their distinctiveness of culture and commitment.'
(Wilson, 1969: 70–3)

At the 1970 AGM, a statement was approved which said that the BSA

> has been concerned at the poor state of staff-student relations at the LSE in view of the body's importance in British sociology.
>
> The particular incident which causes most concern is the dismissal of Robin Blackburn, as this raises crucial issues, apparently unresolved by the Appellate Tribunal, of the freedom of speech of sociologists in universities. The cost of such appeals to the appellant is a further cause of concern.

That was where the matter ended as far as the BSA was concerned. Robin Blackburn did not for many years return to a conventional post in British academic sociology, though he now holds a professorship at the University of Essex, but has held a number of visiting posts and research fellowships in Britain and abroad. He continued to participate in the intellectual life of sociology through editorial roles for the *New Left Review* and its publishing offshoot Verso as well as his own publications, which have included important work on the history of slavery.

The Atkinson affair[8]

Dick Atkinson had been a temporary assistant lecturer in the Birmingham department of sociology in 1968–9, and then moved to Manchester in the same capacity. In 1970, he applied for a permanent post at Birmingham, and was recommended for appointment. The appointing committee included, as was the normal practice, some members from outside the department, and it had been divided 5–4, with the majority of its sociologist members favouring the appointment. The recommendation was, counter to previous practice though not to the university's formal procedure, rejected at a higher level in the university. This rejection was because of the support which Atkinson had given to a student sit-in at Birmingham, and his support there and elsewhere (including the LSE, which he attended as a research student) for the radical student movement.[9] It was argued that this meant that he was likely to be a disruptive influence, and have difficulty in collaborating appropriately with colleagues. (He sees this as a reaction by conservative senior academics who felt threatened by his raising of issues such as the need for better teaching, and for more influence by junior staff in decision-making in professorial fiefdoms.) Parties for and against his candidature had apparently already been formed before the appointing committee met. The party against can be taken to be represented in the meeting of former Deans, called by the current Dean, with the head of the sociology department (W. 'Gi' Baldamus) to discuss criteria for appointment, and in effect to oppose Atkinson's candidature; Baldamus was strongly advised not to advocate his appointment. The party for consisted largely of sociologists, some formally located in other departments, who were said by their opponents to be determined to appoint Atkinson irrespective of the qualifications of other candidates, and possibly to be influenced in this by political considerations. They, however, denied (in a statement circulated at Birmingham by members of the majority on the appointing committee) that they had any shared political position, and said that only one of them had supported his previous 'reformist' activities. Baldamus repeatedly stated that he opposed both Atkinson's political and his intellectual position, but nonetheless favoured his appointment.

The matter was formally drawn to the BSA's attention by members of the Birmingham sociology department in June. Baldamus also asked for support in launching a fund to employ Atkinson 'in a private capacity' at the university. The BSA responded with a statement expressing confidence in the professional judgement of Baldamus and his colleagues, and objecting strongly to the university decision. The objection was both on the ground that only the professional sociologists could evaluate which candidates were competent for a sociological post, and it was improper for them to be overruled by a committee without sociological competence, and also that, even if there were not 'political' grounds for the decision, it rested on inappropriate non-academic criteria. In effect, only purely academic criteria were deemed relevant. BSA members were advised not to apply for posts at Birmingham until selection procedures had been clarified and radically amended, but to be prepared to offer any part-time teaching assistance required. The statement was circulated to all members, and to various organisations. However, it was decided not in any way to sponsor the fund proposed by Baldamus (EC 24 July 1970). Some members expressed concern at the issuing of the statement, while a Teachers' Section meeting had declared its regret that the Association had not set up a fund (EC 2 October 1970). A later request to the Association to give financial support to the fund which was set up at Birmingham was rejected, but it was agreed (by a majority of 6–5) to provide the organisers with a copy of the membership list.

The BSA asked the vice-chancellor of Birmingham for reassurance that its appointing procedures would be amended, and attempted to enter into discussion with him, but he was not prepared to meet them, and the proposal that there should be two independent sociological assessors for future appointments was rejected. The BSA advice to members became that they should not apply for sociology posts at Birmingham in any department. (This action was referred to by participants sometimes as 'ban' and sometimes as 'blacklisting'; their example has been followed below). In response to this and other cases, the EC offered a 'Statement on the Position of the Association in Relation to Matters of Academic Freedom'. This considered how far it was appropriate for the BSA to be involved, responding to the questioning by some members of the appropriateness of the Association taking any stand on such matters, and answered it thus:

> *The BSA is a scholarly association, and its principal object is to advance sociological studies ... The question at issue is whether a concern with academic freedom is closely related to this major scholarly purpose of the Association. In our opinion this is the case, not only because this must be a concern of all scholarly bodies but also because of the controversial nature of sociology. Its subject matter is bound up with ideological and political disagreements, and few sociologists would now want to claim that they are capable of taking a completely impartial and objective view of social phenomena. Moreover, the systematic study of social institutions, especially in one's own society, leads easily to a critical view ... These characteristics of sociology have assumed greater prominence, and have received more public attention, in the last few years, because of the connections between the new political radicalism and certain sociological ideas and theories. It is this situation which has led to the recent 'academic freedom' cases...*

The statement goes on to express concern that those cases should all have involved political radicals, and that a contrast should have been drawn between 'radical' and 'objective' teaching without recognition of the equal possibility of 'conservative' or 'liberal' bias, and to argue that the advancement of sociology emerges from the clash of rival views so that it is 'a *scholarly* duty to ensure that conditions exist in which the free and full exposition and discussion of diverse views is possible' (AGM Report, 15 April 1971) The statement was approved by the AGM, though with many abstentions.

A serious interest in the matter was not confined to the BSA. The Council for Academic Freedom and Democracy[10] set up a commission of inquiry into the affair, whose two eventual members were sociologists John Westergaard and Steven Lukes, and published a pamphlet report on it. This gave a careful and detailed analysis of the facts they had been able to elicit, and reached the conclusion that 'extra-academic considerations' led to the 'preventive non-appointment' of Atkinson for offences he had not yet committed (Lukes and Westergaard, 1971: 28–9).

Meanwhile, at Birmingham a fund had been successfully raised to support Atkinson:

> *what people here invited me to do was as it were to take up the post from which I had been blacked by the university and give the lectures one had been appointed to give ... they then raised a generous amount of money, equivalent to what the post carried, to pay me ...*
> (Atkinson, 1997)

Formally, he was employed by a group of sociologists, but apparently many other people also contributed to the fund; his supporters constituted themselves as a group called Action for Academic Freedom. (This came to be referred to locally as Ack-Ack.) He gave regular lectures, which were well attended despite their unofficial status – by an audience which included 'venerable bureaucrats who took more notes than the students' (Atkinson, 1997). Another former member of the department said that he thought that there were at this time unrealistic expectations about the likelihood that the vice-chancellor would surrender in response to student pressure, and the university would be reorganised. Not everyone, even among Atkinson's original supporters, was enthusiastic about some of the ways in which matters developed among students – for which Atkinson cannot be held responsible. A former member said that to Baldamus 'I think the way things developed had echoes of Nazi Germany; he left in 1937 ... He was in lecture halls full of storm troopers shouting slogans, so what happened here was reminiscent ... ' and, however inappropriate this association may have been,[11] it could have influenced Baldamus' changing views.

At Birmingham, the department of course carried on teaching, with one fewer post than it had expected, and found it hard to recruit the part-time teaching which the BSA had urged members to provide. Atkinson's lectures caused difficulties for Baldamus, since (although Atkinson was in contact with him and had scheduled them not to clash with others in the department) in effect they interfered with normal teaching, including the first-year course which he himself taught for the first term, and in which he took quite a different approach from Atkinson. When with great difficulty he had found a senior person from another university (Norbert Elias) to carry on the course after Christmas, Atkinson at his suggestion contacted Elias and reached an agreement with him that he would give a parallel course covering different aspects of introductory sociology, which left Baldamus with a situation that he was at a loss how to deal with (Baldamus, 1971). He appealed to the BSA to lift its blacklisting so that the two new posts which had now become available could be filled, not just because of the teaching needs but also because of the real threat to the department which he perceived the situation as causing; there had already been some antagonism to sociology as such from the faculties of medicine, chemistry and engineering, and they were using the occasion to undermine sociology further. There was also concern that, if the ban was not lifted, it would affect the range of candidates for the jobs.

The ban was temporarily lifted by the BSA to facilitate the filling of the new posts, but again Atkinson applied and was rejected, and again the procedure (now somewhat changed) was not deemed satisfactory. It is clear that there had been a lot of negotiations and manoeuvring over such matters as the composition of the appointing committee, and some ground for believing that interview dates might have been fixed to make it impossible for some potential members to attend. The vice-chancellor had, contrary to normal practice (and to assurances given to Atkinson by another senior officer that no non-academic considerations would arise this time), attended the interviews, and put questions to Atkinson on his politics which were not put to other candidates. However, Baldamus changed his position, and ceased to support Atkinson, now maintaining a significantly less favourable view on the merits of his work than the one he had advanced the previous year, and putting this forward in the appointing committee to rule Atkinson out on what were ostensibly academic grounds (and as such legitimate in everyone's eyes). This seems to have been done for university-political reasons, to save the situation for the department from the threats to it which he believed would follow from Atkinson's appointment.[12] Thus further divisions among the Birmingham sociologists appeared.

By July 1971, the BSA EC had abolished its existing Professional Ethics Committee, under whose remit the matter had so far appeared in its agendas, and set up instead a Committee on Academic Freedom in Teaching and Research. The members of this were Joe Banks (who withdrew in October and was replaced by Keith Kelsall), Gabriel Newfield and Peter Worsley. Their immediate task was to review the Birmingham situation and to decide on the future of the blacklist, now reinstated, and in pursuit of this they visited Birmingham to investigate matters. In March of 1972, they reported their conclusion that no useful purpose would be served by the continuation of the blacklisting, which prevented some members from applying for jobs at Birmingham but had failed to induce the university to change its procedures. They recommended that the EC should modify its advice to members, simply warning them that there was a risk that applications there would not be evaluated by a body competent to judge them as sociologists. However, the AGM rejected this recommendation by a large majority, voting in favour of the maintenance of the blacklist. One member of the Birmingham department (in a recent interview) described the AGM as he experienced it at the time: 'this mass of people who knew nothing about it, they all voted for the BSA ban without a moment's consideration of what it meant, how it could be enforced, what the consequences would be, there was no real debate, just people chanting almost – I was horrified.' Some Birmingham members were, thus, becoming disaffected from the BSA. In June, the EC declared that the blacklist should be continued, and indeed extended to any participation in teaching or reference writing for Birmingham. This was seen as inappropriate by some members, and it caused some ill feeling and at least two resignations from the Association, one on the ground of the harm caused to students by the ban and another on the ground that 'the Association was not a trade union' (EC 29 September 1972). The general secretary of the AUT sent a letter of protest to the BSA about its intervention in what were general questions of procedure affecting all disciplines, not only sociology, and claimed that the AUT was the appropriate body to represent staff in this connection; it also complained that the BSA had not consulted, or even informed, the AUT about its blacklisting (Sapper, 1972). Baldamus wrote to the BSA:

> *I gather that the intended effects are to impede or to harass my department. For example, we have lost and will continue to lose many of our best students ... .it will be impossible next session to find a competent external examiner ... which of course will lower the value of our degree; I have completely failed to find a replacement for* [temporary lecturer].

> *However, there are also unintended consequences. They converge in one direction: to lower the level of sociological competence in Birmingham. Thus, the boycott is taken more seriously by those applicants who are committed to sociology rather than associated with borderline areas ... [another] unintended effect of the boycott is, understandably, not to allocate further posts to the Sociology Department because they would only be an embarrassment to the Faculty.*
> (Baldamus, 1972)

Atkinson ceased to teach his unofficial course:

> *I thought the Sociology department was going to disappear if I didn't, so I did disappear. I remember the BSA being quite annoyed with me, we've gone to all this trouble blacking it ... if the university's not going to be flexible, neither should we. It's an issue of principle ... I agreed, but pointed out that colleagues were paying me out of their salaries, not out of BSA funds, and that the principle could be applied in other ways.*
> (Atkinson, 1997)

Subsequently, he has made a career which, although not resting on conventional university posts, has drawn heavily on his sociological training, and has included the supervision of research students and formal links of various kinds with Birmingham and other universities. He has been particularly concerned with issues connected with urban renewal and the reform of local government in deprived inner-city areas such as Balsall Heath, and has acted as an advisor on them to central government departments, as well as publishing numbers of related books and journal articles.

Members of the Birmingham department asked, in a document addressed to the 1973 AGM, for the ban to be raised because of the harm it was causing. They reported unacceptably heavy staff workloads, too much teaching by part-timers, optional courses being taught from outside the department, and a petition from students requesting more sociology staff; student numbers in Honours Sociology had fallen. However, an EC resolution to continue the ban was passed at the AGM by a large majority, though on the understanding that the EC could lift it before the next AGM if it saw fit; the outcome of a commissioned report to the university on its procedures from an independent review body chaired by Jo Grimond[13] was awaited. It was lifted at the end of 1973, when it was deemed that the harm it had caused to the department was considerable and that the appointment procedures were being sufficiently modified for similar situations to be very unlikely to arise again.

How effective was the BSA's action in attaining its goals? Views on this varied. The university authorities had consistently refused to meet representatives of the BSA, which it treated as having no standing in the matter. It was, however, invited to submit evidence on issues of general principle to the Grimond review – but it did not do so, on the ground that, as it had not been able to meet the authorities, it did not have sufficient information about the formal situation to address issues outside those apparently raised by this particular case. Clearly, some potential applicants to Birmingham were deterred – but others were not. Of course not all of those were BSA members, but correspondence on file shows some non-members enquiring about the ban as if it concerned them too. Dick Atkinson (1997) himself suggested that 'while the BSA lost that particular battle, because it won the moral argument this meant that it was less likely that it would happen to other members in other departments'. It seems likely that the setting up of the Grimond review was not wholly unconnected with the intervention of the BSA and other bodies and the additional publicity which this generated. However, another Birmingham participant said 'I don't think the BSA had much of a role, it was all very much a local phenomenon on the campus and in people's kitchens and front rooms and bars.' Whether or not the BSA was effective in attaining its goals, it is evident that it did help to cause adverse consequences for the department as such and for its continuing individual members, though the local conflicts were such that some of those would surely have followed in any case. It has to be a matter of personal judgement whether that risk was worth taking, and that price worth paying.

The Gould affair

In 1977, Julius Gould (professor of sociology at Nottingham University) published *The Attack on Higher Education: Marxist and Radical Penetration*, which became generally known as 'the Gould Report'.[14] This collected together a large number of facts which, it was argued, revealed serious intellectual threats to higher education. The report declared its commitment to values of 'open, critical enquiry', 'intellectual diversity and pluralism', freedom to teach in that spirit, the possibility of objective knowledge, the need for 'commitment to logical coherence in argument' and 'systematic use of all available evidence'. Marxist/radical assumptions were seen as opposed to these values; the New Left, in particular, was seen as much inferior to the old left, which did have a commitment to objectivity and did not support relativism. The bearers of those radical assumptions, or at least a minority among them, 'are dedicated political men and women – whose *whole* lives centre upon political ends ... They are adept at building up, using, and diverting for their own ends, a variety of front organisations ... ' (of which the British Society for Social Responsibility in Science and the Council for Academic Freedom and Democracy were given as examples) (Gould, 1977: 5, 45, 46). The argument was both that the positions held were intellectually in error, and that their holders were operating as a network to take over and undermine institutions. Sociologists were not its only targets, but they were prominent among them. Those named in various connections included Robin Blackburn, Hilary Rose, John Rex, M. F. D. Young, John Westergaard, Ron Frankenberg, Paul Hirst and Barry Smart; also mentioned were the BSA study group on the sociology of education, an Open University sociology course 'Patterns of Inequality', and the agenda for a Hull University Sociology department meeting.

Gould (1997) described the report as 'an attempt to get debate going of a reasonably civilised nature', and felt that initially it had some success, although later the debate deteriorated. *Network* in January 1978 reported that it had caused a public furore. It was widely publicised in the press. *The Times Higher Education Supplement* of 23 October 1977 gave it a feature summarising the argument, an article reporting 'fears of a witch-hunt against Marxist academics', and an editorial headed 'Danger of taking the threat from the left too seriously' which criticised Gould's arguments. The *Daily Telegraph* and *The Times* gave it extensive coverage, and debate took place in the letters columns too. Sociologists and non-sociologists on each side accused the other of McCarthyism, and some critics argued that Gould's report did not follow his own intellectual prescriptions. Several of the contributors emphasised the methodological point that the report listed many names of those who had merely participated in public activities such as conferences, some organised under Communist Party or related auspices, with the implication of guilt by association; this did not necessarily indicate the participants' intellectual positions or political activities.

The BSA EC responded by issuing a press statement, carried by a number of papers, which took exception to the use of names on the ground that 'the use of names is ... liable to misuse, particularly if the impression has been gained that the academic probity of those named is in question' (Gould pointed out that, if he had not named names, he would probably have been accused of talking without evidence.) The officers also responded actively to the press follow-up of the Report, defending sociology in general and the Association in particular against attacks. Gould, who was a member of the BSA, was invited to attend a meeting of the Professional Ethics Committee to discuss the issues. He did not, but resigned instead, publicising his resignation in the press; he saw this move by the BSA as interference in an area where they had no jurisdiction. There is clearly room for disagreement on that point but, whatever one's conclusion on it, the BSA did not have much success in this episode. It seems likely that its intervention gave a little more publicity to the report than it would otherwise have received, but failure to intervene would not have prevented whatever public damage was done to sociology.

As a further indication of the levels of conflict at this period, Gould says he received many letters from people unknown to him claiming left-wing bullying and victimisation in their own institutions, especially in some polytechnics. Some of those he had named in the report asserted that their careers had been ruined; the subsequent record suggests that this was not so, although they may have had a shorter-term setback. The drawing of battle lines, and the relatively predictable line-up on each side, is representative of the level of politicisation of discussion at this period.

A somewhat similar public attack was made at a later period by sociologist David Marsland, who had been on the EC and was for a short while secretary. He later became a supporter of the Thatcher government, and in the 1980s published a number of attacks on British sociology's leftism, with titles such as *Neglect and Betrayal* (1985) and *Seeds of Bankruptcy* (1988). (In response to that, the BSA issued a press release suggesting that he slipped 'from advocating an "unbiased" approach to asserting that sociology should be "positive" about existing social arrangements', while 'It is not the business of any scientific discipline to make "positive" or "negative" judgements.') His arguments were widely publicised in the press; the *Daily Mail* had a headline 'Sociologists ... the saboteurs of Britain'. Marsland, however, has remained within the BSA, saying:

> *It doesn't seem right to me not to join in. I'm always very supportive of people who are doing it and actually making the effort. A profession which doesn't have an effective association will be screwed by the other professions. I go to AGMs, and take part when I am at conferences; I feel involved with BSA ... I've always attacked colleagues and friends on the right who withdrew from BSA. Why let our enemies win, I tell them, in there and win. We have a duty.*
> (Marsland, 1997)

These were minority stances among sociologists, though there was and still is a right-wing network to which some sociologists belong[15] as well as a left-wing one. Others supported weaker versions of such positions on some issues, and there were publications advertised, if at all, in more conventionally academic ways which made a right-wing case. At a time when versions of Marxism were extremely influential in intellectual fashion, it was not unreasonable to see the profession collectively as biased, even if the same could not be said of individual members. I do not recall any case where the BSA censured attacks on sociology which came from the left – though this could be justified by the fact that, when these were made, they were not given the newspaper publicity which those from the right attracted, and so were much less likely to affect sociology's general public image.

'Marxism expresses and aids ... the enormous growth in the combativity of the working class and other groups in capitalist society against the established order. Revolutionary marxism has been reborn in the working class movement, with no small amount of help from the student activists of recent years ... The intention of this guide is to aid students in the sociology departments of the universities and colleges to work towards and within this tradition of marxism. Its message is that one does not need to be seduced by the sociological surrogate, however "marxised". There is an alternative tradition ... [this book] is designed for the student who is taking sides against capitalist society ... It is designed first of all to provide an introduction to a theoretical universe distinct from that of academic sociology ... Marxist theory can never be separated from revolutionary working-class politics, which are its practical aim and test ... ' [Shaw, 1974: 1–3]
[Martin Shaw was then lecturer in sociology at Durham University, and a BSA member.]

The BSA can be seen grappling with the question of how to deal with such matters, which were without precedent. In its internal organisation, should the Atkinson or Blackburn affairs be treated as issues of ethics, of academic freedom, or of professional standards? The names and remits of the subcommittees dealing with these matters changed in response to contingencies as they arose. Which parties to the matter should be dealt with? What should the balance of concern be between individual BSA members and the general good of the discipline? To what extent were these matters only for the professional association, and to what extent should the Association defer to bodies such as the AUT, which represented a broader constituency and had a specific remit to defend its members in their employment relations? If the BSA had no power over members such as Gould, or recognition by Birmingham as a legitimate party to its decision-making process, was there any point in trying to intervene? Was it really appropriate to rule out consideration of aspects of Atkinson's behaviour which might reasonably have been seen as in some ways disruptive? (And would the same principle that future actions should not be predicted from past ones have been invoked if his behaviour had been in support of right-wing causes? I think the answer to that has to be that it would probably not have been.)

The BSA does seem to have paid less attention to the real threats to academic freedom of discussion sometimes posed from the left,[16] and to the problems caused when radical *views* led not just to discussion but to radical *action* of kinds previously unheard of in British higher education. (The possible relation between words and action poses an obvious intellectual difficulty in relation to the advocacy of free speech in general.) Of course, not all those who advocated action following from radical intellectual commitments did anything outside existing conventions of political activity. But one of the oddities of the time was that general ideological objections to capitalism were seen as justifying sit-ins in university buildings and the disruption of lectures and exams – institutions hardly regarded previously as central to the capitalist economy and state.[17] There were members of the older left quite thrown by this turn; some urged that it was the first duty of students on the left to work seriously at their studies. The BSA found itself walking an ideological tightrope. It was in the awkward position of wanting to support free speech in academic life, and to maintain that sociology is intrinsically a critical discipline which inevitably and desirably leads to the questioning of existing institutions – but wanting also to deny that sociology had any special prominence in behaviour, following from the views expressed, which many regarded as unacceptable. These positions can perhaps be reconciled if the rationale is the defence of sociology and sociologists against any attacks to which they are exposed, but that is not a rationale likely to convince non-sociologists.

'A revolution is required ... It must not accept the constraints imposed upon action by the world. It must not allow itself to be enervated in its revolutionary force by forms, structures and bureaucracies. It must ... be participative, egalitarian, unrestrained by the sterile confinements of rationality and political appropriateness. Revolutionary action must begin now. It must strike at as many institutions of existing society as possible; and the form of the revolution must be mass-participative direct action at the grass roots. These were the political attitudes that had been reached by many young people of the left in the mid-1960s.' (Crouch, 1970: 31)
[Colin Crouch was president of the LSE Students' Union in 1967–8.]

BSA concern was not only with academic freedom, but also with the more practical defence of its members' jobs and academic status from attack. Threats came from several directions. At the other end of the spectrum from Gould's attack were casual journalistic jokes, like the cartoon caption 'I wanted to be a sociologist, but I failed at the beard' (Rayment, 1991). In the background, there was the continuing prejudice held by some academic groups against sociology as a serious discipline, which meant that defence had to look inwards to the academic community as well as outwards; this affected such matters as the ESRC's success in getting its share of funding in competition with the natural-science research councils. The radical association of intellectual positions with militant action certainly did not help in combating political prejudices; it actively encouraged them, by associating extreme political positions with particular intellectual stands and, as far as the general public was concerned, with sociology as such, even if the positions were only held by a minority. (This makes the later attacks by the Thatcher government on the social sciences less surprising than they might otherwise seem.) The difficulty at the time was to hold a divided profession together, and this made it necessary for the Association to take public positions on ground that was shared, whether or not they fully reflected the personal views of the officers putting them forward. In so far as there was a generational cleavage, it was not one where the middle generation, building careers and new departments, could afford to blow up its bridges.

Notes

1   The eligibility of sociology graduates for Scottish teaching posts was a recurring issue over the years.

2   In addition, it is well established that sociologists have tended to hold more left-wing political views than many other groups; see Lipset and Ladd (1972), Halsey and Trow (1971: 429–33).

3   Blackstone *et al.*'s *Students in Conflict* sketches these events up to 1967, and reports a survey which the authors, all LSE teachers, carried out on the involvement and support of students for them. Colin Crouch (1970), who was president of the Students' Union at the LSE for 1967–8, has also provided an account of the events up to 1969.

4   The letter and the response appear as Document D for item 15(c) in the papers for the EC meeting of 13 June 1969. Other sources, in which student participants give their versions of events, are Crouch (1970) and Hoch and Schoenbach (1969).

5   Long extracts from the formal judgement on Blackburn are given in *Minerva* 8: 100–10, 1970. If Robin Blackburn had really wanted to succeed in his appeal, perhaps he would not have stood by his principles to the extent of addressing a letter to the Director which started 'Dear Adams, we are in receipt of your insolent letter ... ', and went on to say 'It is obvious to everyone why you have made this new move [of setting up an appeal tribunal]. Your own job and ... indeed the position of the entire clique of self-appointed capitalist manipulators on the LSE court of governors, is in grave danger ... ' (Dahrendorf, 1995: 469–70). This could, of course, also be interpreted as showing a touching faith in the judicial impartiality of the appeal tribunal in relation to the LSE authorities.

6   A copy was also submitted to the House of Commons Select Committee on Education and Science for its enquiry into students and their relations with universities and colleges.

7   It is interesting to note the lack of sensitivity to gender issues in a radical group at this stage; in a few years, such a form of words would seem unacceptable.

8   This was a protracted affair, in which many different parties were involved. The facts of the case are not always clear from the available records (as the CAFD report by Lukes and Westergaard on the matter explained in considerable detail at an intermediate stage), and arguably the conflicting perceptions of the matter are at least as important historically as the 'facts'. I have, therefore, presented contrasting perceptions without necessarily making an attempt to resolve their differences. The account is based both on the written record, and on interviews with several participants who played varying roles, including Dick Atkinson himself.

9   An additional factor, which occurred only after the appointing committee had made its recommendation to the higher body, was that his doctoral thesis was referred for revision; this was used as an argument against his suitability for appointment, though at the time a PhD was far from a necessary qualification for an academic post (Platt, 2000), and of course a referral is not a rejection; he did in due course receive his doctorate. Opinions among those who had by then read the thesis differed on its merits, but some, including senior members of LSE staff, thought very highly of it. It had already been accepted for publication, and appeared as *Orthodox Consensus and Radical Alternative* (Atkinson, 1971). Reviews in the British sociological journals were mixed in their evaluations; however, the prominent conservative sociologist Robert Nisbet described it as 'a generally perceptive and scholarly treatment ... [which] Despite (perhaps because of) its tendentious character ... is a first-rate piece of historical analysis of modern

sociology and its tortuous convolutions. Through the author's eyes we can see, as no other book makes us see, the utter bankruptcy of conventional sociological theory ... ' (Nisbet, 1972: 60)

10   This was a body linked to the National Council for Civil Liberties, with the remit to take up cases where academic freedom was threatened and to support the democratisation of institutional structures in higher and further education.

11   Atkinson himself sees the picture of behaviour that this suggests as a distortion.

12   This interpretation is persuasively documented in a detailed account of his statements given in an undated letter, from seven BSA members at Birmingham, addressed to the BSA after these events.

13   Grimond was a respected former leader of the Liberal Party.

14   This was a report of a study group – of the Institute for the Study of Conflict – whose members also included the other prominent sociologists Edward Shils and David Martin. Another sociologist member was Caroline Cox, who was involved in the intense political conflicts at the Polytechnic of North London (on which see Jacka et al., 1975); she contributed to the right-wing 'Black Papers' (Cox et al., 1977), and became a life peer under the Thatcher government.

15   The Social Affairs Unit, founded in 1980 and directed by sociologist Digby Anderson, also had Gould and Marsland in prominent roles. Its current website describes its objective as to 'translate research with a potential to inform public policy from academe into public debate', and goes on to say that 'Many of its authors' ideas then [the 1980s] very controversial especially on schools and higher education – local autonomy, parental accountability, curricular rigour – have now found their way into the policy mainstream ... ' The Institute of Economic Affairs also provides a sympathetic setting and a publication outlet for some sociologists.

16   Exemplified in such matters as actively preventing people characterised, with varying accuracy, as 'racist' or 'militarist', from speaking on campuses.

17   Attempting to explain why this should have been so is well beyond the remit of this book. However, some sociologists did address the topic; see, for instance, Hirst (1973) and Wilson (1969).

Chapter 8
How the organisation has run

A complete picture of the BSA also requires a sketch of its practical running as an organisation – finances, premises, office staff – and how these have responded to and been constrained by external factors such as the changing law, the state of the national economy and the vicissitudes of higher education funding. Decisions made on these practical matters have been affected by the policy priorities of successive ECs and the members who attend AGMs, and have been closely involved with the pattern of provision of services to members.

Finances and premises

First, we sketch a rough chronological outline of some key points in the financial history of the Association, showing how these related to other contingencies. In its first years, only about half the BSA's income came from subscriptions, with the Nuffield grant – thanks to which income exceeded expenditure – as the other main source. (The non-monetary subsidy from the LSE, which was very important in limiting the expenditure needed, is not taken into account here.) Publications and conferences, such as they were, were treated as a service to members and, though charges were made for them, normally ran at a loss. Members' subscriptions roughly covered payable running costs, so the Nuffield grant provided the net cash balance. As the grant was phased out, subscriptions were raised and became a higher proportion of the total income, around 90%. The LSE made it clear that it was not prepared to subsidise the BSA to the same extent indefinitely. In 1956, the first indication of payment to them for secretarial services appears, and soon more was asked for.

In 1956, the first investment was made, in Defence Bonds, and investments started to make a modest contribution to the balance, ranging through the 1960s from 4.9% to 8.9%. In 1958, a subcommittee was set up to formulate a financial strategy to respond to the decline in subsidies, and as a result of its recommendations subscriptions were raised again. It was also decided that publications must be prevented from making a loss, non-members attending meetings should be charged or asked to join, future conferences should be annual and plan a profit, and EC members from outside London should try to get their travel expenses from their own universities (only some universities agreed). In the interim, it was necessary to cash part of the investments. The subcommittee sketched two alternative ideal-type plans for the future of the Association: Plan A, with its keynote retrenchment, and Plan B, with its keynote expansion. It did not propose that either be accepted, but asked the EC to decide where between these extremes policy should lie; the minutes do not record whether any decision was made in those terms. Below, we shall see that the distinction between the Plan A and Plan B approaches became a running theme in BSA affairs. In 1960, a modest surplus was made on the year, and the balance in hand started to rise. The treasurer told the AGM that 'a capital fund had to be built up against the time when the Association became a completely independent, self-supporting organisation'.

The 1962 conference, held in Brighton, was successful in attracting a large number of participants, but a loss was made on it, despite the 1958 decision, because the charges had been fixed at a non-economic rate. In 1963, no conference was held, so a good surplus was made; for 1964, a higher fee was set with the aim of covering expenses – it did not fully do so, but came near to it. Gwen Ayers' resignation in that year led to a review of the situation, and it was agreed that Anne Dix would work for the BSA half-time and be paid half her salary by them, remaining employed by the LSE for the other half of her time. It was minuted at the EC meeting of 1 July that 'ideally, the Association should aim at independence, but it was appreciated that this was not possible in the immediate future owing to the size of the membership and consequent limited income'. By 1965, membership had increased, but so had expenses. The setting up of *Sociology* was under discussion, so to cover its set-up costs there was another rise in subscriptions, from two guineas to three for full members, to whom a combined membership and journal subscription would be offered at a favourable rate. The years 1967–9 showed the first substantial annual deficits, corresponding to the appearance of the first volumes of *Sociology* – and partly due to the subsidised rate for members – although a reasonable balance still remained in hand. There had also been higher costs for the production of the *Register* and a register of research, and a loss on a summer school run without external funding. It was remarked at the AGM that 'it was gratifying to note that although this must not be an annual occurrence, the present deficit was entirely due to the general expansion of the work of the Association'.

Membership was increasing fairly steadily as the discipline expanded, so subscription income held up well, but another rise was required for 1970, and this reduced the subsidy to members' purchase of *Sociology*. More remunerative investments were sought; Defence Bonds were sold, and money placed in unit trusts instead. Inflation now became a strong factor, and yet another subscription rise was needed for 1972 to meet rising costs. However, in that year royalties from the sales of the first conference volume, as well as *Comparability in Social Research* (Stacey, 1969), made the publications balance healthier – and the cancellation of the summer school meant no loss there. But the EC set up a subcommittee to discuss 'all aspects of future policy including facilities which hitherto have not been provided due to lack of funds'. The only financial decision this led to was that a reduced subscription rate was introduced for former student members for two years, to encourage their continued membership. It was felt that the office should remain in London despite the expense – and that buying the Association's own premises there would be difficult, and probably too expensive. The issue of finding a new publisher for *Sociology* who would offer better terms was raised, but this turned out to be unnecessary, since Oxford University Press agreed a more favourable arrangement.

In 1973–4, a long period of serious inflation was starting, and the treasurer correctly anticipated that inflationary cost increases were about to make expenditure exceed income. Income needed to be raised anyway; subscriptions should therefore be raised, he argued, and various economies made and minor services charged for. It might be necessary to leave the LSE and face higher office costs, so negotiations – which came to nothing – started for office space with the Centre for Environmental Studies (EC 26 April). An important strategy decision was made to create the post of development officer in 1974. It was hoped that two-thirds of the cost of the post would be met from the increased membership which it would promote, 10% from a subscription rise, and the rest from reserves. In the event, these hopes were not met.

In 1975, it had been necessary to realise £3,000 of short-term investments to meet the deficit. The controversial decision was made not merely to raise subscriptions for 1976, but to do so substantially for many members, and to introduce an income-related scale. (Two alternative schemes for the rise had been offered to the AGM, and it chose the income-related rather than the flat-rate one.) Several members had written to the treasurer arguing against this, on the ground that the rise was so large in one step that it would provoke mass resignations (Wakeford, 1975), and on the ground of principle that BSA is a learned society, which risks losing sight of its main objectives in the pursuit of solvency – as such, it should have equality of membership and the rate should be the same (Macdonald, 1975). There was, as John Wakeford had predicted, a net loss of almost 500 members in 1976[1] – but total subscription income nonetheless rose significantly (despite the problems caused by many members' failure to change their standing orders to the new figure), from £7,909 in 1975 to £17,119 in 1977. The financial crisis had been met. Figures for the movement in real terms of academic salaries (Cradden, 1998) show that they had been declining, and hit a new low in 1975, which probably contributed to the unfavourable reception of the rise. (This was the period which produced the stirringly militant AUT slogan 'Rectify the Anomaly'.)

By 1977, salaries had risen somewhat and so, correspondingly, had membership. Conferences and *Sociology* had become profitable, and high interest rates meant that investments were doing well; for the first time in four years, a profit was made on the year. A new policy was adopted of diversifying sources of income so that subscriptions would be less dominant in it, and future rises would not be so marked and create such ill feeling. The strategy was to aim for subscriptions to produce around 60% of annual expenditure, the conference 13%, investments 12% and publications 24%. (Those figures add up to 109%, because the generation of a surplus was also envisaged.) At the same time the possibility of the BSA taking over the publication of *Sociology* itself was under discussion, and in 1979 this was indeed done, after which the income from it rose considerably.

By 1978–9, rises in academic salaries meant that people lower down the scale than anticipated were paying the highest subscription rate, and by the end of 1980 virtually everyone in full-time employment would be paying the top rate. A proposal was put to the 1980 AGM for a rise 'to reintroduce the degree of equity into subscription levels which had been intended by the changes in 1975 but was now eroded by pay increases', but the motion was referred back for one to be brought forward with '*more* equity'; the 1981 AGM approved a longer scale, with very low rates at the bottom for students and those unemployed or not fully employed. BSA Publications was set up as a separate limited liability company in 1978; the BSA as a charity was not allowed to make a regular surplus from routine trading, so this was a way of formally avoiding that as publishing activities expanded. The main BSA could then charge it for services – part of the Development Officer's salary was charged to it, reducing the profits to avoid tax liability – as well as receiving donations from it by covenant, which also had tax advantages. (The separation of publications in this way also had the legal advantage that no claims on the BSA's assets could be made for matters such as printing bills or libel claims.)

The early 1980s was the period of 'the cuts' (in university funding), and this influenced the BSA's position. In 1981, the LSE again raised its charges for accommodation and services, to a figure much higher than before, though this was still generous by commercial standards. Additional costs were being incurred by representation at a number of cuts-related meetings, such as those of the working party on proposals for what eventually became ALSISS. The squeeze on departments, which had traditionally been able to use some of their own resources for BSA purposes, meant that more had to be covered by the Association; economies in the running of *Sociology* were needed to sustain its position. In 1983, the 'Support Fund' was started, to provide small sums of money to members in weak financial positions for such matters as conference attendance and research expenses. This was the year of the highest recorded number of higher degrees in sociology, but the cuts meant that there was an extremely unfavourable ratio between those and the numbers of university posts available for their holders (Platt, 2000). There was talk of redundancies as well as unemployment.

In 1982, there was a general EC discussion of membership, services and administration, and it was felt that membership was lower than it should be because the subscription was too high for what members received in return. At the following AGM, therefore, the treasurer argued that, with *Sociology* now profitable and finances on a satisfactory basis, 'While this situation gladdens the heart of a Finance committee, it is clearly unsatisfactory: we ought to be using our resources for the benefit of our members and the discipline... '; spending should be increased. The general strategy became to improve services and so increase membership. *Sociology* became a free membership benefit for full members from 1984, after careful calculation of the (low) marginal cost of the extra copies which would be required. The Publications Committee started to consider the possibility of a second journal, and it was agreed to pursue the proposal for WES, despite the risks if it was published in-house. (A comparison of launch costs showed that they would be similar in-house and commercially, but the return would be much higher in-house, so the risk was taken, though with provisos about a ceiling on expenditure and swift action in case of emergency.) By 1988, WES was breaking even, and a third journal was beginning to be contemplated.

In the 1970s and 1980s, the Association had in effect gone through a long learning process on how to run a body of the size it was reaching and with the aims it held in a changing legal and economic context. One treasurer remarked that in his period of office 'It was a leisurely activity, I'm tempted to say a gentlemanly pastime; the BSA in those days was not businesslike in the way we need to be now.' Some of the learning was through bad experience. In 1991, a possible liability for VAT was discovered:

We had a long crisis over whether we owed back taxes, especially VAT, and apparently we did and had to do all kinds of special pleading that we didn't think we had enough turnover. We made them an offer really, but we still paid about £5000.

Steps were taken to arrange affairs to avoid the liability for the future.

In the later 1980s, some predicted deficits did not occur, because of both unintended economies due to lack of demand for money set aside for some purposes such as the Support Fund and salary rises, and the success of profit-making activities such as the Book Club.[2] An office computer was finally purchased in 1986; it was suggested that the purchase of property should again be considered, and serious consideration of alternative office locations started. In 1990, the BSA had had to move to one small office in the LSE rather than the two formerly occupied, and significant increases in rent were anticipated as well as more realistic charges for such services as post, phones and stationery. The BSA was asked to take over the entire salary of Anne Dix, though she would remain formally an employee of the LSE. In 1992, she reached retirement, and the break with the LSE was finally made. The move was decided on as a result of a substantial report from the Staff and Premises Committee, 'The Next Forty Years', which called this 'the most far-reaching decision facing the BSA in its 40 years' history'. It was clear that other universities did not have space available, or would be unable to offer it at anything less than full-cost charges, so a science park was the next best option. Lower prices for office accommodation were only available outside the South East, so it had to be in the North. At the 1991 AGM, a motion was put to attempt to retain the historic connection with the LSE, but this was defeated. The office was moved to a science park at the University of Durham, where it has remained.

Thus, after the initial period when the Association was establishing itself, the ups and downs of its financial position show the interaction between the internal situation and external factors such as the interest rates available on investments and the level of inflation. Successive treasurers predicted doom – and averted it. Eventually, the more proactive policy was adopted of encouraging membership by improving the services to members, combined with successful efforts to earn profits from publications and conferences and to benefit from investments. Table 26 shows the major shift over time in the balance of sources of income which resulted.

The annual report for 2000–1 shows c.31% of income in 2000 as coming from subscriptions,[3] so the trend has continued in the same direction. But what about the complete financial situation? Inflation makes it hard to see what is really happening over the longer term when the figures are given at contemporary prices. Table 27 uses constant prices to show how the Association has built up its financial position, and shows how has led to a much more satisfactory situation after the serious problems of the 1970s.[4]

Academic sociologists are not the most businesslike group by training or inclination, so this has been achieved despite the lack of interest or support of many members. (It is worth noting that two treasurers who were responsible for important policy shifts had come to academia with a background of some

Table 26 Major components[a] of BSA income

Year	% Contributed by Subscriptions	Investments
1955	63[b]	–
1960	90	5
1965	82	8
1970	89	3
1975	71	10
1980	60	27
1985	56	23
1989[c]	50	23

[a]Other components of income given in the accounts were 'publications' (the meaning of which changed markedly over time), conferences (early conferences usually made a loss and even when there was a charge appear only under expenditure, while for later ones only profits appear as income), and 'other'. Details of these are not included here because of the changing definitions and ambiguity involved.
[b]This figure is so low because of the initial grant received.
[c]All the figures in this table are taken from the annual accounts; 1989 is used here, and is the last date covered, because the accounts from 1990 are in a different format which is not easy to compare with the earlier format.

Table 27 Overall financial situation at 1985 prices (in £s, figures rounded to nearest £100)

Year	Income	Expenditure	Surplus, year	Balance
1955	9,000	7,000	2,000	8,000
1960	8,900	6,400	2,600	10,400
1965	11,800	6,500	5,300	24,200
1970	28,100	26,000	2,400	16,300
1975	31,000	37,900	[–6,900]	9,700
1980	42,200	29,800	12,400	59,900
1985	48,700	31,200	17,400	100,600
1990	72,600	42,400	30,200	137,800

business experience.) The AGM has usually accepted treasurers' proposals, but these have been formulated to take account of the character of the meeting, which has often been concerned to implement egalitarian policies without undue attention to their financial consequences. This is shown in the decisions on subscription scales and the Support Fund, with their special concern for the low-paid and unemployed. Other political themes have also sometimes been relevant; for instance, in 1979, money was withdrawn from an investment fund for charities because it held shares in South Africa.

One of the treasurers with some business experience remarked that

> The tension on the financial side was always trying to be businesslike,
> but also you couldn't call it profits, it had to be a surplus ... there was
> always the tension, should we be dirtying our hands making money, but
> also wanting the social welfare function, funding postgraduates and so
> on, which you couldn't do without it ... The danger always is that someone
> will get up at the AGM and say this is all wrong, why have you got
> £100,000 in the bank and people are starving in Angola ...

On the EC, too, ideological criteria have sometimes been salient. A member
from the 1970s, who took a minority position, reported in a 1997 interview
that:

> the Association had reserves of about £40,000, and it was in some stupid
> local authority account ... they didn't want our money in capitalism. I
> thought it ... irresponsible to our members; what we should do is buy a
> house – it would now be worth £2m! It would have been our HQ, but let
> it to other professional associations and make money out of them. It was
> rejected out of hand on principle, they were against property.

Another treasurer suggested that the long-term issue was not just ideological,
but one of ignorance about good investments and when to buy and sell: 'we
weren't people who knew about the Stock Exchange. Anne [Dix] used to get
advice from the bank'. This led to a very conservative investment policy, avoiding
anything with an element of risk.

A key issue throughout this financial history has been that of how to strike
the right balance between services to members and costs to them. The 'right'
balance is, on the one hand, one such that a fairly large number of members
join and maintain their membership so that the Association can sustain itself
financially and, on the other hand, one such that its claims to represent the
discipline and to speak with authority on its behalf are plausible. What is the
range of services that have been offered to members?

From the Association's earliest days, it provided meetings at which research
was presented, and discounts on journals; soon it also produced the first *Register*
of members. Once its own journal was established, this became first cheaper
and then entirely free to members. Conferences too became regular and cheaper
to members, and started to offer many activities besides research papers,
including ones directly relevant to individual career progress. Spasmodic
newsletters of various kinds appeared, and then were succeeded by the permanent
Network, whose function in providing news and announcements is now
supplemented by e-mail circulation of a wide range of items. For a number of
years, the Book Club provided general academic books at cut prices, in addition
to the discounts available on the books the BSA itself generated. Study groups
have been encouraged to form, and subsidised. All of those services have been
open to every member. Some other services have only been open to a limited
range of members: low membership rates subsidised by other members have
assisted student members and those who are unemployed or low paid, and the
Support Fund has been open to them for such costs as conference attendance;

the Abrams prize is awarded to the authors of first books; the Postgraduate Forum promotes the interests of postgraduates, and summer schools provide an important opportunity for them; support of various kinds has been provided for the teaching function, and at regular intervals a leaflet designed to help in recruiting students to sociology has been made available. In addition, although this is not publicised except when there have been public issues like threats to close departments, or the Atkinson affair, the officers of the Association have from time to time taken up personal – or departmental – cases on behalf of members, and have been available to help in the resolution of disputes between members as well as between members and outside bodies. (For a while from the late 1970s, one of the tasks to be undertaken by a member of the EC was that of Disputes Officer, to deal with any disputes that arose.) Finally, at a level between the universal individual benefit and the discipline-wide public good, there have been the ethical code and other codes which can be invoked for self-defence against demands sometimes made by employers or supervisors, and a document specifying the standards appropriate for departmental resource provision which could be used to support local claims. But different individual members, and categories of member, naturally have different needs and interests, and no member is likely to use the full range of services unless over a long career in the discipline; one member's valued service is another's subsidy to a category to which they do not belong.

The role of representing the discipline (including the free riders who do not join) can only be supported if enough individuals are for their own reasons sufficiently interested to join (and they are predominantly not in the categories whose membership is subsidised). Their own reasons may include simply feeling that it is right to belong to one's professional association, or altruistic and discipline-oriented reasons, but will often also include perception of more individualistic and personal benefits that follow. (One must assume that for potential members who are not professional sociologists, who have always figured among the membership, individualistic reasons will be more salient.) It is in general these more individualistic benefits that treasurers have had in mind when raising the issue. There could be scope for a thesis exploring the relationship between the fluctuating provision of these services, their value to members, academic salaries, and the numbers of members in different categories. Without that systematic work, it can only be a matter for speculation whether a regular and predictable relationship would be found.

Staffing and administrative roles

In the beginning, Gwen Ayers, whose prime employment was as administrative secretary to the LSE's Department of Sociological Research, a post funded by a Rockefeller Foundation grant, was allowed to combine that with acting as secretary to the BSA. When the grant ran out, the department was supported from the LSE general research funds, and a BSA contribution was required to her salary. By 1957, she estimated that she and Anne Dix each spent about three-quarters of their time on BSA work (EC 11 February 1958). In 1963 (EC 1 July), she resigned and, for a very long time after that, Anne Dix essentially did all the office work of the Association, with only occasional ad hoc assistance.

(She said that one of the attractions of the job was that 'some of the honorary officers were very active, though I must say none was very interfering ... you were in a sense your own boss ... and as long as you got the work done you had your own schedule' (Dix, 1992: 3).) It ran on the basis of her close familiarity with every aspect of its activities, and she was the institutional memory as EC members came and went. The workload was often heavy, especially in the run-up to the conference, but she pointed out that when computers became common in academic life far more of the work started to be done by academics themselves rather than in the BSA office. The officers also carried out some of the work of the Association, and frequently received clerical support from their own institutions.[5]

In 1974, Jane Hoy was appointed as Development Officer, and worked from the BSA office at the LSE. She was the first person formally to be an employee of the BSA (rather than the LSE), and it became clear that BSA had no procedure for dealing with employees; Robert Moore, who was then treasurer, reports that he had to find out about National Insurance etc., and go to buy the stamps himself. Jane Hoy did not know who, if anyone, was her line manager. One former chairperson suggests why in remarking that:

> obviously it was the case that the Exec was responsible for the office in some way, I suppose by definition that means that the Chair had some kind of responsibility for it, but it was never formulated that as Chair ... I just remember feeling that the office worked.

Although she talked to various senior members of the EC when they passed through the office, she did not feel that she was given the induction she would have needed to understand the affairs of the organisation and its needs as well as a Development Officer should. The panel of professors who interviewed her for the job were perhaps too impressed by her previous work for the National Union of Mineworkers – 'miners always go down well with sociologists'! – and did not realise that a sociology graduate in her twenties would know very little about professional associations or the politics of universities. In effect, she found that she became another member of staff sharing the tasks of the office, especially around conference time – Anne Dix was surely overloaded – rather than carrying out the development role as had been hoped; she also worked closely with the editor of the new *Network*. 'I think they probably intended my job to be more out there, but the way the organisation was run meant that I was more like somebody who services committees – but that was also because I didn't have the clout to get people involved' (Hoy, 1997). That underestimates her contribution to development work, but indicates the difficulty of the role as conceived.

Meanwhile, however, two more appointments had been made, both part-time ones dealing with the Association's expanding publishing activities. The first, in 1978, was that of Mike Milotte as Publications Officer; he dealt particularly with books and their publishers, both books produced by the BSA and the running of the Book Club, which for a number of years was very successful. By 1988, his work for BSA had become four days a week; then he resigned, and had two successors with short-term contracts before the post was abolished as the move to Durham was planned. Joyce Ward was appointed as business manager for the journals in 1979, and her task gradually expanded from very much part-time to almost full-time employment as they grew. Her husband Robin Ward was a former treasurer of the BSA,[6] and this no doubt helped with what could otherwise have been some of the problems of induction. She worked from her home (in the Midlands, not London), and this dealt in an informal but mutually convenient way with the problem of office space, but the advantageous arrangement by which back stock of the journals filled an increasing area of her loft could not continue indefinitely. Jane Hoy was not totally happy in her BSA job, with 'the kind of flavour you get that you're there to service somebody else's career; you get a lot of thanks, but you're not expected to take an interest in the ideas' and, in 1978, she resigned, and it was decided not to refill the post; some of her former tasks were divided between Joyce Ward and Mike Milotte. (The appointment in 2001 of a marketing and information officer could be seen as reinstating a post with some of the sort of responsibility that she had held.) Joyce Ward eventually retired at the end of 1996, and the journals were returned to a commercial publisher rather than continuing in-house, so her position was not replaced. In 1989, the role of press officer was created, and taken on by an academic sociologist who attended EC meetings. With this enlarged staff, a Staffing and Premises Committee was set up which, to maintain confidentiality, did not report to the EC in the usual way, but could deal with issues in the BSA's role as employer.

When the move from the LSE was under consideration, it was necessary to review staff numbers and tasks to decide what accommodation would be needed. An experienced executive member remarked that

> *Anne was just an exceptionally special person, and her knowledge of the Association and its members was just extraordinary, so some measure of why it ran for so well for so long was down to her special qualities. So even if it had stayed the same there would have been some hiccups and difficulties when she retired.*

The committee decided that it would be preferable to locate all the activities of the Association in one place and, given the degree of overlap between the tasks of existing staff and the complexity of the division of labour which had grown up by gradual accretion, also to review staffing needs. The aim became to concentrate each main activity into one post, to increase the technical expertise available, and to relate the level of responsibility to the level of remuneration and authority of each post. (LSE's staffing policies had meant that Anne Dix, a non-graduate, could not be promoted out of a clerical grade.) Four new posts were created: an executive officer, an administrative officer with special responsibility for financial matters, a clerical officer and a secretary/clerk. Despite the inevitable disruption of the transition period, the change was made fairly smoothly, and the Durham office was safely established.

A shift to greater professionalisation of the organisation came with the move; the office staff was larger, and more outside professional advice was taken rather than relying on the varying knowledge and competence in these matters of lay members of the EC. (It is worth noting, though, how important it was at this stage that several members had considerable experience in senior administrative posts, with responsibility for staff and budgets, in their own institutions.) In 1992 and 1993, there were new Charities Acts, which stressed accountability. Members of the EC now found they had became 'trustees', and had personal civil liability for the Association's debts and criminal liability for breaches of the law by it. New internal procedures were necessary, and this meant an increasing need to draw on external professional advice. In addition, it became necessary for the office to take on an increasing amount of work, as the financial pressures on universities meant that tasks which used to be done by volunteers with institutional support for no charge were no longer willingly undertaken on that basis. A crisis arose in 1999, when it emerged that some of the Association's formal obligations had been neglected. BSA Publications was removed from the Companies Register because it had not filed the full set of documents legally required, and similar irregularities had arisen in matters related to charities legislation; the consequences were sorted out, but at the cost of a fine and a large amount of work for the officers and staff.

There was a major review of the organisation, led by an external consultant recommended by the National Council for Voluntary Organisations. The aim was to identify how far existing systems supported the Association's requirements and where they were deficient. It was concluded that 'the systems were unduly complex, there was unnecessary duplication and paper chasing, too many committee meetings were being held, there were too few people dealing with too many functions, and there was a serious danger of staff overload' (Minutes of AGM, 2000). (One of those involved suggested that this was partly due to the larger number of smaller committees created in 1997.) As a result, the financial software used was to be replaced, additional staff were to be employed at peak times, and the committee structure was to be simplified. The decision was also made to convert the Association from an 'unincorporated association' into a company limited by guarantee, and in 2000 this change was implemented on the basis of proposals developed with the help of a consultant. Thus the Association, while retaining its charitable status, became for the first time from a legal point of view an organisation rather than a group of individuals acting personally. This meant that the office staff could be formally employed by the Association rather than the individual who happened to sign their letter of appointment, members could pay their subscriptions electronically or by direct debit, and members of the EC were no longer personally liable legally in respect of their assets for the BSA's financial affairs. One EC member remarked that 'the BSA has grown from a one-person, back-room voluntary group into a complex, professional organisation with a small professional staff within ten years and without anyone really noticing' (EC 24 September 1999) – but now it had been noticed, and action was accordingly taken.

Committee structures

The office is one part of the BSA's organisational structure, but the executive and its subcommittees is another, so to complete the picture we also need to outline the major changes there in roles and structures. The EC itself has changed rather little in its structure since the 1950s, when provision was made for some members to retire early so that there would be continuity despite turnover, and the position of president was added. For many years, the working officers were the chair, vice-chair, honorary general secretary and treasurer, and a less formal provision was made for deputies to assist the secretary and treasurer and potentially succeed them; other tasks were taken on ad hoc. (Some presidents have accepted the role as primarily honorific, while others have taken an active part in the executive's work.) In addition, however, there have been many ex officio members, who have reported on their spheres of work and could also choose to take part in the general business. In the 1990s, the post of honorary vice-president was introduced for ex-presidents; this does not give EC membership, but it is understood that the holders will be available for suitable specific tasks. There have been many working parties, and longer-term subcommittees, often composed of both EC members and non-members. It would be intolerably complex to describe every change in these matters, and no attempt will be made to do so. But there have been repeated general reviews of activity which have often initiated deliberate shifts in practice, and we shall concentrate on these, which typically have concerned both structures and policies.

The 1958 subcommittee has already been mentioned above. At the end of 1972, a Future Policy Subcommittee: Long Term Planning reported to the EC (Doc B, item 11, EC 15 December 1972). The issues it considered were membership, the relationship with other professional bodies, the location of the Association's HQ, and relations with government and decision making. The growth of the ATSS and other such bodies was felt to indicate a failure of the BSA to recruit potential members, and the possibility was raised of exploring the incorporation of ATSS into the BSA, 'where it belonged'.[7] Other disciplinary associations were seen as more successful, and discussion with them might be helpful. Development in the direction of a professional association was seen as worryingly likely to ossify the curriculum. It might become necessary to split the Association between a learned society and a professional qualifying association, with the aim of promoting and supporting standards and competence both inside and outside academia, but if so this should not be allowed to prevent diversity and conflict within the discipline. In relations with political decision-makers, it was agreed that 'we would make little progress ... until we are incorporated with our own top brass', but the Association should speak for sociologists in general, so a modus vivendi was also needed with more radical groups.

In 1974, the EC initiated another major review of the Association's organisation, and put proposals for change to the membership, at a special meeting as well as two AGMs. These proposals, aimed at both moving to 'a further stage in professionalisation' and expanding the Association's public activities, included the institution of two classes of membership: full, for people with qualifications in sociology or employed as sociologists, and associate, for anyone else interested in sociology, possibly with reduced rights to vote and hold office. This was a response to the growth of sociology and interest in it, outside the universities as well as inside them. It was at this meeting that the issue of relations with other bodies of sociologists was raised, and reports were circulated from the ATSS, SIP and the NATHFE Sociology branch.

It was agreed at the meeting to close the Teachers' Section. The motion for two classes of membership, however, only received a narrow majority, 13–11, among the small attendance; the EC therefore decided to take the views of the whole membership by postal questionnaire. The first question was 'Should the BSA seek to strengthen its claim to be a professional association by requiring that in future only those persons with higher educational qualifications in sociology and/or employed as sociologists be admitted to full membership?' The questionnaire also asked whether there should be two subscription rates for varying levels of service, and whether subscriptions should be related to income [LSE Box A7]. Four hundred members responded to the questionnaire, and a clear majority supported each of the proposals made. In addition to the items on which the membership was consulted, it was recommended to the incoming EC to decentralise business by introducing a system of subcommittees (Teaching, Research, Membership, Programmes, Finance, Publications and Ethics; only the last two already existed.) and to appoint a Development Officer. The new EC acted accordingly though, by the 1976 AGM, experience had led to the amalgamation of the Membership and Finance subcommittees, and by the 1977 AGM Teaching and Programmes were amalgamated. Difficulties had been found in getting enough candidates to stand for election to the subcommittees. A new structure was put in place: Publications, Programmes and Teaching, Research, Finance and Membership, Equality of the Sexes, Professional Ethics, (and the Working Party on Education Cuts). Each subcommittee had two members nominated by the EC, two elected by the membership, and three from defined interest groups; some also had many ex officio members such as editors of *Sociology Network*, book series, and conference volumes, and summer school and conference organisers. But in 1979, insufficient nominations were received for any of the subcommittees, and soon those for Programmes and Teaching, Research and Ethics were disbanded, but a Standing Committee on Conferences was set up.

In 1991, Bob Burgess (then president) put forward proposals, which were implemented, designed to streamline EC meetings, and to get informed decisions made faster with less circulation of paper. The main ones were that agendas and minutes should be in a standard form, that EC agendas should distinguish clearly between items to be considered and those merely for report, and that there should be a new office of chair of Publications Committee, who should report on all publications matters, rather than editors attending the meetings.

In 1997, Finance and Membership was split into two; Membership and Services will 'take a more strategic role in relation to the development of services to members and to monitor trends in recruitment.' Publications was also divided into Publications and Publications Management and Policy Group, with the aim of reducing the burden on editors, and allowing more scope for creative thinking. But after a year's experience showed that it created extra work, this reverted to the old single committee pattern. Committees on Race and on Teaching and Learning were created.

Finally, the Annual Report for 2000–1 shows the most radical new structure. This introduced an Academic Affairs Committee (with the remit of developing initiatives to promote and enhance the intellectual profile of sociology), and a Professional Development Committee ('to develop and implement initiatives aimed at supporting members of the BSA in personal and career growth'). This was done in response to soundings about what was important to members. The Equality of the Sexes Committee, Publications Committee, Race Committee and Scotland Committee were retained, and the old Finance and Personnel Committees were combined to create a Finance and General Purposes Committee. In parallel with this, every elected member of the EC was given a formal role; those who were not officers of the Association acted as chair or vice-chair of the new committees, or filled the new roles of link officer for study groups and for departmental representatives and postgraduates. A report on progress since incorporation adds that, since most tasks formerly carried out by the secretary now fall to the office, that post is to be abolished. The term of office on the EC was increased from two to three years to improve continuity and experience, and to stimulate members' interest and participation the direct election of the three remaining officers (chair, vice-chair and treasurer) was to be introduced from 2002.

There does not seem to be a clear overall direction of change in the development of the way the EC has worked, at least in intermediate periods; indeed, similar reforms seem to have been made several times, addressing similar problems. That is in part simply because some problems are permanent ones; for instance, more participation by members and devolution of detail to subcommittees always seems a good thing, but it is almost always difficult to recruit enough people to take the jobs on. But perhaps there are also traces of what Anne Dix observed – that after four years there would always have been a complete turnover in EC membership, and the new members would not know what had been discussed and tried before and so would almost inevitably start considering whether it might not be a good idea to invent the wheel. This supports the natural wave pattern which arises when one tries a new way of doing things, after a while discovers its drawbacks and institutes reforms, whose disadvantages after a time emerge … and so on. However, despite some elements of recurrence, there is no doubt that the developments of the 1990s have made a break with the less formal working of the past.

Thus, the BSA started as an in-house sideshoot of the LSE, grew to an organisation with a small office and employees of its own supported by a high input of voluntary effort but with no real management, and then transformed itself into a more formally structured body which could meet the demands of both a much larger membership and a more complex and demanding external situation.

Notes

1   See Chapter 5 for the details.

2   This started in 1977; in 1987, 171 titles were offered, and 2,370 books were bought; in 1989, it was 266 titles and 3,287 sales (Reports to AGM). It lapsed with the move to Durham, was revived in 1995, and then was abandoned as too much work for the office.

3   The figure given in the Report is 21%, but that includes in the base a large amount of Medical Sociology Group income, almost all of which was spent on MSG purposes.

4   I am indebted to my father Kit Platt for his advice as a chartered accountant on the analysis of these accounts.

5   When Margaret Stacey took over the secretaryship, it became necessary to make a payment to her department in Swansea in recognition of this; that was apparently the first time this was done.

6   Anne Dix (1992: 15) reports another example of informal practice and personal involvement. In the early days of the Book Club, Robin Ward used to get a list of the conference delegates expected, check it against the list of Book Club orders, and fill his car with their books to take to the conference in order to avoid the BSA having to pay postage on them.

7   It is not clear whether this idea was taken any further at this stage, but the report to the 1978 AGM mentions that agreement to the eventual amalgamation of BSA with SIP, ATSS and NATHFE had not been gained.

Chapter 9

The BSA in its organisational context

The BSA in its structure, organisation and pattern of activities is not just an independent body responding to its own internal concerns, but a member of a set of organisations which can be seen as making up a loosely linked system. This chapter looks at some of the more salient other organisations in the set, and how the BSA has related to them. These include other international and national organisations of sociologists, learned societies from other disciplines, and the ESRC. Other bodies with which BSA has had less continuous dealings have included national educational policy makers such as the Higher Education Funding Councils and government departments, academic trade unions, research funding bodies other than the ESRC, public examination boards and single universities when issues have been raised about individual cases (for some instances, see Chapter 7). These are mentioned in other chapters when an issue involving them is discussed.

Organisations of sociologists

The specifically sociological subset of related organisations includes the ISA and the European Sociological Association (ESA), of which the BSA is a collective member, and other British groupings less inclusive than the BSA which have had various forms of affiliation with it: Sociologists in Polytechnics (SIP), the Association for the Teaching of the Social Sciences (ATSS), the Sociology Section of the Association of Teachers in Colleges and Departments of Education (ATCDE) and the Sociology HoDs body.

International Sociological Association

To understand the BSA's relations with the ISA, a little explanation of its working is needed. The ISA was founded in 1949, at the instance of the Social Science Department of UNESCO, and initially followed a United Nations organisational model, with only collective members, wherever possible national sociological associations. Its remit was to concern itself with the world-wide development of sociology in both teaching and research. This was part of the post-war settlement, with social science seen as an instrument for the promotion of democracy, peace and understanding how to prevent circumstances encouraging the growth of fascism.[1] Its collective members were represented in its Council, from which was elected an Executive Committee with officers. The Council consisted of representatives nominated by the national associations. It maintained an office with a secretariat, which moved every few years; the executive secretary was normally an academic working part time. (Since 1987, the secretariat has been based in Madrid, and headed by a professional administrator.) World Congresses were held from 1950 onwards, and a Research subcommittee was established which actively promoted research.

As the organisation, and sociology, evolved, the initial structure changed considerably. The Research Committee subdivided into groups with specialist interests. At first, members of these were still recruited individually from known researchers, and there were limits on the number who could belong from any one nation, so these were small elite working groups. It became evident that it was in these groups that there was more real internationalism of approach than came from national representatives. In response to growing dissatisfaction with the formal structure, it was radically changed in 1970: individual membership of the Association was introduced, Research Committees (RCs) became open, and the EC was no longer elected from within the Council. (It has always been informally understood that major geographical and political constituencies such as the Soviet bloc or the Third World should be represented on the EC, whatever their numbers of sociologists.) Since 1970, there have been further moves to represent the RCs in the structure of governance, reaching the point now where there are parallel Councils for RCs and for national associations, and they are equally represented on the EC. These changes have, of course, meant that the role of national associations as such has become much reduced, although there is far more scope for participation by their individual members.

The BSA, when it was in turn founded, joined the ISA. The leading figures then in British sociology were active in the ISA's foundation, and as individuals figured prominently in its earliest development: Morris Ginsberg was one of the two first vice-presidents, David Glass played the leading role on its Research Committee, and T. H. Marshall was president from 1959 to 1962. From 1949 to 1998, Britain has been second only to the USA in the number of representatives it has had on the ISA executive. Table 28 shows every British representative on the executive, plus holders of editorships and the executive secretaryship, in chronological order of start, with details of major positions held in the BSA by these people.

How has it come about that these people have occupied those positions? The answer varies in different cases. T. H. Marshall was head of UNESCO's Social Science Department from 1956 to 1960, and that was closely involved with the ISA as part of UNESCO's general social-scientific activity, so his emergence as president probably came about through that network of connections as much as via the BSA; it is not referred to in BSA minutes. Others had no special prior ISA connections,[2] and a decreasing concern with ISA matters is suggested when in 1961 [EC 2 October] it was proposed that BSA delegates be appointed when it was known who would be attending the World Congress at which the Council would meet. But by the later 1960s, the climate of the times was in favour of greater democracy, and it was agreed (EC 19 April 1968) that, in future, BSA representatives should be elected by ballot of the membership and (EC 5 December 1969) that the ISA representative should be an ex officio member of the BSA EC; the notice of the AGM explained to members why the choice of representative was important. If this plan had been implemented with

Table 28 British ISA EC members and their main BSA roles

EC member	ISA roles	BSA roles
Morris Ginsberg	Vice-President 1949–56	Chairman 1951–4; president 1955–7
David Glass	Research Committee member, 1950-	EC member 1951–3, 1959–60
Tom Bottomore	Executive secretary 1953–9; Editor, *Current Sociology* 1957–62; vice-president 1970–4; president 1974–8	President 1969–71 (Invited to attend EC meetings when president of ISA)
W. J. H. Sprott	EC member 1956–62	Treasurer, 1954–9
T. H. Marshall	President 1959–62	EC member, 1951–4; chairman 1954–7; president 1964–9
Charles Madge	EC member 1962–70	Vice-Chairman 1957–8, 1960–2; chairman 1962–, 1966–8
Margaret Archer	Editor, *Current Sociology* 1973–81; EC member 1982–6; president 1986–90	EC member 1972–4
James Beckford	Editor, *Current Sociology* 1982–9; vice-president 1994–8	
Martin Albrow	Editor, *International Sociology* 1984–90	Editor, *Sociology* 1982–4; president 1985–7
Deniz Kandiyoti	EC member 1986–90	
William Outhwaite	Editor, *Current Sociology* 1989–93	
Jennifer Platt	EC member 1994–2002	Editor, *Sociology*, 1985–7; president 1987–9; EC member 1990–2

full participation, there might have been a more active relationship with the ISA. However, in 1970 [EC 27 February], it was reported that no nominations had been received for the post of ISA representative, so Tom Bottomore, the current BSA president, was nominated. While he was president, the question of ex officio membership did not arise. However, he ceased to be a member in 1972, and no replacement ISA representative seems to have been recruited. In 1974, with another ISA World Congress coming up, it appears that an ISA representative was elected. That was Tony Marks, who had been elected to the BSA EC in any case; he resigned in 1975 when his term on the EC came to an end. Bottomore was then asked to provide a 'job description' for the post, and in view of that it was agreed [EC 8 July 1975] that, instead of election by the membership, the position should be held ex officio by the president. Subsequently, the normal arrangement appears to have become that the president acts if planning in any case to attend the World Congress but, if not, recruits some other member of the EC who is attending to be appointed as an alternate representative.[3]

'It was a very interesting reflection on the BSA ... each national association nominated its representative to the ISA Council. There was the most lethargic, laid-back approach to it – the issue was punctiliously placed on the [EC] agenda, but approached in the same way that in a department you scrabble around saying "oh, we need a safety officer". Nobody on the executive wanted to do it; I was just about to volunteer when somebody said "why don't we ask Sami Zubaida" ... somebody had heard that Sami was going ... it was really not on the BSA agenda.'
(Archer, 1997)

The idea of Council membership as a continuing commitment with activity in between World Congresses may once have been a realistic one, but it has long ceased to be so; this corresponds to the ending of the system where ISA EC members had to be national representatives, and the more general declining centrality of national associations in the ISA's affairs. Thus, later British ISA activists were not necessarily recruited via the BSA: Margaret Archer was always much more active in the ISA than in the BSA, Deniz Kandiyoti is not recorded as even a BSA member in the Membership Registers of 1982 or 1988, and Jennifer Platt was recruited through ISA channels because of her activity as secretary of a Research Committee. For the appointive positions as editor, intellectual networks independent of organisations have often played a key role, and Tom Bottomore's long involvement made his knowledge and influence important. (Heavy British involvement has also been promoted by the importance of English language in ISA publications.) Those BSA members who have become really active appear to have been so in ways related to their personal interests and/or wider international connections at least as much as because of the BSA nomination;[4] correspondingly, many of those active within the BSA, including its officers, have had little or no participation in the ISA.

In addition to the holding of formal posts, British sociologists have also been quite prominent in rank and file activities such as participation in World Congresses and the open Research Committees. Figures are not available for all years,[5] but we note that 52 British participants attended the 1956 Congress and 82 the 1959 Congress, constituting 10% and 9.2% of the total attendance; it is not known how many of those were BSA members, but those figures are equivalent to 9.5% and 15.3% of the total BSA membership at the time. This was probably assisted by the fact that, in the 1950s, BSA conferences took place only irregularly, while ISA ones were initially at three-year intervals. (After 1962, the interval was four years.) The state of development of world-wide sociology – and long-distance transport – was such that the ISA was at this stage very much centred on Europe, and the network of international bodies based in Paris, though there was also active US involvement. However, as times have changed, British participation has remained relatively prominent; the equivalent of more than 10% of the BSA membership attended the Congresses of 1982 and 1990, and constituted 3.2% and 5.4% of the total attendance.

In the early days of both BSA and ISA, their affairs were quite entangled, in ways which centred on the LSE, then the undoubted heart of British sociology. The ISA secretariat, with Bottomore (an assistant lecturer at the LSE) as executive secretary, was located at the LSE from 1953 to 1959, in Skepper House, the same research building as the one in which the BSA then had its office. Glass was responsible for the programme of research on stratification and social mobility by the Research Committee, which held a working conference as early as 1951 (see Rinde and Rokkan, 1951) and led to the initiation of several national studies comparable to the British work already completed (Glass, 1954). When the ISA sought volunteers for ad hoc tasks, the BSA was sometimes the formal channel of recruitment, though the cross-connections, and the degree to which everything revolved around the LSE, were such that it was not necessarily clear in which capacity individuals such as Ginsberg or Glass were acting. As early as 1951, it was reported to the BSA EC that the LSE department was cooperating in the production of an international bibliography of sociology, subsidised by UNESCO, to appear at regular intervals under the auspices of ISA; later, this would be available to BSA members at a reduced rate.[6] The report by MacRae – a lecturer at the LSE – on the teaching of sociology (mentioned in Chapter 2) was commissioned by UNESCO (UNESCO, 1953) and, in 1961, John Smith, also a lecturer at the LSE, produced a work on the teaching of industrial sociology for the same series (Smith, 1961). Similarly, later in the 1950s, UNESCO promoted a social science dictionary in English and French, and Julius Gould, then a junior lecturer at the LSE, was recruited to play a lead working role in this, though he says (Gould, 1997) that was not at the request of the BSA. At any rate, the BSA EC set up a subcommittee to oversee the work [EC 7 December 1954], and received regular reports on progress; eventually representatives of the Association of Social Anthropologists and the Political Science Association were also involved. (This project led to Gould and Kolb, 1964.) Bottomore's textbook *Sociology* (1962) was commissioned by the ISA in 1957 to provide a text suitable for Indian students. When the UNESCO Social Science Department became less active, such activities became less salient; in addition, of course, as sociology developed internationally, any one national association was likely to have responsibility for a smaller share of the total.

Equally, as BSA developed its own activities more, it became less reliant on the ISA/UNESCO link to provide the material for them. After the 1950s, when ISA matters appeared regularly on BSA EC agendas, attention to them became more spasmodic. Relations between ISA and BSA at the organisational level have not always been entirely positive, and seem to have become less good as the two organisations and their leading personnel became more distinct. In 1965, the EC expressed concern at its lack of information, and eventually the secretary wrote to the ISA office complaining at the lack of the annual report and other information on its activities; it turned out that the Annual Report had actually been sent, but not presented to the committee. However, the letter expressed a more general feeling:

> *Our feeling as an EC, which reflects the feelings of many of our members, is that the ISA is a very remote and inaccessible body and we should like to act as an intermediary to put an end to this very unfortunate state of affairs.*
> (Banks, 1965)

At the next meeting, the secretary was able to report that he had now been 'inundated with literature', including a copy of the constitution, with which he appears not to have been familiar previously (EC 17 December 1965). (It is very unlikely that the BSA did not have an official copy in its office, but the secretary was based in Liverpool, several hours' train journey from the office in London, so there were practical problems then in keeping in touch.) EC interest in the earlier 1960s appeared to be mainly in the practical aspects of World Congresses and their organisation. In 1968, several letters were received from American sociologists involved in discussions of the ISA arising from the 1966 World Congress, and expressing dissatisfaction with various aspects of the ISA's structure and operation, including the way in which members of its Research Committees were recruited, and these were received sympathetically. Support was given to the proposal that the ISA should be more democratic; this would imply not just that the Research Committees should become more open, but also that the nominating process for office should involve elected members and lead to elections with alternative candidates, and that representatives of organisations such as those from the Soviet sphere, which were not true voluntary associations of sociologists, should not be eligible for its Council membership. (It was against this background that the decision – not successfully implemented – to elect the BSA representative to the Council was made.) Charles Madge, the BSA's current representative, attended the EC meeting on 1 November 1968 to clarify ISA matters, and explained the general problems in ISA administration caused by the inadequacy of its funds. A subcommittee was set up to consider the proposals for reform expected from the ISA, and put a resolution, passed without opposition at the 1970 Annual General Meeting, which opposed the proposed introduction of individual ISA membership except in special circumstances, declaring that:

> The national associations are the proper bodies to exert some degree of democratic control, through their representatives on the ISA Council, over the affairs of the ISA ... It [BSA] advocates other methods of improving ISA finances such as fixing the contributions from national associations in accordance with the volume of their membership.

The BSA's then representative on the ISA Council, Sami Zubaida, reported that he had argued against the proposal that Research Committees should be represented on Council, on the ground that, in practice, this would give greater power to senior academics from countries with resources for travel, mainly the USA. On both these points, the BSA view was defeated. At this period in particular, the ISA was seen by many as an arena in which more general political concerns could appropriately be expressed; Zubaida described the 1970 situation:

> The main politics was Cold War politics, there were the blocs, and I remember one Council meeting I attended there was an election for President of the ISA, and there was an unknown American from some obscure place and the other was Belgian or Dutch. They were both from the Western camp ... the whispering around was which of the two reactionaries to elect!
> (Zubaida, 1997)

and added that political left meetings were held at the Congress. (It is interesting to note that at this time of Cold War politics Reuben Hill – the 'unknown American' from the 'obscure place' of the University of Minnesota in Minneapolis, and clearly as such an ex officio reactionary – who had been a very active internationalist for many years in the ISA RC on the Family, was greeted on election, his wife recounts (Hill, 1998), with welcoming chants from the floor of 'Hillski! Hillski!' because of his good relations with members from the Soviet bloc.) Around this period, another cause of dissatisfaction was the BSA's repeated, but unsuccessful, attempts to get the ISA to take up publicly the cause of sociologists in various parts of the world who were oppressed and persecuted on political grounds for their sociological work. The ISA was extremely reluctant to do this, both because its remit required it to be non-political, and because of the international diplomatic implications; internally, though this was not necessarily clearly communicated to member associations, the officers often felt that quiet work behind the scenes was more likely to be effective, and it is evident that some did take place.

Through most of the 1970s, the ISA was not at all salient in BSA EC meetings. A detailed report is, however, on the record as made after the Council meeting at the 1970 World Congress and, again in 1973, it was decided that the Council representative should report on its meetings to the following February EC meeting. But that took place only in 1975 – and then the representative had been unable to attend the meeting, and no alternate appears to have been arranged; presumably the decision had been forgotten by 1979. Tom Bottomore, then ISA President, was invited in 1974–5 to attend the EC meetings, but is not recorded as actually having done so, though once some information from him was reported. In the 1980s, the situation was similar; the only reference to ISA affairs around the 1982 Congress is a resolution deploring the consequences of the Polish government's suspension of its national sociological association,[7] so that it could not be represented at the Congress (EC 9 July 1982). A discussion document put to the BSA executive said 'The ISA, and our relations with it, are a longstanding scandal, and our representatives on it have a lot to account for because they never have.' It does not, however, look as though it was only the ISA, or the BSA's representatives to it, who were responsible for this.

In 1985, the possibility was raised of supporting a bid from Warwick to host a future World Congress, but this lapsed for practical reasons. A report was made from the 1986 Council meeting, and merely noted in the EC minutes; there was a written report on the 1990 Council and Congress, with recommendations for action on a variety of organisational points where provision had been unsatisfactory, but there was much more discussion around that time of the process of creating what became the ESA, in which the BSA was actively represented. The 1998 Council and Congress make no appearance in the minutes. In the early 1990s, some proposals for change in the ISA were greeted unenthusiastically, both because they raised the BSA subscription and because they were seen as potentially undemocratic. The organisers of the 1994 BSA conference were to be asked to include on the programme space for a session on the ISA, with speakers actively involved in it, but this does not appear actually to have taken place. The BSA representative reported back to the EC on her experience as a Council delegate at the 1994 World Congress [EC 24 February 1995]; she noted that 'it was difficult to act for the BSA when she had not been previously aware of the internal politics of the ISA', and suggested that BSA should be more proactive and do more to draw on the knowledge of those who were actively involved. This was agreed, though it is not evident that any particular action was taken to follow it up. The discussion also raised the question of whether BSA should continue its ISA membership, or perhaps focus more on the ESA, though no decision to that effect was made.

These rather fragmentary notes of issues raised in the EC indicate the extent to which its concern with ISA has been fragmentary and spasmodic, and often little informed by direct personal knowledge of the organisation and its activities or formal structure, let alone its informal politics. Although that is bound to seem somewhat unsatisfactory, it is not at all surprising given the nature of the practical relations between the two. Recurring complaints have been made in the BSA executive that they receive no information from ISA, that they are not consulted on policy issues, and that their representatives on its Council cannot truly represent its views because the agenda is not known sufficiently in advance for them to gather opinion on it. The BSA's complaints have sometimes been justified, but sometimes have merely shown its lack of adequate internal mechanisms for dealing with the participation that is permitted by the ISA structure. But that provides opportunities for organisational participation at such infrequent intervals that it is very hard for those not immediately involved for other reasons to have any share in the organisational memory, or sense of continuity of business – especially when holders of key national roles always change between ISA meetings – and hence to understand what goes on; this is not likely to produce well-informed representative national participation.

The BSA does not now have a strong need for the ISA, either practically or as an indicator of status, as perhaps national associations in countries with less developed sociology do, and there have been many national issues, such as those connected with university expansion, student unrest and the changing policies of government and funding bodies, which have taken up a lot of its time and effort and left little for international issues. However, its individual members continue to make heavy use of the ISA's provision, though that is only by chance represented within the BSA's formal structures; this is a natural consequence of the shift to individual membership. The ISA's attention has now started to turn once again to the national associations, some of which have felt neglected, and perhaps this will lead to new developments. Ironically, though, the globalisation of intellectual communities makes the system of formal national representation – designed to promote internationalism – less relevant.

European Sociological Association

The ESA was only formally founded in 1995, although that was the culmination of a process started at the First European Conference of Sociology in 1992. Its activities are mainly intellectual: the holding of conferences, support of research networks, running a journal (*European Societies*) and a newsletter (*European Sociologist*), and initiating a book series. However, its conferences have shown considerable interest in policy-related issues, and its formal statement of purpose includes 'to give sociology a voice in European affairs ... in the midst of massive changes, including the transformations in east and central Europe and the increasing integration of the European Union'. As the ISA responded to the historical moment of the post-war settlement, this could be seen as in part a response to the historical moment of emergence of a new Europe in the wake of the break-up of the Soviet Union. (A latent function is to make it possible for sociologists from Eastern Europe, who find it hard to pay for attendance at more distant meetings, to play a full part, as many have been doing.) Perhaps it also reflects an increased interest in comparative European research encouraged by the availability of European Union funding.

The formal structure of the ESA has some similarity to that of the ISA. There is a Council of National Associations, with one representative from each member national association. This has an advisory role, it appoints the nominating committee for the EC, and its chairperson is an ex officio member of the EC without voting rights. But although there are formally constituted research networks, they have no role in governance. Instead, there is a General Assembly of individual members, which meets during conferences and makes the major decisions. The EC is elected by the General Assembly, and elects its own officers from among its number. Thus, this appears to be a sort of compromise between the usual structure of a national association, and the 'United Nations' model of national representation. How this works in practice it is too early to say, except that its conferences appear to have been large and successful.

The BSA was among the national sociological associations which participated actively in the founding of the ESA, and British sociologists have taken part in its committees and its research-related activities; however, of those who have done so, only the official national representatives have acted in a representative capacity, and they have not necessarily been prominent in BSA affairs. Again, therefore, the pattern of personal interests appears at least as important as formal organisational relations in determining involvement and, from a BSA point of view, the ESA should perhaps simply be regarded as a good additional opportunity for members to take part in conferences, research networks etc.

SIP, ATSS, ATCDE

These bodies have to be treated here collectively to some extent, since they often acted and were treated collectively in relation to the BSA. What they had in common was that each organised a group of sociology teachers who were not affiliated with universities (or, in the case of university departments of education, commonly came from non-university backgrounds). A short account of each is given below before going into the history of their dealings with the BSA.

Sociologists in Polytechnics (SIP) was, as its name indicates, a body whose membership remit was covered by that of the BSA. It came into existence, however, because, in the earlier stages of development of polytechnic sociology, many of those employed there worked under different conditions from the universities, and felt that the BSA was more oriented to the needs of universities.[8]

The polytechnics, created on the basis of existing colleges in 1966, were under the central auspices of the Council for National Academic Awards (CNAA), which approved their syllabuses and awarded their degrees, rather than the UGC, which did not control universities so tightly. CNAA validating groups were often headed by senior university teachers and, in some ways, this followed on from the old pattern of the London University external degrees, with a more formally hierarchical relationship. As well as degrees, the polytechnics offered more part-time and sub-degree level courses, and they were not expected to award higher degrees; their staff members had lower average qualifications than those in universities. Polytechnics were more focused on teaching, because research was not initially part of their formal remit, even though some certainly took place. They were intended to be heavily vocational, and to emphasise science and technology. However, they rapidly expanded, developed research and higher degree work and, in response to student demand, expanded their range of degree courses beyond science and technology. By 1973, the numbers of their students in social and business studies matched those in science and technology (Stewart, 1989: 203–4) and, by 1974, there were more sociology teachers employed in polytechnics than in universities. Thus they rapidly became more like the universities – and, in 1992, officially joined their number. SIP was most active in the later 1970s, when it held a number of conferences; at these, most papers were on organisational and teaching topics; its conferences were small and brought together people in similar situations who felt less confident and at home in BSA's larger and more diverse conferences. It also initiated a series of Working Papers, printed at Hatfield Polytechnic, intended to be written by sociologists in polytechnics and cognate institutions and to be focused on topics of particular interest to that group.[9] As the initial situation changed as they became more established, the need that was felt for a separate organisation faded.

One of the problems to which the polytechnic expansion at first led was that the new institutions had senior staff whose experience was from the less academic pre-polytechnic era, and the heads of sociology departments sometimes had little or no background in sociology. A similar problem could be found in colleges of education, the membership base of the Sociology Section of the ATCDE. ATCDE was a professional association which performed some of the functions of both a trade union and a learned society, and it had a number of disciplinary sections. The Sociology Section was formed in December 1967, by which time there was a lot of sociology taught in the colleges which trained school teachers. Its aim was 'the discussion of the teaching of sociology in teacher education', and its members were concerned with teaching sociology both to prospective teachers of social science and as part of the general teaching of educational method. It ran courses in conjunction with the relevant government department, held conferences on topics such as the submission of syllabuses to new validating bodies, and published material of related interest (Reid, 1974). These activities responded to a need that was felt which was not met elsewhere, though numbers of its members also belonged to the BSA. Its inaugural meeting was attended by an invited representative from the BSA EC, who reported back to the EC on it. In the mid-1970s, the traditional teacher training colleges were abolished by merger, closure or change of function. At the beginning of 1976, the ATCDE merged, in response to these changes, with the Association of Teachers in Technical Institutions, to form the new National Association of Teachers in Higher and Further Education (NATHFE), which was more straightforwardly a trade union (Stewart, 1989: 196–7). Inter-organisational relations at that level gradually lapsed.

The ATSS was founded in 1965 at the initiative of Charmian Cannon, a lecturer in the sociology of education at the London University Institute of Education; the aim was to provide support for the non-specialists catering for the growing demand for sociology in schools and technical colleges (Cannon, 1966). The ATSS has always included among its functions the circulation of useful teaching materials, as well as the discussion of teaching issues; it has also aimed to promote the role of social science in schools, and to maintain standards there, especially in the less specialist teaching. Its primary constituency is those involved in teaching to groups of school age, largely but not exclusively in sociology and for A levels, though a few members have come from other groups with an interest in the matter. A levels in sociology started in 1964 and, by the end of the 1970s, were being taken by over 17,000 candidates per year (Stewart, 1989: 151), and there were also well-established O-level courses and interdisciplinary work in 'social studies'. Given that these courses led on to university work in sociology, liaison with university teachers was seen as desirable from the point of view of both sides; contact with the BSA has been almost entirely on issues of syllabus and national examinations. Traditionally, the presidency of the ATSS alternated between prominent university sociologists and those drawn from the 'education' world, and numbers of people also active in the BSA have held the Presidency. There have also been less formal contacts from cross-membership – and Ms Cannon mentions, in the letter drawn on above, that it was via her husband, a polytechnic sociologist then a member of the BSA EC, that she had been approached to keep the BSA informed of ATSS activities. The EC in 1966 discussed the possibility of corporate membership of ATSS, but it was decided that not all BSA members might approve and so a donation was made instead – of the same value (Banks, 1966).

That start of BSA's formal relations with this set of organisations was rapidly followed up towards the end of the 1960s. In 1967, Joan Abbott was sent to represent the BSA at an ATSS conference in York, on which she made a lengthy report to the EC. It was reported to the 1968 AGM that the EC had been discussing how to deal with the colleges of education. A conference was held jointly with the social anthropologists in July 1968 to discuss the contribution university departments could make to teaching in schools; it emerged that there was much ignorance of sociology at the school level, and a subcommittee was set up to take the matter further. There was concern about the A-level syllabuses so far available, and informal discussions with the anthropologists continued. This led to discussions with the Oxford and Cambridge Exam Board about the development of an alternative syllabus. By September of 1969, the appointment of a part-time research assistant to collect source material for this was agreed and, in 1970, a proposal was made to the Board; the minutes do not indicate whether this was accepted. Meanwhile, by 1969, the Teachers' Section had co-opted to its executive (of only five other members) representatives from a polytechnic, a technical college, a college of education and Goldsmiths (then only a college 'institution with recognised teachers' within the University of London); it is not clear whether this was at the initiative of the main EC, or an independent decision. In 1972, Asher Tropp declared that if no member of the ATCDE were elected to the BSA EC, he would make proposals for the formal representation of minorities there; after the election, a member of the ATCDE was co-opted to the EC, which presumably met his immediate concern. It is of interest, in view of that reference to 'minorities', what the composition of BSA membership was at the time, and this was given in the January 1972 edition of *News and Notes*:

Last recorded place of employment of UK non-student members:		
	All current members (%)	Recent entrants (%)
University	54	50
Polytechnic		9
Technical college	23	13
College of education, school		13
Other, no record	23	15

We can see that the minorities were indeed substantial. In the 1973 AGM report, it was remarked that 'For a variety of reasons, many fortuitous, the current Executive is more representative of the membership than many of its predecessors',[10] and a constitutional amendment related to the issue was anticipated. This came forward and was approved at the 1974 AGM. It opened the possibility of corporate membership of the BSA[11] for appropriate organisations of sociologists; the membership fee suggested for SIP was only £10 per annum, and it joined. In the same year, regular meetings with SIP, ATSS and the NATHFE Sociology Section, plus the British Association's Section N,[12] started as the Standing Committee of Sociologists (SCOS).

Later in the year, the 'Which Way for the BSA' meeting had papers from each of these groups, and was introduced by a discussion paper from the executive which suggested that 'other professional groups, in the absence of an initiative from the BSA, have made incursions into fields which the Association might consider its own ... '. (For more on this meeting, see Chapter 8.) Mike Rustin of North East London Polytechnic responded to the discussion of professionalisation at this meeting by giving a paper to SIP, also published in *Network*, which strongly criticised the BSA and the conception of sociology as a profession which it was seen as representing; his comments arose from discussions in the SCOS. He saw BSA's dominant activity as 'to service the research activities of academics, and especially university teachers', with a latently individualistic approach encouraging competition rather than cooperation and a stratified conception of knowledge. The BSA EC is described as 'liberal and incorporative to a fault' [fair comment!], but the outcome as 'well-intentioned co-option of leaderships rather than deeply-worked changes in structure and attitudes' (Rustin, 1976: 2) The desired alternative was the creation of an intellectual community which would be more egalitarian and inclusive of sociologists and sociology graduates outside universities, more concerned with teaching, more concerned with the relevance of sociology to public policy and to professions such as medicine, social work and law. Some of the themes are typical of thought on the left at the time, while others are obviously addressed to the specific situation within sociology. His views certainly had some support,[13] though there were also critical responses (Miller, 1976; Deem, 1976) which, among other things, saw part of the problem as sectarian divisions within academic sociology rather than the BSA as such. Talking about this recently (Rustin, 1997), he said that at the time he did not have a strong sense of himself as a social scientist, not seeing a real difference between social scientists and political intellectuals, while in the BSA he encountered other people with a strong identity as social-science intellectuals; that is, of course, a point about the period as much as about one individual, and suggests one of the lines of potential cleavage within the discipline.

In 1976 and 1977, representatives of SIP, ATSS and the NATHFE Sociology Section were co-opted to the BSA EC. By 1977, the SCOS had run out of steam, attendance shrank, and it was terminated. One member, in a letter accepting the termination, remarked 'we have been beaten by that large immovable block the BSA' (Reid, 1977), but the outcome could be interpreted in an opposite sense. A system of exchange of observers between the BSA and other members' ECs was set up, and the BSA also invited observers for particular items on the agendas of its sub committees. The possibility of some form of merger of memberships was raised by the BSA (report to AGM, 1977), but does not seem to have got further. In 1979, five of those associated with the SCOS were members of the BSA Teaching and Programmes Committee, and in subsequent years several of those most active in the SCOS and its other member bodies became individual members of the BSA EC. (Later developments in representation from non-university institutions on the EC, which became substantial, are described in Chapter 5.) In the late 1990s, a formal system of affiliated membership was added to the BSA's constitution in order to allow ATSS members to join at reduced rates, with a corresponding arrangement for BSA members within the ATSS. Given the history of the SIP and what became NATHFE, it is not surprising that as organisations they gradually ceased to figure within the BSA. One interviewee suggested that one reason why polytechnic teachers participated less in the BSA in the 1970s was simply that they were so busy with the expansion and validation of new courses – which also meant that they had no time for personal research. Some of the dissatisfaction with the BSA probably owed as much to dissatisfaction with a work situation in non-university settings, which improved over time as sociology became more institutionalised there. It seems likely, too, that some of it arose from the rapidly changing labour market situation, which meant that the ratio of university jobs to those potentially interested in them deteriorated very sharply in the 1970s (Platt, 2000) and so forced some who had hoped for such jobs into other settings with less favourable circumstances.

The ATSS, however, has continued to be active and to represent a constituency which has survived educational change, and it has continued to have relations with the BSA, though their significance has fluctuated. In 1976,

BSA ceded A-level issues to the ATSS (ATSS EC 19 June 1976, LSE Folder 35), but this cession did not last. A long-term strand of connection has been the shared concern with national exams and, for the BSA, this has been part of its relationship to the exam boards, with which regular meetings have been held. In 1988, for instance, both BSA and ATSS representatives attended a meeting with members of exam boards, called to consider the contexts of sociological work in schools and colleges and their (dis)continuities (EC 2 December 1988, document N). In the later 1980s, representatives were still exchanged but, in 1991 (41st AGM Report), it seemed necessary to agree again that a BSA representative should attend ATSS meetings. In 1992, BSA and ATSS representatives met to explore modes of cooperation, in particular in spreading knowledge among teachers of the curriculum at other levels from the one where they work themselves; it was agreed that each body should arrange a panel at the other's forthcoming conference. Within the BSA, the practical relationship has repeatedly been resurrected in such ways, and has depended to some extent on the interest of particular individuals active in both bodies. In the later 1990s, it became less salient, probably both because the EC happened to have no such member, and because other concerns were very pressing, while pre-university issues had become less problematic.

Heads of Departments

The final group(s) of sociologists with which the BSA has had relations is the organisations of heads of department. Initially, the university (Professors and Heads of Department – PHoDs) and polytechnic (Sociology Heads in Advanced Further Education – SHAFE) groups met separately but, in November 1992, they merged, when the polytechnics became new universities, to become simply HoDs. Its constitution stated that in the first instance one of the officers (chair and secretary) should be drawn from the former 'public' sector and the other from the old university sector and, since then, some such balance, as well as that by region and gender, has been understood. It has played an important role not just in representing departmental concerns to the outside world, but also in promoting communication between departments and providing information about external developments.

The university group started meeting in 1981, at the initiative of Asher Tropp (in his role as head of department), in response to the serious educational cuts of the time, which potentially affected departments as such directly; in 1982, the BSA also set up two meetings of heads of department in the maintained sector (Report to 1982 AGM). Initially, the agenda was the immediate response to cuts and the threat to SSRC, and the meeting did not become an established body until it was agreed in 1982 to place it on a more permanent footing, and it gradually became more formalised and broadened its effective range of concerns. The BSA chairperson was invited to attend meetings of PHoDs, to make a link with other parts of the profession; when HoDs was founded, its constitution said that a member of the BSA EC should if possible always be present, though the degree of overlap between the two might make a formal arrangement unnecessary. In 1985, the BSA agreed to a request from PHoDs for a small annual subsidy to meet its organisational expenses – and allocated one to SHAFE too without being asked (EC 6 December 1985). By 1989, however, it was suggested that the heads of departments meetings had become rather separate from the BSA, and something should be done about this (EC 22 March 1989); the chair suggested that in relation to the UGC review of sociology both university and polytechnic groups [the latter were not covered by the review] 'ought to be seen as under the rubric of the BSA'. In the following year, it was reported that PHoDs had agreed to close liaison with the BSA, but not a direct link (EC 16 February 1990). There was sometimes friction over which of BSA and heads of departments should be seen as representing sociology nationally, with each side in danger of seeing the other as encroaching on its territory. In addition, the egalitarian tradition of BSA activists meant that they could be reluctant to give much support to a body representing the hierarchy. On more than one occasion, concern was shown at the possible conflicts of interest between the two bodies on some points, despite their overlap in membership. (In a general discussion of strategic planning, where the desirability of recruiting more senior members of the discipline to the BSA was raised, the EC minutes (8 July 1994) record that 'Some reservation was expressed about the encouragement of members of HoDs Council [the plenary meeting of the Heads] to be active in the BSA in case that led to the institutionalisation of elitism within the BSA', as opposed to the present pattern where the diversity of BSA membership was reflected in the composition of its subcommittees and other groupings.) However, HoDs was gradually drawn into a closer formal relationship with the BSA. Since 1990, it has become the regular practice for a HoDs meeting to be held at each BSA conference, timetabled as part of the conference programme. In 1996, the BSA secretariat took on the contract to service HoDs, and an office representative attends HoDs conferences with material on BSA activities. It remains a formally separate body, but is thus now closely linked with the BSA.

We can see a pattern by which various groups of sociologists have formed when circumstances arose to which they felt a need to respond, and may initially have been dissatisfied with the BSA as a medium for dealing with their needs. Over time, however, the BSA has been actively supportive to each of them, and has taken steps to involve these groups and their representatives in the BSA mainstream. As a result, their activities have become absorbed into the BSA to the extent that their remits overlapped with its remit; this has, of course, been very much influenced by the national changes made in the structure of the system of higher education.

Other learned societies

There has been ad hoc cooperation with other learned societies at various points in the BSA's history. In the 1950s, the Association of Social Anthropologists figured relatively prominently, perhaps because of the importance of the LSE department as well as the membership of several leading holders of posts in anthropology on the BSA EC; there were cooperative responses to various external issues. Equally, members of the LSE's 'social science' (social policy) department were often members of the EC, though the issues are blurred here by the fact that several of them were generally regarded as sociologists anyway.[14] The first BSA conference was on the theme 'Social Policy and the Social Sciences', while the second, in 1955, was on 'Political Behaviour in Contemporary Democratic Society', and organised jointly with the PSA, though political scientists seldom appeared on the EC. Much later, the BSA Book Club became open to members of several other associations too: initially the ATSS, and later the SPA and the Social Research Association. In 1968, the SSRC initiated informal discussions with some learned societies about their activities and problems and, having found that there were shared problems and only limited contacts, a Joint Working Party of Social Science Societies and Associations was set up in 1970, serviced by the SSRC, and was joined by the BSA. A report was produced (Joint Working Party of Social Science Societies and Associations, 1974) which reviewed the situation, and made recommendations for cooperation on administrative facilities and accommodation, and for the setting up of a forum in which they could continue to meet, share experience and plan cooperation. This does not appear to have happened, at least not involving the BSA, whose records reveal no sign of interest in it. That was one of several points, usually when there were current or anticipated problems with the office accommodation at the LSE, when the possibility of sharing accommodation with other learned societies was raised, though this never came to anything in the end.

However, much the most important and systematic cooperation with other societies has been through the establishment of ALSISS.[15] This was formally founded in 1982, after a founding meeting the previous year; that was not an official move of the BSA, but it was on the initiative of sociologist John Eldridge, president of the BSA from 1980 to 1982, who became its first president; Margaret Stacey was also heavily involved. Its members were learned societies, and BSA was one of the 21 founding members; by 1992, this number had risen to 29. For most if not all of its history, the BSA was represented on its executive by people active in the BSA, who normally started their term while BSA EC members. ALSISS was originally part of the social-scientific response to 'the cuts' of the period, although it continued its activities for the promotion of a favourable policy response to social science after that particular emergency was over. Early activities included representations about the proposed change of name of the SSRC, the allocation of 'new blood' university posts, and the number of student places at universities. One of its most important continuing activities was the organisation of an 'All Party Group', which held seminars for MPs showing the relevance of social-scientific work to topics of current parliamentary concern ranging from road pricing to political Islam in the Middle East. At election campaign periods, attempts were made to influence future government policy by diffusing information to candidates about the social sciences, and to universities about the parties' policies for social science. Between elections, there was regular pressure to influence governmental and quango policy, on matters ranging from postgraduate research training to the improvement of official statistics and the need for more evaluation research. In 1988, a formally separate group was set up, the Social Science Forum, which dealt with promotional rather than professional issues, and was jointly supported by the Association of Social Research Organisations. It launched a 'Campaign for the Social Sciences'; this employed a firm of parliamentary consultants, and advised member societies on how to work in Westminster. Activities which faced inwards to the social-science community, such as meetings on topics of general interest including research funding and dealing with the media, were also held, and there were briefings on issues in the practical running of societies such as the effects of VAT and charities legislation. There was also liaison with other bodies whose interests in some way overlapped with those of ALSISS; these included the British Academy, the BAAS and Save British Science (a parallel body for the natural sciences).

ALSISS is now dead; long live ALSISS! It has successfully transformed itself into the *Academy* of Learned Societies for the Social Sciences, launched in November 1999. This responded to the need that was felt to fill the gap left for social scientists by the Royal Society and the British Academy. It has 42 societies as members, and is gradually creating Academicians, 'distinguished scholars and practitioners drawn from academia and the private and public sectors', for whom selection is an honour. BSA leaders were active in the transformation process – Nigel Gilbert led the Academy Implementation Group – and a number of BSA people have become Academicians. The Academy's objectives include promotion of the development of social science, its representation to government and other agencies, the provision of comment on policy issues and the dissemination of information about social science.[16] Note that its membership is not purely academic, so that these aims are supported by the recruitment of others who work for some of the same goals, and may have access to contacts useful in achieving them.

It was important to the practical organisation and impact of ALSISS Mark 1 that it worked in what was effectively an alliance with the ESRC. The ESRC provided modest funding for the parliamentary seminars, gave grants for some other ad hoc activities, and held regular meetings for members of ALSISS societies at which future research initiatives were discussed. However, the president of ALSISS felt it appropriate, in her report for 1991–2, to say that, while the relation with the ESRC was very welcome,

> *It is important that our independence from all bodies supported with*
> *public funds is maintained so that we can make constructive criticisms*
> *of any changes taking place which we feel would be detrimental to the*
> *development of the social sciences ...*
> (Lewis, 1992: 10)

and ALSISS certainly did not simply follow ESRC leads. It may be presumed that, from the ESRC's point of view, the connection was worthwhile both because ALSISS figured as an independent representative body supporting some of its goals, and because it provided an economically collective way of consulting the opinions of its academic constituency. But that indirect relationship is far from the only way in which the ESRC has figured in BSA affairs.

SSRC/ESRC

Initially as the Social Science Research Council,[17] the ESRC has been prominent in BSA concerns ever since it was founded in 1965. This is not surprising given its key role in the provision of studentships giving financial support to research students, and of grants for faculty research.

The ESRC's internal organisation has changed over time; at first there was a specific Sociology Committee (though originally paired with Social Administration), and then the committee structure became formally cross-disciplinary, though the Social Affairs Committee could have been regarded as the lead one for sociology, and more generic committees such as the Training Board, covering the whole range of social-science disciplines, became important. The BSA's direction of attention has shifted accordingly, after its opposition to the removal of a clear disciplinary focus was unsuccessful.

Many of the sociologists represented in whatever parts of the ESRC structure have also been active in BSA; they include Michael Young, who played a role in the founding of each, and nine BSA presidents. In some cases, BSA EC and ESRC committee memberships have coincided, as they did for T. H. Marshall in 1967, Tony Coxon in 1971, Sheila Allen in 1973, Paul Rock in 1978, Sara Arber in 1986, Jennifer Platt in 1988 and Bob Burgess in 1991, while in many others they have been consecutive.[18] Thus informal liaison has often been easy, although a member of one part of the ESRC structure need not know what is going on in another part. There has, however, been a longstanding system of more formal liaison. Sociologists from ESRC committees have regularly been invited to meet the BSA EC; this appears to have been initiated in 1972 by the ESRC's Sociology and Social Administration Committee – it was not a general ESRC policy – and there were two or three meetings a year in the early 1980s, while more recently this has become one.[19] Since 1977, there has also been a 'Meet the ESRC' slot in every conference timetable, where ESRC administrators and academic members attend – and have, by tradition, been fiercely criticised by the audience. The BSA's vice-chair has held the responsibility for general liaison with the ESRC since 1976. Raymond Illsley, in a very interesting general report to the joint meeting when he retired as chair of the Sociology and Social Administration Committee, suggested that the BSA had shown greater interest in the ESRC and had more contacts with it than other professional associations, because sociology was almost totally dependent on the ESRC for research funds [EC 8.12.78; Box A13, Folder 111]. Certainly *Network* and EC minutes show a very active and continuing concern to be informed about, and to respond to, developments within the ESRC.

For many of the EC/ESRC meetings, minutes have been kept, so that the issues discussed can be followed. The general tone of BSA representations is egalitarian, at both the individual and the departmental level, with arguments put against any selection of the departments to receive studentships and in favour of choice of ESRC committee members for their representative character rather than seniority;[20] there is continuing suspicion shown of any constraint on the availability of research money irrespective of topic, method or location, and resistance to what a January 1987 *Network* editorial saw as a drift to *dirigisme*. One can trace the development of the discipline in the changing emphases from the BSA on different parts of the ESRC's role. At the stage of massive expansion, when those building departments had little time for research, numbers of studentships and their distribution was a dominant concern, and a higher proportion of the Sociology Committee's money went on those than for other ESRC committees. (This no doubt contributed to the very strong BSA response to the cutbacks in numbers of studentships which followed from the start of the national funding cuts in 1979.) The ESRC, correspondingly, deplored the standard of grant applications from sociologists, and was anxious to promote methodological improvement – probably with good cause, given the limited training of many of those then in faculty positions; the BSA repeatedly asked for more guidance on how to write successful applications, and more feedback on reasons for failure, and expressed anxiety at the perceived possibility of methodological bias against non-positivist applications. [A 1970 report on the work of the Sociology and Social Administration Committee deplored such rumours, for which it saw little foundation in its experience (Anon, 1970: 15).] When the ESRC committee structure became less disciplinary, there was anxiety at the possibility that some sociological applications would be referred to committees with few sociologists on them and rejected for that reason. Gender issues were also regularly raised.

These discussions show BSA representing its constituency, but it has also had relations with the ESRC on its own organisational behalf. The longest-standing and most successful example is the Summer School for research students, which has run annually since 1965; initially, this was run by the Teachers' Section and had funding from the Nuffield Foundation and other sources but, since the early 1970s, it has received ESRC financial support and that, although from time to time threatened, has become a routine for BSA. The ESRC has also funded research projects carried out on behalf of the BSA: work directed by Joe Banks in the early 1970s on the employment of sociology graduates (see Webb, 1972; Banks, 1974), and work directed by John Wakeford in the late 1970s on the process of postgraduate research (see Scott, 1984). The important 1979 conference on 'Graduate Research Methodology Teaching in Sociology', papers from which were published as a special issue of *Sociology* in November 1981, was funded by the ESRC, as was the production of a register of postgraduate theses in 1975.

Thus there has been considerable support from the ESRC for BSA activities, some of which would surely not have been possible without it, as well as a continuing dialogue. That dialogue has often reflected important disagreements, though one must assume that the input of BSA views has been taken into account by the ESRC when it has not been directly acted upon.

The system of organisations

The material presented above shows the network of relationships within which the BSA is embedded, and the extent to which its activities have depended upon support from other bodies, have responded to their actions, and have been undertaken jointly with them. The argument that it makes sense to consider the set as a loose social system depends not merely on the elaborate structure of relationships between them as organisations, but also on the considerable overlap of personnel, which ensures that informal as well as formal channels of communication create significant links. (Naturally, one depicts the system as centring on the BSA when writing the BSA's history but, from the point of view of other organisations in the set, each is at the centre of a slightly different but overlapping network.) We cannot understand the BSA without placing it within this wider social system. How the BSA has acted within the system has been strongly influenced by the external challenges it has had to deal with, which have suggested relevant alliances. An interpretation in terms of organisational self-interest has considerable plausibility, though how self-interest is conceived has been influenced by disciplinary and broadly political ideologies, and the boundaries of self-interest have changed in response to external developments.

Notes

1   For a general historical account of the ISA, see Platt (1998).

2   David Glass was not nominated in 1959 (EC 11 May), because he was already an ISA Council member in another capacity.

3   Each representative could have an alternate, who could also attend meetings, and vote if the lead representative was absent, so that there might in practice be two representatives at any one time.)

4   For instance, Margaret Archer had done postdoctoral work at the École Pratique des Hautes Études, and her early research was heavily oriented towards France, as was Martin Albrow's towards Germany; Tom Bottomore had spent 1951–2 in Paris on a research fellowship, after war service in India and Austria, and made many connections there.

5   These figures are based on ISA reports, which have not been produced in consistent formats for every Congress. Some of the bases to which the percentages are calculated are round-number estimates, not precise counts, but there seems no reason to believe that this would make the British proportion calculated misleading.

6   Initially, this was published with the ISA's *Current Sociology*, which also contained 'trend reports', later to become its sole content. The central organisation was undertaken by UNESCO's International Committee for Social Science Information and Documentation. In 1989, the bibliographical enterprise was taken over by the LSE's BLPES (Anon, 1962).

7   The Polish association was a focus of political opposition to its government (Sulek 2002). Poles had been very active in the ISA, and provided two members of its 1978–82 executive.

8   Not all of these drew the conclusion that a separate body was the way to go. One said that in his first job 'there was little initial interest in the BSA, even without invoking an acute sense that many of us had of being only second best to the "real" universities, whose sociologists "owned" the BSA ... [but there was a group] of aspirant upwardly mobiles who wanted to be "proper academics". These people began to acquire the badges for publication, higher degrees, seminar attendance at neighbouring universities, and conference attendance ...: ', and they oriented themselves to the BSA.

9   These include Jary (1979), which gives a useful general account of sociology in polytechnics at that period.

10 Its membership included three people employed in polytechnics, two from research units and one from the Civil Service College.

11 This entitled one officer of the association to the rights of an ordinary BSA member, and all members of the association to participate in BSA study group activities as though they were individual members.

12 This is another body in which the BSA has taken a continuing interest, with reports made to the EC on developments and a concern to ensure that sociology is well represented in the BA's important public forum, though the inter-organisational relationship has not been a formal one.

13   A paper by Len Law to the same conference puts forward an overlapping argument, criticising the structure of sociology as reflecting the hierarchical nature of the wider society and urging that sociologists at 'higher' levels should bear in mind those working at other levels, and should write so that not merely lower-level sociologists but those they teach and who constitute their subjects can understand them (Law, 1976).

14   A Social Administration Association (later renamed Social Policy Association) was only formed in 1967, apparently, it was reported to the EC, as a result of people meeting at a BSA conference.

15   Another body with some resemblance to ALSISS was the Standing Conference of Arts and Social Sciences (SCASS), founded in 1984. Although several prominent sociologists were active in it, departments and faculties were the prime members here and learned societies were only eligible as associate members, so the BSA as such, though affiliated, was not so active in it.

16   The material in this paragraph is drawn from the Academy's website, at http://www.the-academy.org.uk

17   For a general account of its early history, see Nicol (2000).

18   In addition, Cyril Smith went in 1975 directly from chairing the BSA to become secretary of the ESRC.

19   The BSA has, of course, also participated in a variety of meetings organised by the ESRC which were open to wider groups.

20   The names on a list proposed by the BSA in 1982 for membership of the range of ESRC committees look remarkably like the usual suspects! It includes a number of people who had already served on the ESRC, and four future vice-chancellors. Some of those listed were, however, then relatively young – in their middle thirties – and there is a skew towards people who had been active within the BSA in one way or another, as well as a close approach to gender equality. Of those nominated, some were indeed selected; one cannot tell what weight the BSA's support had in the process [EC 19.2.82, Item 5b].

Chapter 10

The BSA's trajectory: an overview

How can we characterise the BSA's development over time?

First, it has grown very much larger, and its range of activities has grown too. This growth means that it has been essential to have a larger office staff with greater division of labour, and for the organisation to operate in a more formal way. What was originally very much a London-based body, centred on the LSE, has now become a national one as higher education, and sociology, have expanded and spread. When the discipline was small, and a high proportion of its members had also been educated in the same places, everyone could know almost everyone. Inevitably, expansion changed that, and its speed and the pattern of recruitment from other backgrounds which that made necessary created a much more scattered and divided disciplinary community. The rapidly changing demographics of academic sociology have been of overwhelming importance in the development of the discipline, and in consequence for the BSA's membership and development. However, the generational cleavages so marked before the 1980s no longer seem of much significance.

One of the most noticeable long-term patterns is the tolerance and inclusiveness which the BSA has shown, both in its membership policy and towards its critics and to group interests which could have led to the creation of rival bodies: former-polytechnic teachers and the Heads of Departments now work within the BSA, the Women's Caucus has achieved many of its goals and is no longer an external critic, study groups which are far from purely sociological in composition have remained within the fold, even if in some ways deliberately choosing to be marginal, and groupings which take distinct intellectual positions can all find places in study groups and conferences. The internal diversity which this creates could be seen as a manifestation of declining levels of social integration, but it could equally be seen as a successful response to the needs of a wide range of constituencies. Concern has often been expressed at the fragmentation and dispersal of sociology, with many people who would formerly have seen themselves as sociologists now defining their work as, for example, cultural studies or women's studies, but the openness of the BSA means that they can, and often do, stay within it.

However, this has not been achieved without a price. It goes with the egalitarianism which, while of great importance to some members, has led to disaffection among other (potential) members at what they see as a disregard for high disciplinary standards. This has probably disadvantaged the BSA in its relations with external bodies which look for a more elitist style of representation.[1] Despite that, however, it has become successfully integrated into, and influential within, the network of institutions which represent the social sciences more generally, and which make policies affecting the social sciences.

Women are now thoroughly integrated into the BSA at all levels, and supported by gender-equality policy and some special services. It is not easy to be sure how far the shift towards this pattern has been directly due to political decisions, individual and collective, and how far demographic changes in the gender composition of the discipline have also played a role. Although women are the most prominent special group within the Association, there have also been other groups seen as disadvantaged, and so in need of compensating support; in the past, the unemployed were salient while, more recently, concern has turned to racial and ethnic minorities. These focuses follow the political movements of the wider society, and the changing historical situation of the discipline. Simpson (1988: 123), Simpson and Simpson (1994) and Demerath (1981) describe the very similar pattern of change in the ASA and the (US) Southern Sociological Society, in response to similar movements in their wider society, and see this as part of a shift away from the concerns of the discipline as such to concern with the occupational interests of its members. That could be seen as a move away from being a learned society in the direction of a professional association, and the issue of whether or not the BSA should be, or should be regarded as, a professional association has quite often been raised. Whether the BSA 'should' be regarded as a professional association, a learned society or something else is a different question from how the participants have regarded it, although their perceptions and aims will have affected how it has evolved. We address the second issue first.

'Professionalism' as an idea within the BSA

Some sociologists have discussed the idea of 'profession' and 'professional association' with sophisticated technical detail, but many of those active within the BSA have not had a research interest in the matter, and have probably had little familiarity with that literature. It cannot be assumed, therefore, that when the terms have been used within the BSA, the matters at stake can be understood in the light of the literature. This means that we need also to observe the meanings that the words have been given in the contexts of their use to understand their significance. We start, therefore, by considering the use of the term within the BSA, before going on to relate its form to ideas in the literature.

The idea of professionalism was current in discussion within the BSA in the 1950s, especially among the post-war cohort of LSE graduate students. For them, it was a focus of concern in two ways. In their own lives, they saw themselves as undergoing training as professional sociologists, and entitled to expect that they would find jobs as such – and that others without that training would not get such jobs, at least if there was any competition from those with the training. In the organisation of the BSA, they saw the participation of members who were merely 'interested' in sociology as leading to discussion which did not meet professional standards.[2] Both those concerns were to some extent connected with the growing disaffection from the older, Ginsbergian, conception of sociology as a synthetic social science rather than as a specialism (Banks, 1967). It was these concerns which led them to initiate study by the BSA of the employment of sociology graduates and, some years later, to found the Teachers' Section.

Between those initiatives, they also succeeded in leading the BSA to hold a conference in 1956, with attendance by invitation only, on 'The Present State of Professional Sociology'. Asher Tropp's report on this described it as concerned with 'the broad relationship between the application of sociological knowledge and the university teaching of sociology as well as with the more specific problems of the recruitment, training and employment of sociologists' (Tropp, 1956: 2). There were three panels, one of people (such as Mark Abrams, of the market research firm Research Services Ltd) involved in the application of sociology, the second of university teachers of sociology, and the third bringing them together to consider the possibilities of application of sociology and the employment of trained sociologists. Members of the first panel said they found sociology graduates inadequately trained for independent empirical research. The second panel rejected the idea that the degree should be 'narrowly vocational', and thought that it should include social philosophy as much as research methods. There is an underlying ideological friction here between the critical and the vocational. By the end, however, there was apparently a consensus that the undergraduate course should be 'broad and humane', while serious research methods should be taught at the postgraduate stage (Tropp, 1956). This suggests a division of the category of 'professional sociologist' into the more and less trained. The initially strait 'gates' of the Teachers' Section soon became less narrow, but remained seriously intended to exclude those who were not professionals in the sense of being employed in sociological teaching or research. It did not include everyone who met that criterion, but the *Register of Professional Sociologists* (1965) aimed to do so, though it did not succeed in creating a complete list. It was published with the intention of distinguishing between those who were and were not professionals. But the fact that it included some names of people who, while very respectable and professional colleagues, were not by any usual criterion 'sociologists' (see Chapter 3), suggests that the key underlying distinction was still professional/amateur rather than sociologist/ non-sociologist. It was perhaps partly as a result of these efforts that the issue rapidly came to seem less pressing.

The idea of professionalism as appropriate training appeared in the wording of the 1968 'Statement of Ethical Principles … ', which is on 'the responsibilities of the sociologist acting in his professional capacity', and asserts that 'The professional sociologist, while insisting that only persons properly trained or skilled should undertake social research, should himself recognise the boundaries of his professional competence', and that 'When a professional sociologist is working in a non-academic organisation, it should be made plain that he has a right to decide what comes within his area of professional competence'. Shortly afterwards, the BSA argued strongly, in its criticism of Birmingham University over the Atkinson affair, that only 'professional sociologists' had a right to evaluate sociological competence; here, though, the 'professional' status invoked was in effect simply being a member of the relevant discipline, since that was the distinction relevant to the circumstances of the case. Both those instances are ones where sociologist/non-sociologist is the distinction made.

Another form which the theme of professionalism took was the various proposals, at periods from the early 1950s to 1974, to distinguish different categories of member. The categories proposed normally included what was in effect a distinction between professional sociologists and others. After the very early experience of the difficulty of deciding who should fit into which category led to the abandonment of the initial structure, this was never again implemented, although the idea recurred from time to time. The last such proposal came from the EC in 1974, and resulted from a review of where the Association was going. The discussion document circulated to members identified the problems as being the expansion in sociology not adequately reflected in BSA membership, a limited range of activities, a small secretariat and an overloaded EC. It described the broad line of its proposals as being that 'the Association must now move to a further stage in professionalisation but, in doing this, it should seek to sustain and, indeed, expand the public activities of the Association'; the specifics were to abolish the Teachers' Section but introduce two main forms of membership, 'professional' and 'associate', as well as creating a number of subcommittees, and appointing a Development Officer. One of the officers of the time, in a letter to colleagues, said that the rationale of the two-class membership system was meant to be 'image', though this was not stated in the meeting (which rejected the proposal). The 'image' may refer to common conceptions of what a professional association should be like, but otherwise the 'professionalisation' seems more like improving the efficiency of the running of the Association.

An obvious difficulty until the 1980s[3] was that many of those holding university jobs in sociology, including professors and widely respected colleagues, had limited formal qualifications in it, or were appropriately qualified but in other fields. This meant that criteria based on employment would often conflict with criteria based on formal qualifications. It was perhaps in response to this difficulty that the 1968 AGM agreed to the setting up of a subcommittee with the remit to enquire into the definition of the professional sociologist, 'who should be one whom the Association would support in his professional activities'. The subcommittee considered the character of BSA activities which might suggest restricted membership or be of interest to special categories of member, and also its possible role as 'the protector of the employer and of the public from incompetent and unethical sociologists'. It eventually concluded that the issue had been raised prematurely, given the BSA's lack of control over syllabuses and the limited resources available, and that 'the further professionalisation of the BSA seems ... to depend on decisions about administration, finance and organisation as these are related to the functions it can carry out for its membership'. (All quotations from 1969 AGM Report: 9–10.) The recommendation was, therefore, that there should be a number of working parties to deal with particular issues, and that the question could then be raised again in the light of their progress. The EC decided that the officers would deal with complaints by or against sociologists, and that working parties on survey procedure and on model contracts should be set up (EC 25 April 1969), but difficulties were found in recruiting members, so in the end nothing came of that.

John Rex, in his Chairman's Report to the 1970 AGM, reviewed the developments, especially in the huge expansion of sociology teaching, which had been leading to concern about standards, and the BSA's efforts to respond to them. He concluded that it remained 'an Association which is open to all who wish to join ... [but] the question has been raised as to whether it should become a closed professional organisation or promote within itself the formation of such a closed professional organisation'. He suggested that the new EC might have to give attention to this question – but it does not appear to have done so, perhaps because it faced so many pressing specific matters to deal with.

Soon after this, many of the younger generation rejected, on broadly political grounds, at least some forms of the idea of professional exclusivity. Philip Schlesinger in 1976 (LSE) urged the BSA that the idea that non-members should be charged for attendance at study group meetings 'should be opposed in principle as part of the growing attempt to professionalise the sociological community. This notion of professionalism is an unacceptable brand of exclusivism.' Geoffrey Hawthorn (1975), explaining why he had resigned from the BSA, objected to the attempt to distinguish professional sociologists as confusing self-interest with intellectual progress, and argued that:

> There is obvious sense in trying to stop amateurs and adventurers practising engineering, medicine or law. Otherwise, great damage can be done. But what conceivable grounds other than pride or selfishness can there be for trying to stop a non-sociologist ... practising sociology? There are no skills peculiar to the trade.

This lack of concern to maintain boundaries was also reflected in the pressure to treat sociologists not employed as such as continuing members of the sociological community, though it is not clear what the criteria were for defining people as 'sociologist'; it seems likely that it was, with some risk of inconsistency, their possession of degrees training them in sociology. The women's movement too, in a different way, cut across the boundaries between sociologists and others. These were political commitments and solidarities which did not arise from disciplinary identities.

Who or what was the 'other' from whom the criterion of professionalism distinguished one? The 'others' with whom the claim to professionalism was a mode of competition were other occupations or disciplines which threatened to take sociological jobs, or to make unsatisfactory decisions on sociological departments, appointments or curricula. The 'other' from whom the claim to professionalism dissociated one were amateurs, the untrained, and we may perhaps take it as implicit that this dissociation was not only because they made weak contributions to discussion, but also because association with them weakened the claim to recognition as a serious discipline like, say, physics or classics.[4] It is understandable that these matters became of less concern when there were more than enough jobs for those with qualifications, and sociology, if not precisely treated as an equal by physicists, had become an established discipline with departments in many universities. More cynically, one might also suggest that the attraction of claiming one's place by attacking one's elders naturally diminished when the age structure of the discipline had moved on. However, some interview respondents saw different parties as defined on a less explicit basis:

Three post-war LSE graduate students:

- *What happened to professionalism within the sociological group which had started* Sociology *as a journal, as a highly professional thing representing the best standards, was that eventually they were outflanked and undermined by other people who saw sociology much more in terms of being a voice for society ... 'Professional'? ... it was a slogan to express our outlook. Ginsberg would have wished me to write about the idea of equality ... but I wanted to do empirical work. Behind the move to be professional was our desire to do empirical work; if anybody got in our way we wanted to push them aside, not to exclude them.*

- *... the idea some of us wanted, what we would call a professional sociology, which meant that all sociologists should be trained in both theories and methods.*

- [Re the introduction of income-related subscriptions] *... somehow it was thought that the BSA was not just a professional association, but was engaged in wider issues of inequality, and people being hard up and so on.*

Two younger members first active in the 1970s:

- *There are those who think sociology should be like a campaign, and those like* [other names] *and me ... who think it's a profession, where research skills are important – and we've won.*

- *... the idea of a critical sociology was very strong, and if you were professional you couldn't be critical and vice versa ... [it] was not interested enough in areas like methodology ... there was too much taking up political stances ... I don't think I've ever seen the BSA as a social movement, as* [leading feminist] *seemed to ... my impression is that BSA is something worth being a member of, from which one can gain as a sociologist, but as far as I'm concerned I wish it had become more of a professional organisation, though that's a dirty word with many sociologists.*

There is a set of ideas here which link professionalism with empirical research and taking methods seriously, and counterpose that both to a concentration on theory – possibly of a normative kind – and to a concern with goals for the wider society, rather than with ones specific to sociology as a discipline. This could be seen, rather confusingly, as associating the idea of professionalism with something more like the learned-society than the professional-association model.

In more recent times, the interest in 'professionalism' as a term either of praise or of abuse seems to have died away in general discussion within the Association, although it has cropped up from time to time in EC discussions – for example:

- ... *agreed* [a propos of departmental cuts] *that the BSA should be actively involved in taking a stand for the profession and not become involved in trade union activities.*
(EC April 1982)

- *The Association should aim to increase its professional activities* [such as those associated with research] *and have a less defensive profile.*
(EC July 1984)

- *It was agreed that future membership drive leaflets should include provision for the name of a sponsor in order to comply with the status of a professional association.*
(EC July 1985)

- *A propos of pressure for the accreditation of teaching, a risk was seen that Quality Assurance Agency consultation would push the BSA towards the role of a professional association rather than a learned society.*
(EC February 1998)

These are, though, spasmodic references made in passing rather than representing a stable ideological stance or a continuing concern in relation to which more general action was contemplated or taken.

A professional association?

The discussion over whether the BSA should or should not be professional, or confined to 'professional sociologists', however defined, does not precisely address the question of whether it is, or should be, a professional association. That has not been so explicitly addressed, though some members have taken normative stances about it, as quotations in Chapter 5 illustrate. Martin Albrow, in an article about the role of sociologists in planning matters, contrasts the 'professional' with the 'sociologist':

> *the professional is bound to espouse values over and above those of science if he puts his knowledge to the service of clients ... But the sociologist regards such values simply as the properties of the groups he studies.*
> (Albrow, 1970: 11)

He sees professional associations as ones which have 'developed autonomous codes of practice and methods of corporate discipline', and points out that

> *The codes of practice which sociological associations have developed are binding on individuals only through voluntary accession ... expulsion of individuals from the BSA for 'unprofessional' conduct is unknown, and there is little recognition of the right of that body to speak for sociologists in official circles, to negotiate terms of employment, or indeed to define what the role of a sociologist is.*
> (Albrow, 1970: 4)

At around the same time, a meeting was held between representatives of the BSA and the Sociological Studies Board of the CNAA. The BSA had expressed anxieties about narrower courses being approved as 'sociology', and staff being appointed without the participation of sociologists. The report on the meeting says that 'In reply to a question about ways in which the BSA could help the Board, the Chairman, Prof. MacRae [of the LSE Sociology department], said that he regarded the BSA as a learned society and not a professional association' – the implication being that it should not concern itself with vetting syllabuses (LSE, Folder A 40).

John Barnes suggested, in a general discussion of professionalism in the BSA, that in so far as that involved 'supervision of credentials', it was being done more by the SSRC than by the BSA (Barnes, 1981: 16). He contrasted a learned society and a professional association:

> A learned body exists to seek truth and promote scholarship, unsullied by material and ephemeral considerations ... The professional association ... is then left free to concentrate its energies on the defence and furtherance of the mundane interests of the professionals, their remuneration, legal protection and the like ...
> (Barnes, 1981: 17)

(This implies that a discipline should have both, which it is clear that British sociology has never had, at least as separate bodies. In so far as the great majority of those generally recognised to be working as sociologists are in academic life, however, they are mainly represented in that way by the AUT and other academic trade unions.) He concludes that there is a case for 'professionalism' in relation to empirical research, but is concerned that an emphasis on empirical work and its methods should not detract from sociology's critical role. Sociologists need a collective body to protect them from 'critics and paymasters', but the BSA 'functions best as an association of persons interested in the study of society, irrespective of qualifications, even if most of its members do happen to have qualifications', and he doubts 'if there is any place in sociology, as we know and enjoy it in this country, for a learned society to define orthodoxy and generate professional respectability' (Barnes, 1981: 23–4).

Neither of those, however, attempts a full definition of a profession or a professional association. This is not the place to attempt a review of the extensive literature on that, so we rely on sources which have undertaken it for us. Millerson (1964: 4–5) provides a useful tabular summary of the themes in earlier writers' definitions, revealing a consensus that the essential features of a profession are that it has a skill which requires training and education and is based on theoretical knowledge, that competence must be demonstrated by passing a test, there is a code of professional conduct which is adhered to, there is an organisation, and the ethos is one of professional service seen as done altruistically for the public good. He goes on to suggest that 'the term professional organisation refers to any association, which directly aims at the improvement of any aspect of professional practice: for example, by providing a qualification, by controlling conduct, by co-ordinating technical information, by pressing for better conditions of employment' (Millerson, 1964: 33), and distinguishes four basic types of organisation, though particular cases may not be pure types. The types are prestige association, study association, qualifying association and occupational association. He places the BSA as a study association, one that aims to study and promote a specific subject, which may be highly specialised or may be accessible to the general public, and for which the requirement for membership is only interest in the subject and recommendation by one or more existing members. We note that his category 'study association' includes – listed in an appendix – a large number of what are generally recognised as learned societies, as well as some less plausible candidates for that status, and so blurs the conventional distinction. He suggests that study associations are particularly likely to be found when there is a strong and expanding theoretical base (so that what is wanted is not simply the demonstration of an established level of knowledge), and when the subject is not so technical that it cannot be treated on an amateur as well as a full-time employment basis.

Table 29 shows how the BSA has rated on the most conventional standards for constituting a professional association. This tabular presentation conceals many nuances, as well as ignoring some changes which have taken place over time, so a little commentary is appropriate:

(a) There would be general agreement that this is true in principle of sociology as a discipline but, in practice, there have been respected practitioners with little or no formally sociological education, and the BSA has certainly not excluded them.

(b) This would apply only if at least a first degree in sociology were required; in addition, it is not clear what jobs other than those in academia would count as practising sociology, and BSA's rather half-hearted attempt to define this in the early 1970s was certainly not successful.

(c) True, but somewhat diluted by the fact that if the applicant has no nominator a member of the EC usually performs that function even without personal knowledge of them.

(d) Very occasionally an application has been rejected, but that is most unusual.

(g) The only 'enforcement' which is in practice available, when normative controls fail, is where the BSA itself directly controls the activity in question; it can, for instance, be required that sexist language be not used in BSA journals, and editors have immediate power over the matter. But where the issue is one such

Table 29 BSA as 'professional association': characteristics present

(a)	Theoretically grounded skill requiring education	Yes
(b)	Test to be passed to permit practice	No?
(c)	Require nomination by existing member	Yes
(d)	Qualifications required for membership	No[5]
(e)	Confers qualifications	No
(f)	Code of conduct	Yes
(g)	Enforcement of standards in code of conduct	No
(h)	Lack of concern with material benefits	Yes
(i)	Altruism	Yes?

as how graduate students, research officers or respondents are treated, that is entirely beyond its control, except in the sense that individual complaints may be investigated and moral pressure exerted on those complained against – and this only applies when the parties are BSA members. The 'Gould affair' reported in Chapter 7 illustrates the lack of leverage the Association has had, even when attempting to deal with a member; the strongest available sanction, apart from unfavourable publicity, would be termination of membership, and I do not know of any instance where that has been used.

(h) The BSA has not shown any active concern with members' earnings, or attempted to control the fees they charge for services; it has, though, been very much concerned with their employment levels and with the funding of their academic activities.

(i) Clearly, the BSA has in general assumed that sociology is a good thing for society, and so its support for the conditions which it sees as good for sociologists and sociological research and teaching could be seen as – somewhat indirectly – altruistic. Unfortunately, though, it has not always been wholly successful in the ideological campaign to persuade even academic colleagues from other disciplines of the benefits conferred by sociology.

The description of the BSA as 'a professional association only in the sense that it tries to promote and preserve a standard of professional conduct amongst those who teach sociology and carry out sociological research' (Banks and Webb, 1977: 10) has some merit.

Macdonald (1995: 32–5), in his much more recent review, emphasises the importance in recent thinking on professions of 'the professional project', a conception which does not simply accept occupations' public views of themselves, but treats those as often part of a bid for social recognition and closure pursued in the interests of their members. It is clear that the bodies he is primarily concerned with are those which succeed in making a 'regulatory bargain' which secures a monopoly for their members, and can defend their jurisdiction. One can see what might be regarded as a clear 'professional project' among the Young Turks of the BSA in the 1960s, though they certainly did not go so far as to propose a formal monopoly of sociological services, but since then there has not been anything that one could identify as the classic project. The attempt to relate the classic criteria to the BSA's activities brings out that it has more often wished to control things *outside* its own membership: ESRC policy, institutional treatment of sociology departments, unsatisfactory syllabuses in public examinations, and so on.[6] Rather than social closure, therefore, the issue for the BSA has been more one of legitimacy and recognition by those with power over matters outside its boundaries.

There is no literature, analogous to that on professions, on the correct identification of a learned society, or the processes of claiming that status, and the mere failure to be a full-blown professional association does not of itself make a body a learned society. We need, therefore, to propose criteria for qualifying as a learned society. I suggest, in accordance with Barnes' distinction cited above, that the general idea of a learned society is that it is one concerned with the advancement of a discipline as a body of knowledge rather than as an occupation. Functions appropriately connected with that role are the oversight and improvement of syllabuses, the encouragement and provision of advanced training, the creation of intellectual networks and forums for discussion, the promotion of research, the dissemination and critical analysis of new ideas (and support for the maintenance of conditions which make these things possible). It is clear that all these functions have been performed by the BSA, in its annual conferences, one-off meetings on teaching and research topics, study groups, summer schools, journals and involvement in wider discussions of syllabuses and research resources. There can be no doubt that it is a learned society – but the learned-society functions do not describe anything near the whole range of what it has done. In the end, it seems more appropriate to say either that it has been a body with mixed functions, drawn from more than one of the ideal types current, or that it is a body of a type for which a name and a description have not yet been developed.

One reason why its functions have been so mixed may be the absence of any parallel society with a clear place for amateurs. As Chapter 2 showed, such bodies existed in the past for sociology; their great period in the social sciences was the nineteenth century. Some other disciplines have retained their earlier associations longer, and created new ones alongside them. Ron Johnston, in his work in progress on the history of British geography, shows how, while the Royal Geographical Society continued, the Institute of British Geographers was founded in 1933 to represent the research concerns of academic geographers;[7] David Mills' work in progress on the history of British anthropology (on which see Mills, 2001) shows a somewhat similar relationship between the Royal Anthropological Institute – which long had both a scholarly journal and a section for contributions from amateurs – and the Association of Social Anthropology (founded 1946) which was exclusive to professional (social) anthropologists from an approved tradition.[8]

But there may be other instances of the same type as the BSA. How does it compare with other disciplinary associations? Unlike the BPS, with which respondents commonly contrasted it, the BSA does not control syllabuses or provide a licence to practise.[9] This reflects the fact that 'sociologist' has not been regarded in Britain as an occupation outside academia in the same way that 'psychologist' has. In some Latin countries, 'sociologist' is regarded in that way, and there are parallel national associations of more and less academic character.[10] In the USA, it is interesting that the American Sociological Association did attempt to establish formal qualifications for practitioners in some fields, but that was done in response to state legislation which gave psychologists priority for a range of jobs for which it was felt that sociologists should be equally eligible[11] – and it was soon found that the demand for these qualifications was so low that the enterprise was abandoned. However, the ASA goes further than the BSA in the direction of occupational concern by providing an Employment Bulletin advertising jobs, and opportunities for recruitment interviews at its annual conference. The BSA has been more preoccupied with the consequences of the policies of national bodies for its members. These differences reflect national differences in the social context: the USA is a larger and geographically more scattered society with a tradition of recruitment through networks rather than by advertisement, while Britain has more centralised national control of its educational system.

Some countries have had associations with much less open membership than the BSA; for instance, the German Deutsche Gesellschaft für Soziologie (DGS) started in 1909 as an association of professors recruited by invitation only; later, it expanded to admit anyone with a doctorate in sociology. Many others, including France with its major sociological tradition, have had disciplinary associations with more narrowly learned-society functions, not extending much beyond conferences, journals and study groups. In countries with fewer social scientists, there has often been only an association which grouped several social sciences. It would be very interesting, but is not appropriate here, to explore how it has come about that different countries have developed their associations in different ways.[12] It is evident, though, that this reflects not merely national cultural and structural differences in the system of higher education, but also the historical moments at which different associations originated.[13] Some associations older than the BSA have changed considerably over their history, and there does seem to be some tendency to convergence of pattern over time; the DGS is now more like the ASA than it used to be, and some of the changes that have taken place in the ASA can also be seen in the BSA.

These examples provide a far from comprehensive list of the potentially relevant comparators. Perhaps, however, they are sufficient to establish that the BSA is, like most other cases, both a member of a wider category with which it has much in common, and the only instance of its own historical type.

Notes

1   Simpson and Simpson use as one index of a shift in the ASA away from disciplinary concerns the decreasing representation of elite graduate departments among its officers, showing that an increasing proportion of officers have been elected for reasons other than disciplinary eminence. (The argument is both that it is the departments producing significant numbers of graduate students which are in effect responsible for the intellectual continuity of the discipline, and that they contain the most distinguished faculty members.) For BSA data on this issue, see Chapter 4.

2   When in October 1962 the Teachers' Section requested the status of a self-funding section within the BSA, the letter sent presented this from a slightly less abrasive angle: 'Of course we appreciate that by virtue of its constitution the BSA contains many members who have a general interest in sociology but are employed in other fields of activity, and we feel that it would hardly be fair to expect such people to finance meetings which are too specifically professional to be of interest to them' (Banks, 1962).

3   By then, many of the younger people recruited in the great expansion had completed the higher degrees which they had not held when first appointed.

4   Strong (1983) points out that one of sociology's felt needs is to distinguish itself from common sense and everyday knowledge, since everyone can claim some direct knowledge of its subject matter. He also suggests that literature and journalism may be regarded as rival sociological trades, though his interest is in co-opting or learning from them, rather than in competing with them or establishing a claim to superiority over them.

5   Surprisingly, though, the 1999 *Register of Learned and Professional Societies* (Foundation for Science and Technology, 1999), the material for entries in which must have been provided by the societies, lists it as having membership not open to the public.

6   These activities fit into Simpson and Simpson's (1994: 265) category of adaptive functions, 'that relate the association to the socio-political environment'.

7   In 1995, however, the two merged, while the former IBG continues as the research arm of the merged society.

8   Its 'others' were both the amateurs of the colonial service, and Americans in the tradition of Boas and the 'culture and personality' approach of such authors as Ruth Benedict.

9   For a historical account of how this situation has developed, see Lovie (2001).

10   These do not include only schoolteachers, so the ATSS is not a very good parallel.

11   Some interest has been taken in the BSA in the possibility of pressing for a Civil Service job category of 'sociologist' in parallel with the existing one of 'economist', but that has not gone very far or had success.

12   For a step in that direction, see the March 2002 issue of *International Sociology* on national associations.

13   For an interesting brief discussion of change within the American Sociological Association, see Demerath (1981).

Notes on sources

British sociologists

The *Commonwealth Universities Year Book* (CUYB), an annual reference book which lists every member of university teaching staff by name, rank and qualifications, is the source used for identifying numbers and some characteristics of academic sociologists. This is much less than perfect for our purposes. An important historical deficiency is that it has only covered 'universities', thus omitting large numbers of academic sociologists for the period when polytechnics existed as a separate administrative category (for which no comparable source was published). A considerable practical difficulty in using it is that its material is arranged by department within institution, so that to identify sociologists can be extremely laborious – a task not assisted by the variety of departmental names under which they can appear, and were especially likely to figure in the earlier part of the period covered, when many departments had titles such as 'social studies' or were joint ones with social work or social anthropology.

What has been done is to compile lists of university sociologists identified from the CUYB for years which can be related to the BSA data (see below), adding years to provide background information to fill the larger chronological gaps in that; the years covered are, thus, 1950, 1955, 1960, 1964, 1968, 1972, 1976, 1981, 1987, 1992 and 1997, so these are the ones used for any figures cited in the text.

BSA membership

The basic sources on the numbers and characteristics of members of the BSA are the published and unpublished membership lists and figures produced by its office. Until the mid-1960s, the office compiled good-quality lists of names, addresses and posts held for all members and, in the 1950s, from time to time summarised for the EC the characteristics of members so far. These detailed listings appear to have ceased when total numbers became higher, but *Registers* started to be published. These, however, relied on members filling in forms, which many of them failed to do, or did only in part. This meant that, for those who did complete the forms well, there is a rich source of data, including such matters as employment history and research interests. But for those who did not complete them, there is often nothing but a name and address; the name may be given only with initials, the address is not necessarily that of a workplace, and there may be no basis for inferring sex. The social practice of always identifying women by their full first names and/or a gendered title may have been sexist, but is very helpful to the researcher; unfortunately it gradually died out, so that as gender became a recognised issue it is harder to compile full data on it.[1]

Full *Registers* were published in 1973,[2] 1977,[3] 1982, 1988[4] and 1997, so many of our data refer to those dates or is related to them when drawn from other sources.

Executive Committee

For details of members of the EC, the situation has not been as much easier as one might expect. The list provided has, thus, been compiled with effort from a range of sources, and data on the social characteristics of members are at some points incomplete. The BSA's records such as annual reports and minutes do not always list the members and, when they do list them, the increasing egalitarianism and informality of the times means that the absence of titles can leave sex, and rank even for professors, unspecified, while places of employment are not always given, and it is not always clear which members have been elected and which are co-opted or ex officio. Ages have in many cases been gained from *Register* information but, where that does not help, the main additional source has been personal request by e-mail; the response rate to this somewhat impertinent request has been 100% for those successfully contacted, but in a number of cases – especially for recent years – I have been unable to obtain an e-mail or current address.

Annual conferences

Each conference has generated a programme, of which a copy has been obtained, and this always contains a list of accepted papers with the names of their authors. That does not indicate who actually attended (only one of multiple authors may attend), or which papers were actually given (some are cancelled too late for the programme). Some, but not all, programmes give a separate complete listing of speakers with affiliations. There has also usually been a less formal 'list of delegates' (i.e. those attending, whether or not they are giving a paper), produced shortly before the conference on the basis of registrations so far; this does not include those who register on the spot, and may include a few who did not actually make it in the end; fewer of such lists have been located. All these lists have varied over time in the fullness of the information they provide, and in particular the problems of identifying gender recur. (We have sometimes been able to go through the list with one of the organisers to identify those not otherwise known.) Various committee sources give figures for the total numbers attending particular conferences, but those are sometimes improbably round numbers, or only presented as estimates, so they are not always a source of whose accuracy one can be confident.

Documents on events in BSA history

The Association's formal archives are deposited in the BLPES at the LSE. However, the papers there are not a complete set up to the present, but consist of what was in the office that could be spared at the point when it moved to Durham, supplemented by some donations from individuals. All these have been left, in accordance with archival principle, in the sequences in which they were found, which are often incomplete or distributed across files in ways no longer rational to the researcher, though no doubt meaningful to the people who originally worked with and filed them. Considerable delays occurred in using these materials because several crates, including some of the earliest material, had accidentally been left in a hut on the LSE roof, uncatalogued, so that it was not obvious that they were missing from those actually available. Once the gaps had been noticed and investigated, it took months to get the crates down. Once down, I was kindly allowed to check through the crates to record what there was in each. On my next visit, I found that the papers had all been moved to files, so that my notes on location had become useless. At the time of writing, they have not yet been catalogued.

Such problems apart, the archival material is of course of varying character and quality. Minutes of meetings can be incomprehensible without background material; this seems most likely to be absent when a matter was so important that everyone knew about it at the time. Some useful correspondence is on the record, but certainly does not cover all we should like to know. Some study groups have left copious documentation, others almost none, and this does not necessarily relate to their levels of intellectual activity, though it may often do so. Most of the papers are from the routine work of the office and the EC, but there are some letters not originally intended to be of a public nature. Where any of these are used, the identity of the individuals concerned is concealed unless I have their permission to use their names; where they are directly quoted, the effort has been made to contact all the authors to ask their permission, though some are dead now, and others could not be located.

In the course of work on this history, a very considerable amount of working material has been collected; this includes minutes, conference programmes and other documents which are not available in the BLPES collection. Some of this comes from my own records, but a lot has been donated by colleagues – whose contribution has been invaluable – or provided by the current BSA office. It is hoped, when this work is completed, to deposit these materials at the BLPES, which will improve the collection for research purposes. Once that has been done, there will be easier ways of locating some key materials there, since we have, for instance, filed all the EC minutes that we have in chronological order in one place.

For these reasons, the conventional system of citing archival papers by their box and file location has not been followed in most cases. Where the document comes from a sequence such as the EC minutes, it is cited simply as 'EC [date]', which will be sufficient to locate it once the near-complete sequence is there in order. Where it comes from the so far uncatalogued part of the papers, it is described simply as 'LSE' plus the nature of the particular document. Only where the paper comes from some other part of the LSE archival collection, or is not from a sequence and is in the catalogued part of the BSA papers, is the citation given in the conventional form.

Finally, there are BSA publications which are useful sources; the newsletter *Network* and its shorter-lived predecessors are particularly valuable, and information on journals is of course contained in the journals themselves.

Notes

1   Many of the data reported on gender would be considerably worse if they had relied only
     on the published sources. Since I have a large background of personal knowledge of
     those involved, this has been drawn on wherever it was relevant and supplementation
     was needed. This inevitably gives some bias in the direction of better identification of
     people who have been around for longer, or are more prominent in the discipline, as well
     as those who work in areas of interest to me; that seemed a price worth paying when
     the alternative was to have larger numbers of unidentified cases.

2   In the 1973 *Register*, full names are given for members who have provided details on
     themselves, while there are only titles and initials for the large number who did not. It
     looks as though women have always been given a title but, in the case of those for
     whom it is Professor or Dr, there is no indication of sex; in the many cases where I know
     of the person, I have acted on that knowledge and, where I do not, it has been assumed
     that it was a man. There were relatively few doctorates at this period. The net effect is
     that the proportion of women is likely to have been slightly underestimated. (24% of
     those on the detailed list, as compared with 28% of the others, were identified as
     female.) Students were not listed separately so, given the likelihood that they are
     concentrated in the list of those without details but cannot be distinguished there, it was
     not worth counting the very few identified as such.

3   In the 1977 *Register*, the previous convention of indicating sex by always giving women
     their first name or a title has not consistently been followed, except for students, and
     some people who are known to be women appear with only their initials. It follows that
     others whose sex is not independently known are very likely to be concealed within that
     category, so that a confident complete count cannot be made.

4   Again in the 1988 *Register*, sex is not indicated in the list without details for those with
     the title Dr or Professor, though otherwise both sexes are given titles; those with non-
     gendered titles are assumed to be male unless known not to be, so the proportion of
     women is probably again somewhat underestimated here. (39% of those on the detailed
     list, as compared with 38% of the others, were identified as female.) Students were not
     separately listed.

Appendix

Table A1 Members of the Executive Committee (women's names are in italics)

Year	Role	Name
1951–2	Chair	M. Ginsberg
1951–2	Vice-Chair	T. H. Pear
1951–2	Secretary	R. J. Goodman
1951–2	Treasurer	T. S Simey
1951–2		V. G. Childe
1951–2		R. Firth
1951–2		M. Fortes
1951–2		D. V. Glass
1951–2		T. H. Marshall
1951–2		W. J. H. Sprott
1951–2		R. M. Titmuss
1951–2		*B. Wootton*
1952–3	Chair	M. Ginsberg
1952–3	Vice-Chair	T. H. Pear
1952–3	Secretary	R. J. Goodman
1952–3	Treasurer	T. S. Simey
1952–3		A. Carr-Saunders
1952–3		V. G. Childe
1952–3		M. Fortes
1952–3		D. Glass
1952–3		T. H. Marshall
1952–3		J. M. Mogey
1952–3		W. J. H. Sprott
1952–3		R. M. Titmuss
1952–3		*B. Wootton*
1953–4	Chair	M Ginsberg
1953–4	Vice-Chair	T. H. Pear
1953–4	Secretary	J. Madge
1953–4	Treasurer	T. S. Simey
1953–4		M. Fortes
1953–4		*R. Glass*
1953–4		R. J. Goodman
1953–4		C. Madge
1953–4		T. H. Marshall
1953–4		J. M. Mogey
1953–4		W. J. H Sprott
1953–4		R. J. Stansfield
1953–4		R. M. Titmuss
1954–5	Chair	M. Ginsberg
1954–5	Vice-Chair and Treasurer	T. H. Pear
1954–5	Secretary	J. Madge
1954–5		T. Burns
1954–5		R. W Firth
1954–5		M. Fortes
1954–5		*R. Glass*
1954–5		C. A. Mace
1954–5		T. H. Marshall
1954–5		T. S. Simey
1954–5		W. J. H. Sprott
1954–5		R. M. Titmuss
1954–5		*B. Wootton*
1955–6	President	M. Ginsberg
1955–6	Chair	T. H. Marshall
1955–6	Vice-Chair	J. Madge
1955–6	Secretary	W. J. H. Sprott
1955–6	Treasurer	T. H. Pear
1955–6		T. Burns
1955–6		T. E. Chester
1955–6		R. J. Goodman
1955–6		C. A. Mace
1955–6		C. Madge
1955–6		R. T. McKenzie
1955–6		J. C. Spencer
1955–6		A. Tropp
1955–6		*B. Wootton*
1956–7	President	M. Ginsberg
1956–7	Chair	*B. Wootton*
1956–7	Vice-Chair	T. H Pear
1956–7	Secretary	John Madge
1956–7	Treasurer	W. J. H Sprott
1956–7		Joe Banks
1956–7		P. S. Florence
1956–7		R. J. Goodman
1956–7		D. G. MacRae
1956–7		C. Madge
1956–7		R. T McKenzie
1956–7		W. H. Scott

(Continued overleaf)

Table A1 (continued)

Year	Role	Name	Year	Role	Name
1956–7		J. C. Spencer	1960–1	President	B. Wootton
1956–7		A. Tropp	1960–1	Chair	R. M. Titmuss
1957–8	Chair	B Wootton	1960–1	Vice-Chair	C. Madge
1957–8	Vice-Chair	C. Madge	1960–1	Secretary	R. K. Kelsall
1957–8	Secretary	R. K. Kelsall	1960–1	Treasurer	O. R. McGregor
1957–8	Treasurer	W. J. H Sprott	1960–1		R. Fletcher
1957–8		J. A. Banks	1960–1		R. Glass
1957–8		P. S Florence	1960–1		R. Illsley
1957–8		D. G. MacRae	1960–1		C. A. Mace
1957–8		J. Madge	1960–1		J. Madge
1957–8		R. T. McKenzie	1960–1		I. Schapera
1957–8		T. H. Pear	1960–1		W. H. Scott
1957–8		I. Schapera	1960–1		T. S. Simey
1957–8		J. C. Spencer	1960–1		R. Stewart
1957–8		A. Tropp	1961–2	President	B. Wootton
1958–9	Chair	B. Wootton	1961–2	Chair	R. M Titmuss
1958–9	Vice-Chair	R. M. Titmuss	1961–2	Vice-Chair	C. Madge
1958–9	Secretary	R. K. Kelsall	1961–2	Secretary	W. H. Scott
1958–9	Treasurer	W. J. H Sprott	1961–2	Treasurer	O. R. McGregor
1958–9		J. A. Banks	1961–2		O. Banks
1958–9		R. Fletcher	1961–2		R. Fletcher
1958–9		P. S. Florence	1961–2		M. Freedman
1958–9		A. H. Halsey	1961–2		R. Glass
1958–9		F. M. Martin	1961–2		A. H. Halsey
1958–9		O. R. McGregor	1961–2		R. Illsley
1958–9		I. Schapera	1961–2		D. Lockwood
1958–9		J. C. Spencer	1961–2		T. H. Marshall
1958–9		A. Tropp	1961–2		T. S. Simey
1959–60	President	B. Wootton	1962–3	President	B. Wootton
1959–60	Chair	R. M. Titmuss	1962–3	Chair	C. Madge
1959–60	Vice-Chair	C. Madge	1962–3	Vice Chair	T. S. Simey
1959–60	Secretary	R. K. Kelsall	1962–3	Secretary	W. H. Scott
1959–60	Treasurer	O. R. McGregor	1962–3	Treasurer	R. K. Kelsall
1959–60		J. A. Banks	1962–3		O. Banks
1959–60		P. S Florence	1962–3		P. Collison
1959–60		D. Glass	1962–3		R. Fletcher
1959–60		A. H. Halsey	1962–3		R. Glass
1959–60		C. A. Mace	1962–3		J. H Goldthorpe
1959–60		D. G. MacRae	1962–3		D. C. Marsh
1959–60		J. Madge	1962–3		T. H. Marshall
1959–60		I. Schapera	1962–3		I. Neustadt
1959–60		A. Tropp	1962–3		P. Townsend

(Continued)

Table A1 (continued)

1963–4	President	*B. Wootton*	1966–7	President	T. H. Marshall
1963–4	Chair	T. S. Simey	1966–7	Chair	C. Madge
1963–4	Vice-Chair	J. H Goldthorpe	1966–7	Vice-Chair	W. H. Scott
1963–4	Secretary	W. H. Scott	1966–7	Secretary	J. A. Banks
1963–4	Treasurer	R. Fletcher	1966–7	Treasurer	J. Madge
1963–4		*O. Banks*	1966–7		M. Abrams
1963–4		P. Collison	1966–7		R. Blackburn
1963–4		*J. Floud*	1966–7		I. Cannon
1963–4		R. K. Kelsall	1966–7		S. Holloway
1963–4		J. Madge	1966–7		D. Lockwood
1963–4		D. C. Marsh	1966–7		J. B. Mays
1963–4		T. H. Marshall	1966–7		D. S. Riddell
1963–4		I. Neustadt	1966–7		*M. Stacey*
1963–4		P. Townsend	1966–7		R. G. Stansfield
1964–5	President	T. H. Marshall	1966–7		P. Worsley
1964–5	Chair	R. K. Kelsall	1967–8	President	T. H. Marshall
1964–5	Vice-Chair	D. C. Marsh	1967–8	Chair	C. Madge
1964–5	Secretary	J. A. Banks	1967–8	Vice-Chair	W. H. Scott
1964–5	Treasurer	J. Madge	1967–8	Secretary	J. A. Banks
1964–5		M. Abrams	1967–8	Treasurer	R. K. Kelsall
1964–5		*O. Banks*	1967–8		D. S. Riddell
1964–5		P. Collison	1967–8		*M. Stacey*
1964–5		J. H. Goldthorpe	1967–8		P. Worsley
1964–5		C. Madge	1967–8		S. Zubaida
1964–5		F. M. Martin	1967–8		M. Abrams
1964–5		J. B. Mays	1967–8		M. P. Carter
1964–5		O. R. McGregor	1967–8		D. Lockwood
1964–5		P. Townsend	1967–8		J. B. Mays
1965–6	President	T. H. Marshall	1967–8		J. Rex
1965–6	Chair	R. K. Kelsall	1967–8		S. Holloway
1965–6	Vice-Chair	W. H. Scott	1968–9	President	T. H. Marshall
1965–6	Secretary	J. A. Banks	1968–9	Chair	W. H. Scott
1965–6	Treasurer	J. Madge	1968–9	Vice-Chair	J. Rex
1965–6		M. Abrams	1968–9	Secretary	*M. Stacey*
1965–6		P. Collison	1968–9	Treasurer	R. K. Kelsall
1965–6		J. H. Goldthorpe	1968–9		F. Bechhofer
1965–6		D. Lockwood	1968–9		R. K. Brown
1965–6		C. Madge	1968–9		A. P. M. Coxon
1965–6		D. C. Marsh	1968–9		N. Dennis
1965–6		F. M. Martin	1968–9		*E. Gittus*
1965–6		J. B. Mays	1968–9		D. Lockwood
1965–6		P. Worsley	1968–9		C. Turner

(Continued overleaf)

Table A1 (continued)

Year	Role	Name	Year	Role	Name
1968–9		P. Worsley	1971–2		*E. Gittus*
1968–9		D. T. H. Weir	1971–2		S. Lukes
1968–9		S. Zubaida	1971–2		R. Mapes
1969–70	President	T. B. Bottomore	1971–2		A. H. Marks
1969–70	Chair	J. Rex	1971–2		A. Tropp
1969–70	Vice-Chair	J. G. H. Newfield	1971–2		D. T. H. Weir
1969–70	Secretary	*M. Stacey*	1972–3	President	P. Worsley
1969–70	Treasurer	R. K. Kelsall	1972–3	Chair	J. A. Banks
1969–70		F. Bechhofer	1972–3	Vice-Chair	J. G. Newfield
1969–70		R. K. Brown	1972–3	Secretary	A. H. Marks
1969–70		A. P. M. Coxon	1972–3	Treasurer	R. Moore
1969–70		N. Dennis	1972–3		*J. Abbott*
1969–70		*E. Gittus*	1972–3		P. Abrams
1969–70		*M. McIntosh*	1972–3		*S. Allen*
1969–70		J. Peel	1972–3		*M. Archer*
1969–70		A. Tropp	1972–3		R. K. Kelsall
1969–70		D. T. H. Weir	1972–3		R. Mapes
1969–70		S. Zubaida	1972–3		S. R. Parker
1970–1	President	T. B. Bottomore	1972–3		J. Peel
1970–1	Chair	J. Rex	1972–3		C. S. Smith
1970–1	Vice-Chair	J. G. H. Newfield	1972–3		A. Tropp
1970–1	Secretary	J. Peel	1973–4	President	P. Worsley
1970–1	Treasurer	R. K. Kelsall	1973–4	Chair	C. S. Smith
1970–1		*S. Allen*	1973–4	Vice-Chair	J. E. T Eldridge
1970–1		J. A. Banks	1973–4	Secretary	A. H. Marks
1970–1		F. Bechhofer	1973–4	Treasurer	R. Moore
1970–1		R. K. Brown	1973–4		P. Abrams
1970–1		A. P. M. Coxon	1973–4		*S. Allen*
1970–1		*E. Gittus*	1973–4		*M. Archer*
1970–1		*M. McIntosh*	1973–4		J. A. Banks
1970–1		A. Tropp	1973–4		H. Cohen
1970–1		D. T. H. Weir	1973–4		R. K. Kelsall
1970–1		S. Zubaida	1973–4		R. Mapes
1971–2	President	P. Worsley	1973–4		S. R. Parker
1971–2	Chair	J. A. Banks	1973–4		*C. Riddell*
1971–2	Vice-Chair	J. G. H. Newfield	1973–4		D. T. H. Weir
1971–2	Secretary	J. Peel	1974–5	President	P. Worsley
1971–2	Treasurer	R. Moore	1974–5	Chair	C. S. Smith
1971–2		*S. Allen*	1974–5	Vice-Chair	J. E. T. Eldridge
1971–2		F. Bechhofer	1974–5	Secretary	J. Wakeford
1971–2		R. K. Brown	1974–5	Treasurer	R. Moore
1971–2		A. P. M. Coxon	1974–5		P. Abrams

(Continued)

Table A1 (continued)

Year	Role	Name	Year	Role	Name
1974–5		H. Cohen	1977–8	Secretary	A. Waton
1974–5		R. K. Kelsall	1977–8	Treasurer	R. Ward
1974–5		R. Mapes	1977–8		M. Bulmer
1974–5		A. H. Marks	1977–8		J. Hall
1974–5		H. D. R. Miller	1977–8		A. H. Marks
1974–5		S. R. Parker	1977–8		D. Marsland
1974–5		C. Riddell	1977–8		H. D. R. Miller
1974–5		K. Thompson	1977–8		H. Moorhouse
1974–5		D. T. H. Weir	1977–8		B. Smart
1975–6	President	S. Allen	1977–8		K. Thompson
1975–6	Chair	J. E. T. Eldridge	1977–8		J. Wolff
1975–6	Vice-Chair	M. Stacey	1977–8		A-M. Wolpe
1975–6	Secretary	J. Wakeford	1978–9	President	R. K. Kelsall
1975–6	Treasurer	R. K. Kelsall	1978–9	Chair	M. Stacey
1975–6		P. Abrams	1978–9	Vice-Chair	H. Rose
1975–6		H. D. R. Miller	1978–9	Secretary	A. Waton
1975–6		S. R. Parker	1978–9	Treasurer	R. Ward
1975–6		C. Riddell	1978–9		J. Hall
1975–6		H. Rose	1978–9		D. Marsland
1975–6		T. Shanin	1978–9		B. Moorhouse
1975–6		C. S. Smith	1978–9		H. Roberts
1975–6		K. Thompson	1978–9		P. Rock
1975–6		A. Waton	1978–9		G. Salaman
1975–6		D. T. H. Weir	1978–9		B. Smart
1976–7	President	S. Allen	1978–9		J. Wolff
1976–7	Chair	J. E. T Eldridge	1978–9		A-M Wolpe
1976–7	Vice-Chair	M. Stacey	1978–9		D. Woodward
1976–7	Secretary	J. Wakeford	1979–80	President	J. E. T Eldridge
1976–7	Treasurer	R. Ward	1979–80	Chair	J. Wakeford
1976–7		M. Bulmer	1979–80	Vice Chair	S. Allen
1976–7		A. H. Marks	1979–80	Secretary	D. Marsland
1976–7		H. D. R. Miller	1979–80	Treasurer	H. Moorhouse
1976–7		K. Thompson	1979–80		M. Cain
1976–7		C. Riddell	1979–80		D. Leonard
1976–7		H. Rose	1979–80		R. Moore
1976–7		T. Shanin	1979–80		H. Roberts
1976–7		A. Waton	1979–80		H. Rose
1976–7		D. T. H. Weir	1979–80		G. Salaman
1976–7		A. M. Wolpe	1979–80		R. Towler
1977–8	President	R. K. Kelsall	1979–80		R. Ward
1977–8	Chair	M. Stacey	1979–80		A-M Wolpe
1977–8	Vice-Chair	J. Wakeford	1979–80		D. Woodward

(Continued overleaf)

Table A1 (continued)

1980–1	President	J. E. T Eldridge	1982–3		J. Wakeford
1980–1	Chair	J. Wakeford	1982–3		A. Waton
1980–1	Vice-Chair	R. Moore	1982–3		J Westergaard
1980–1	Secretary	*H. Roberts*	1983–4	President	R. K. Brown
1980–1	Treasurer	H. Moorhouse	1983–4	Chair	*J. Finch*
1980–1		*S. Allen*	1983–4	Vice-Chair	F. Bechhofer
1980–1		R. Burgess	1983–4	Secretary	R. Burgess
1980–1		*R. Deem*	1983–4	Treasurer	A. Waton
1980–1		*J. Finch*	1983–4		N. Abercrombie
1980–1		*D. Leonard*	1983–4		*R. Deem*
1980–1		D. Marsland	1983–4		*E. Gamarnikow*
1980–1		N. Parry	1983–4		D. H. J. Morgan
1980–1		G. Payne	1983–4		G. Payne
1980–1		D. Robbins	1983–4		R. Towler
1980–1		R. Towler	1983–4		J. Urry
1981–2	President	*M. Stacey*	1983–4		R. Ward
1981–2	Chair	R. Moore	1983–4		J. Westergaard
1981–2	Vice-Chair	*J. Finch*	1983–4		*E. Wormald*
1981–2	Secretary	*H. Roberts*	1984–5	President	R. K. Brown
1981–2	Treasurer	R. Towler	1984–5	Chair	F. Bechhofer
1981–2		R. Burgess	1984–5	Vice-Chair	J. Westergaard
1981–2		*R. Deem*	1984–5	Secretary	D. H. J. Morgan
1981–2		D. H. J. Morgan	1984–5	Treasurer	A. Waton
1981–2		O. Newman	1984–5		P. Brannen
1981–2		N. Parry	1984–5		*C. Davies*
1981–2		G. Payne	1984–5		*R. Deem*
1981–2		*D. Taylorson*	1984–5		A. Giddens
1981–2		J. Urry	1984–5		P. Glasner
1981–2		J. Wakeford	1984–5		*K. Purcell*
1981–2		A. Waton	1984–5		*S. Scott*
1982–3	President	*M. Stacey*	1984–5		J. Urry
1982–3	Chair	R. Moore	1984–5		R. Ward
1982–3	Vice-Chair	*J. Finch*	1984–5		*E. Wormald*
1982–3	Secretary	R. Burgess	1985–6	President	M. Albrow
1982–3	Treasurer	R. C. Towler	1985–6	Chair	F. Bechhofer
1982–3		*E. Gamarnikow*	1985–6	Vice-Chair	J. Westergaard
1982–3		D. H. J. Morgan	1985–6	Secretary	P. Glasner
1982–3		O. Newman	1985–6	Treasurer	*R. Deem*
1982–3		G. Payne	1985–6		*M. Barrett*
1982–3		*S. Scott*	1985–6		P. Brannen
1982–3		*D. Taylorson*	1985–6		*J. Busfield*
1982–3		J. Urry	1985–6		*R. Crompton*

(Continued)

Table A1 (continued)

Year	Role	Name	Year	Role	Name
1985–6		C. Davies	1988–9		J. Busfield
1985–6		E. Ettorre	1988–9		A. P. M. Coxon
1985–6		A. Giddens	1988–9		R. Crompton
1985–6		M. Maynard	1988–9		E. Ettorre
1985–6		K. Purcell	1988–9		D, Lane
1985–6		S. Scott	1988–9		R. Lee
1986–7	President	M. Albrow	1988–9		M. Maynard
1986–7	Chair	R. Deem	1988–9		G. Payne
1986–7	Vice-Chair	M. Barrett	1988–9		S. Walby
1986–7	Secretary	P. Glasner	1989–90	President	R. Burgess
1986–7	Treasurer	J. Busfield	1989–90	Chair	M Cross
1986–7		S. Arber	1989–90	Vice-Chair	G. Payne
1986–7		F Bechhofer	1989–90	Secretary	J. Scott
1986–7		P. Brannen	1989–90	Treasurer	S. Arber
1986–7		A. P. M. Coxon	1989–90		C. Bryant
1986–7		R. Crompton	1989–90		A. P. M. Coxon
1986–7		M. Cross	1989–90		M. David
1986–7		E. Ettorre	1989–90		·B. Harrison
1986–7		M. Maynard	1989–90		D. Lane
1986–7		C. Smart	1989–90		R. Lee
1986–7		C. Wallace	1989–90		A. Murcott
1987–8	President	J. Platt	1989–90		J. Purvis
1987–8	Chair	M. Barrett	1989–90		T. Rees
1987–8	Vice-Chair	A P. M. Coxon	1989–90		C. Wallace
1987–8	Secretary	C. Wallace	1990–1	President	R. Burgess
1987–8	Treasurer	J. Busfield	1990–1	Chair	G. Payne
1987–8		S. Arber	1990–1	Vice-Chair	A. Murcott
1987–8		P. Brannen	1990–1	Secretary	J. Scott
1987–8		C. Bryant	1990–1	Treasurer	T. Rees
1987–8		R. Crompton	1990–1		P. Abbott
1987–8		M. Cross	1990–1		J. Bailey
1987–8		E. Ettorre	1990–1		C. Bryant
1987–8		P. Glasner	1990–1		C. Buswell
1987–8		M. Maynard	1990–1		M. David
1987–8		G. Payne	1990–1		B. Harrison
1987–8		C. Smart	1990–1		D. Lane
1988–9	President	J. Platt	1990–1		J. Platt
1988–9	Chair	M. Barrett	1990–1		J. Purvis
1988–9	Vice-Chair	M. Cross	1990–1		R. Scase
1988–9	Secretary	C. Wallace	1991–2	President	J. Westergaard
1988–9	Treasurer	S. Arber	1991–2	Chair	J. Scott
1988–9		C. Bryant	1991–2	Vice-Chair	J. Bailey

(Continued overleaf)

Table A1 (continued)

Year	Role	Name	Year	Role	Name
1991–2	Secretary	P. Abbott	1994–5	President	M. Barrett
1991–2	Treasurer	B. Harrison	1994–5	Chair	R. Deem
1991–2		K. Brehony	1994–5	Vice-Chair	D. Jary
1991–2		C. Buswell	1994–5	Secretary	F. Webster
1991–2		J. Chandler	1994–5	Treasurer	K. Brehony
1991–2		M. David	1994–5		I. Bowler
1991–2		D. Jary	1994–5		J. Chandler
1991–2		D. Lane	1994–5		D. Chalcraft
1991–2		J. Platt	1994–5		G. N. Gilbert
1991–2		R. Scase	1994–5		S. Lyon
1991–2		F. Webster	1994–5		C. Mann
1992–3	President	J. Westergaard	1994–5		S. Outram
1992–3	Chair	J. Scott	1994–5		S Roseneil
1992–3	Vice-Chair	J. Bailey	1994–5		S. Scott
1992–3	Secretary	P. Abbott	1994–5		S. Westwood
1992–3	Treasurer	B. Harrison	1995–6	President	S. Hall
1992–3		I. Bowler	1995–6	Chair	R. Deem
1992–3		K. Brehony	1995–6	Vice-Chair	G. N. Gilbert
1992–3		C. Buswell	1995–6	Secretary	S. Outram
1992–3		D. Chalcraft	1995–6	Treasurer	S. Lyon
1992–3		J. Chandler	1995–6		S. Allen
1992–3		M. David	1995–6		I. Bowler
1992–3		A. Drewett	1995–6		S. Cunningham-Burley
1992–3		D. Jary	1995–6		S. Jackson
1992–3		D. Owens	1995–6		G. Jones
1992–3		F. Webster	1995–6		R. Mallett
1993–4	President	M. Barrett	1995–6		C. Mann
1993–4	Chair	P. Abbott	1995–6		S. Scott
1993–4	Vice-Chair	J. Bailey	1995–6		A. Warde
1993–4	Secretary	F. Webster	1995–6		S. Westwood
1993–4	Treasurer	K. Brehony	1996–7	President	S. Hall
1993–4		I. Bowler	1996–7	Chair	A. Warde
1993–4		C. Buswell	1996–7	Vice-Chair	G. N. Gilbert
1993–4		D. Chalcraft	1996–7	Secretary	R. Mallett
1993–4		J. Chandler	1996–7	Treasurer	S. Lyon
1993–4		R. Deem	1996–7		S. Allen
1993–4		A. Drewett	1996–7		S. Cunningham-Burley
1993–4		D. Jary	1996–7		R. Deem
1993–4		S. Lyon	1996–7		S. Jackson
1993–4		S. Roseneil	1996–7		G. Jones
1993–4		S. Westwood	1996–7		S. Scott

(Continued)

Table A1 (continued)

1996–7		J. Scott	1998–9		*H. Thomas*
1996–7		A. Spybey	1998–9		*R. Thomson*
1996–7		R. Towler	1999–2000	President	*S. Arber*
1996–7		*S. Westwood*	1999–2000	Chair	G. Payne
1997–8	President	D. H. J. Morgan	1999–2000	Vice-Chair	A. Blaikie
1997–8	Chair	A. Warde	1999–2000	Secretary	*P. Abbott*
1997–8	Vice-Chair	G. N. Gilbert	1999–2000	Treasurer	B. Goldfarb
1997–8	Secretary	*G. Jones*	1999–2000		*M. Aldridge*
1997–8	Treasurer	J. Scott	1999–2000		*K. Deverell*
1997–8		*P. Abbott*	1999–2000		*C. Farquhar*
1997–8		A. Blaikie	1999–2000		S. Jeffers
1997–8		*S. Cunningham-Burley*	1999–2000		R. Jenkins
			1999–2000		T. May
1997–8		*S. Jackson*	1999–2000		J. Scott
1997–8		S. Jeffers	1999–2000		A. Spybey
1997–8		*R. Mallett*	1999–2000		*E. Stanley*
1997–8		*C.. Roberts*	1999–2000		*H. Thomas*
1997–8		*S. Scott*	2000–1	President	*S. Arber*
1997–8		A. Spybey	2000–1	Chair	G. Payne
1997–8		*R. Thomson*	2000–1	Vice-Chair	*M. Aldridge*
1998–9	President	D. H. J. Morgan	2000–1	Secretary	*P. Abbott*
1998–9	Chair	*G. Jones*	2000–1	Treasurer	B. Goldfarb
1998–9	Vice-Chair	A. Blaikie	2000–1		J. Bailey
1998–9	Secretary	*P. Abbott*	2000–1		A. Blaikie
1998–9	Treasurer	J. Scott	2000–1		*J. Chandler*
1998–9		*S. Cunningham-Burley*	2000–1		S. Jeffers
			2000–1		R. Jenkins
1998–9		*S. Jackson*	2000–1		T. May
1998–9		S. Jeffers	2000–1		*L. McKie*
1998–9		*R. Mallett*	2000–1		*E. Stanley*
1998–9		G. Payne	2000–1		S. Taylor
1998–9		*C. Roberts*	2000–1		*H. Thomas*
1998–9		A. Spybey			

Table A2 Editors of Sociology

Dates	Names	Institution
1967–9	Michael Banton	University of Bristol
1970–2	John H. Goldthorpe	Nuffield College, Oxford
1973–5	Gordon Horobin	MRC Medical Sociology Unit, University of Aberdeen
1976–81	Philip Abrams	University of Durham
1982–4	Martin Albrow	University College Cardiff
1985–7	Jennifer Platt and William Outhwaite[a]	University of Sussex
1988–91	Janet Finch and Nick Abercrombie	University of Lancaster
1991–4	Liz Stanley and David Morgan	University of Manchester
1994–6	Joan Busfield and Ted Benton	University of Essex
1997–9	David Mason and Joan Chandler	University of Plymouth
2000–	Maggie O'Neill and Tony Spybey	University of Staffordshire

[a]*William Outhwaite was deputy editor.*

Table A3 Editors of Work, Employment and Society

Dates	Name	Institution
1987–9	Richard Brown	University of Durham
1989–92	Bert Moorhouse	University of Glasgow
1993–5	Rosemary Crompton	University of Kent
1996–8	Paul Edwards	University of Warwick
1999-	Theo Nichols	University of Cardiff

Table A4 *Study groups: dates active*

Study group	1955	1957	1959	1961	1963	1965	1967	1969	1971	1973	1975	1977	1979	1981	1983	1985	1987	1989	1991	1993	1995	1997	1999–
	–6	–8	–60	–2	–4	–6	–8	–70	–2	–4	–6	–8	–80	–2	–4	–6	–8	–90	–2	–4	–6	–8	2000
Education	×	×	×	×	×	×	×	×	×	×	×	×	×	×	×	×	×	×	×	×	×	×	
Industrial Sociology, Work and Industrial Relations	×	×	×	×	×	×	×	×	×	×	×	×	×	×	×	×	×	×	×	×			
Urban	×	×	×	×	×	×	×	×	×	×	×	×	×				×	×					
Theoretical and Comparative, Theory		×			×			×	×	×	×	×	×	×	×	×	×	×	×	×	×	×	×
Law			×	×																			
Language (Communication)				×		×			×	×	×	×	×	×	×	×	×	×	×	×	×	×	×
Asian					×																		
Design					×	×	×	×															
Political Sociology						×	×	×	×	×	×	×	×	×	×	×	×	×	×	×			
Social Policy							×	×	×	×	×	×	×										
Religion						×	×		×	×	×	×	×	×	×	×	×	×	×	×	×	×	×
Maths, Computing and Statistical Applications, Quantitative Sociology[a]								×	×	×	×	×	×										
War and Peace[b]								×															
Art, Art and Literature									×	×	×	×	×	×	×	×							
Development								×	×	×	×	×	×	×	×	×	×	×	×	×	×		
Family and Kinship								×	×	×	×	×	×	×	×	×	×	×	×	×			
Mass Communications								×	×	×	×	×	×	×	×	×	×	×	×	×	×		
Medical								×	×	×	×	×	×	×	×	×	×	×	×	×	×	×	×
Race, Race and Neo-Imperialism, Race and Ethnic Relations																			×				

(Continued overleaf)

Table A4 Study groups: dates active (continued)

Study group	1955 -6	1957 -8	1959 -60	1961 -2	1963 -4	1965 -6	1967 -8	1969 -70	1971 -2	1973 -4	1975 -6	1977 -8	1979 -80	1981 -2	1983 -4	1985 -6	1987 -8	1989 -90	1991 -2	1993 -4	1995 -6	1997 -8	1999- 2000
Science								×	×	×	×	×	×	×	×	×	×						
Sports and Games[c]								×	×	×											×	×	×
Welfare								×	×	×													
Computers in survey analysis									×														
History and Sociology										×	×	×											
Social Psychology									×	×	×												
Socialist Societies								×	×	×	×	×	×	×	×	×							
Socio-legal									×	×													
Political Economy, State and Economy											×	×	×										
Revolution											×	×											
Deviance											×	×											
Gay Research												×	×										
Sociology and Psychoanalysis												×	×										
Labour											×	×	×	×	×	×	×	×	×	×			
Leisure and Recreation															×	×	×	×	×	×	×	×	×
Human Reproduction													×	×	×	×	×	×	×	×	×	×	×
Sexual Divisions													×	×	×	×	×	×	×	×	×	×	×
Survey Research											×	×	×	×	×								
Libraries and Information												×	×										
Architecture, the Spatial World, Environment and Architecture.														×	×	×	×	×	×	×	×	×	×
Urban Poverty and the Labour Process													×	×	×								

(Continued)

Table A4 Study groups: dates active (continued)

Study group	1955	1957	1959	1961	1963	1965	1967	1969	1971	1973	1975	1977	1979	1981	1983	1985	1987	1989	1991	1993	1995	1997	1999–
	-6	-8	-60	-2	-4	-6	-8	-70	-2	-4	-6	-8	-80	-2	-4	-6	-8	-90	-2	-4	-6	-8	2000
Childhood													X	X	X	X							
Ethnography													X	X	X	X	X	X	X				
Fatherhood													X	X				X					
Rural Economy and Society													X	X	X	X	X						
State and Economy													X	X	X	X							
Teaching Sociology													X	X	X	X	X						
Aspects of Popular Music														X	X								
Humour														X	X	X	X						
Sociology and Social Research														X	X	X	X						
Class Formation and the Third World[d]															X	X	X	X					
Social Networks																X	X	X					
Youth																X	X	X	X	X	X	X	X
Emotion																	X	X	X	X	X	X	X
Figurational Sociology																	X	X	X	X	X		
Public Policy and Politics																	X	X					
Family Studies																		X	X	X	X	X	
Max Weber																		X	X	X	X	X	X
Class Formation and the Labour Process																	X						
Violence Against Women																		X	X	X	X	X	X
Auto/Biography																			X	X	X	X	X
Food and Eating																		X	X	X	X	X	X

(Continued overleaf)

Table A4 Study groups: dates active (continued)

Study group	1955 -6	1957 -8	1959 -60	1961 -2	1963 -4	1965 -6	1967 -8	1969 -70	1971 -2	1973 -4	1975 -6	1977 -8	1979 -80	1981 -2	1983 -4	1985 -6	1987 -8	1989 -90	1991 -2	1993 -4	1995 -6	1997 -8	1999- 2000
HIV and AIDS																			×	×	×		
Music																			×				
Risk and the Environment																				×	×		
Lesbian Studies																×					×	×	×
Protest and Social Movements																×					×	×	×
Consumption																						×	×
Gender, ('Race') and Ethnicity																				×		×	×
News Media																							×
Disasters																							×
Number of SGs	3	4	5	6	8	8	8	17	22	24	31	27	33	29	28	29	23	22	24	22	24	20	22

[a] Merged with Survey Research.

[b] This group is reported to have existed formally for a number of years, with little or no activity; an attempt to revive it was made in 1988–9, but was unsuccessful.

[c] This became Leisure and Recreation, which then subdivided to recreate Sport.

[d] Merged with Development.

Table A5 BSA annual accounts – Total income and expenditure, surplus on year, and balance (Values at constant [1985] prices are given in italics)

	Income	1985 index	at 1985 prices	Expend- iture[a]	at 1985 prices	Surplus on year	at 1985 prices	Balance	at 1985 prices
1951	682	9.7	7,031	296	3,052	469	4,835	469	4,835
1952	842	10.5	8,019	553	5,267	289	2,752	709	6,752
1953	933	10.9	8,560	859	7,881	74	679	806	7,394
1954	731	11.1	6,586	827	7,450	−97	−874	691	6,225
1955	1,047	11.6	9,026	820	7,069	227	1,957	944	8,138
1956	703	12.1	5,810	784	6,479	−81	−669	798	6,595
1957	878	12.6	6,968	755	5,992	122	968	920	7,302
1958	749	13.0	5,762	968	7,446	−193	−1,485	757	5,823
1959	1,110	13.0	8,538	835	6,423	275	2,115	1,032	7,938
1960	1,178	13.2	8,924	840	6,364	338	2,561	1,370	10,379
1961	1,265	13.6	9,301	836	6,147	429	3,154	1,799	13,228
1962	1,364	14.2	9,606	1,117	7,866	247	1,739	2,046	14,408
1963	1,441	14.5	9,938	1,003	6,917	438	3,021	2,884	19,890
1964	1,534	15.0	10,227	1,455	9,700	79	527	2,963	19,753
1965	1,847	15.7	11,764	1,015	6,465	832	5,299	3,795	24,172
1966	2,647	16.3	16,239	1,891	11,601	756	4,638	4,575	28,067
1967	3,067	16.7	18,365	3,354	20,084	−287	−1,719	4,287	25,671
1968	3,482	17.5	19,897	4,631	26,463	−1,149	−6,566	3,168	18,103
1969	4,329	18.4	23,527	4,799	26,082	−470	−2,554	2,713	14,745
1970	5,509	19.6	28,107	5,036	25,694	473	2,413	3,186	16,255
1971	5,838	21.4	27,280	4,746	22,178	1,092	5,103	4,278	19,991
1972	6,891	23.0	29,961	5,324	23,148	1,567	6,813	5,845	25,413
1973	8,511	25.1	33,908	8,287	33,016	224	892	6,069	24,179
1974	9,942	29.1	34,165	10,013	34,409	−71	−244	5,998	20,612
1975	11,190	36.1	30,997	13,683	37,903	−2,493	−6,906	3,505	9,709
1976	22,042	42.1	52,356	14,665	34,834	7,377	17,523	10,882	25,848
1977	24,962	48.8	51,152	18,598	38,111	6,364	13,041	17,246	35,340
1978	22,394	52.8	42,413	16,252	30,780	6,142	11,633	23,388	44,295
1979	27,381	59.9	45,711	17,196	28,708	10,185	17,003	33,573	56,048
1980	29,865	70.7	42,242	21,085	29,823	8,780	12,419	42,353	59,905
1981	33,494	79.1	42,344	27,070	34,223	6,424	8,121	48,779	61,668
1982	41,430	85.9	48,231	25,274	29,423	16,156	18,808	64,935	75,594
1983[b]	37,956	89.8	42,267	32,352	36,027	5,604	6,241	72,189	80,389
1984	46,821	94.3	49,651	35,893	38,063	10,928	11,589	83,084	88,106
1985	48,682	100	48,682	31,238	31,238	17,444	17,444	100,599	100,599
1986[b]	54,194	103.4	52,412	38,890	37,611	15,304	14,801	116,090	112,273
1987	57,977	107.7	53,832	55,080	51,142	2,897	2,690	119,184	110,663
1988[b]	62,372	113.0	55,196	59,790	52,912	2,582	2,285	121,721	107,718

(Continued overleaf)

Table A5 BSA annual accounts – Total income and expenditure, surplus on year, and balance (Values at constant [1985] prices are given in italics) (continued)

	Income	1985 index	at 1985 prices	Expend-iture[a]	at 1985 prices	Surplus on year	at 1985 prices	Balance	at 1985 prices
1989	70,237	*121.8*	*57,666*	56,507	*46,393*	13,730	*11,273*	135,389	*111,157*
1990	91,537	*126*	*72,648*	53429	*42,404*	38,108	*30,244*	173,583	*137,764*

[a]*NB For these dates, data are from the following year's accounts, which in some cases give figures differing from those in the year-end ones, presumably because more payments credited to the previous year have by then come through? 1968, 1969 accounts show 3,074, 4,631, –1,149, 3,168; 1969, 1970 accounts show 3,698, 4,168, –470, 2,713; 1971, 1972 accounts show 6,891, 5,324, 1,567, 5,845; 1972, 1973 accounts show 6,329, 4,762, 1,567, 5,845; 1974, 1975 accounts show 8,577, 8,648, –71, 5,998; 1975, 1976 accounts show 9,854, 12, 347, –2,493, 3,505; 1977, 1978 accounts show 21,900, 15,536, 6,364, 17,246; 1978, 1979 accounts show 20,189, 14,047, 6,142, 23,388; 1995, 1996 accounts show 124,707, 119,328, 5,379, 279,130.*
[b]*Until 1956, conference costs appear as expenditure, while after that only any net loss was treated as expenditure; this means that the earliest figures are artificially high in this column in relation to the later ones.*
1985 prices have been calculated from the General Index of Retail Prices, for all items, as given in the CSO Economic Trends, Annual Supplement, 1991 edition (HMSO).

Problems in achieving consistency over time:

- In the early days, 'publications' refers to things published by other bodies and bought in to sell to members; since this was run as a service, selling at a reduced rate, rather than to make a profit, it usually made a modest loss. Sometimes this appears entirely under the 'expenditure' column in the accounts, and sometimes it does not. Later on, the BSA started to have its own publications, and later still 'BSA Publications' was set up as a separate company for tax purposes, and its accounts appear to some extent separately – but payments are made between the two, at least notionally.

- Early conferences were also generally run at a loss, and even when a charge was made tend to appear only under expenditure. For later ones, it became standard to budget for a profit, and the net profit is entered under income.

- Some figures used by treasurers in working papers do not appear consistent with the audited accounts – or they are using different definitions; this leads to differences from them in calculating the percentage subscriptions are of income, where I have stuck to the figures from the accounts.

Bibliography

Abbott, J. (1969) 'Employment of Sociology and Anthropology Graduates 1966–7', British Sociological Association, mimeo

Abrams, P. (1968) *The Origins of British Sociology: 1834–1914*, Chicago: University of Chicago Press

Albrow, M. (1970) 'The role of the sociologist as a professional: the case of planning', in P. Halmos (ed.) *Sociological Review Monograph 16, The Sociology of Sociology*, Keele: Sociological Review, pp. 1–19

Allen, S. and Leonard, D. (1996) 'From sexual divisions to sexualities: changing sociological agendas', in J. Weeks and J. Holland (eds), *Sexual Cultures*, London: Macmillan, pp. 17–33

Anon. (1962) 'The International Committee on Social Sciences Documentation: Ten years of activity', *International Social Science Journal*, Vol. 14, pp. 177–91

Anon. (1970) 'Sociology and Social Administration Committee', *SSRC Newsletter*, June, pp. 14–17

Archer, M. (1997) Interview with Platt

Atkinson, D. (1971) *Orthodox Consensus and Radical Alternative*, London: Heinemann

Atkinson, D. (1997) Interview with Platt

Atkinson, P. (1974) 'Editorial', *Medical Sociology Group Newsletter*, Vol. 1, No. 3, Spring

Bakke, E.W. (1933) *The Unemployed Man: A Social Survey*, London: Nisbet

Baldamus, W. (1971) Letter to John Peel, Secretary of BSA, 15 January

Baldamus, W. (1972) Letter to Joe Banks, Chairman of BSA, 27 June

Banks, J.A. (1958) 'Employment of sociology and anthropology graduates: final report', *British Journal of Sociology*, Vol. 9, pp. 271–83

Banks, J.A. (1962) Letter to BSA, 1 October, LSE

Banks, J.A. (1965) Letter to Girod, 14 October, BSA Folder, Box 31/1, ISA

Banks, J.A. (1966) Letter to Mrs Noble, Secretary of ATSS, 25 October; Folder 35, ATSS, LSE

Banks, J.A. (1967) 'The British Sociological Association: the first 15 years', *Sociology*, Vol. 1, pp. 1–9

Banks, J.A. (1974) 'The vocational orientations of sociology graduates', *Sociology*, Vol. 8, pp. 297–304

Banks, J.A. (1989) 'From universal history to historical sociology', *British Journal of Sociology*, Vol. 40, pp. 521–43

Banks, J.A. (1996) Interview with Platt

Banks, J.A. and Webb, D. (1977) 'Ideas or People: The Vocational Dilemma for Sociology Graduates', British Sociological Association, mimeo

Banks, O., Deem, R. and Earnshaw, S. (1980) 'Some perceptions and reappraisals of teaching and learning in sociology 1950–1980', paper given at the BSA's 1980 conference

Banton, M. (1997) Interview with Platt

Barnes, J.A. (1981) 'Professionalism in British sociology', in P. Abrams *et al.* (eds) *Practice and Progress: British Sociology 1950–1980*, London: Allen & Unwin, pp. 13–24

Barrett, M. (1986) 'The soapbox', *Network*, Vol. 35, p. 20

Bartlett, F.C. *et al.* (eds) (1939) *The Study of Society: Methods and Problems*, London: Routledge & Kegan Paul

Bell, C. and Newby, H. (1977) *Doing Sociological Research*, London: Allen & Unwin

Berger, B.M. (ed.) (1990) *Authors of Their Own Lives*, Berkeley, CA: University of California Press

Bhopal, K. (1997) 'BSA Standing Committee on the Equality of the Sexes', *Women's Caucus Newsletter*, p. 2

Bibby, J. (1972) 'University expansion and the academic labour market', *Higher Education Review* Vol. 4, pp. 23–43

Blackburn, R. (1969) 'A brief guide to bourgeois ideology', in A. Cockburn and R. Blackburn (eds) *Student Power: Problems, Diagnosis, Action*, Harmondsworth, Middx.: Penguin, pp. 163–213

Blackstone, T., Gales, K., Hadley, R. and Lewis, W. (1970) *Students in Conflict: LSE in 1967*, London: Weidenfeld & Nicolson

Bott, E. (1957) *Family and Social Network*, London: Tavistock

Bottomore, T.B. (1962) *Sociology*, London: Allen & Unwin

Bouchier, D. (1983) *The Feminist Challenge*, London: Macmillan

Boyne, N., Emslie, C., McKee, L., New, C., Quinn, J. and Williams, C. (1999) *Writing and Publishing*, Durham: British Sociological Association

Bradbury, M. (1975) *The History Man*, London: Secker & Warburg

Branford, V. (1928) 'James Martin White', *Sociological Review*, Vol. 20, pp. 340–1

Brown, R.K. (1967) 'Research and consultancy in industrial enterprises: a review of the contribution of the Tavistock Institute of Human Relations to the development of industrial sociology', *Sociology*, Vol. 1, pp. 33–60

Bryce, J. (1904) 'Introductory address', in Galton, F. *et al.*, *Sociological Papers 1903*, London: Macmillan, pp. xiii–xviii

Bulmer, M., Bales, K. and Sklar, K.K. (eds) (1991) *The Social Survey in Historical Perspective*, Cambridge: Cambridge University Press

Bunn, G.C., Lovie, A.D. and Richards, G.D. (eds) (2001) *Psychology in Britain*, Leicester: BPS

Burgess, R.G. (ed.) (1986) *Key Variables in Social Investigation*, London: Routledge

Burgess, R.G. (ed.) (1989) *Investigating Society*, London: Longman

Calder, A. (1985) 'Mass-Observation 1937–1949', in M. Bulmer (ed.) *Essays on the History of British Sociological Research*, Cambridge: Cambridge University Press, pp. 121–36

Canaan, J. and Griffin, C. (1989) 'Men's Studies: part of the problem or part of the solution?', *Network*, Vol. 43, pp. 7–8

Cannon, C. (1966) Letter from Cannon to J. Banks, 15 September; Folder 35, ATSS, LSE

Carr-Saunders, A.M. and Jones, D. (1937) *A Survey of the Social Structure of England and Wales*, 2nd edn, Oxford: Clarendon Press

Chamberlain, M.K. (ed.) (1988) 'Women's groups in professional associations', in *Women in Academe*, New York: Russell Sage Foundation

Cherns, A. and Perry, N. (1976) 'The development and structure of social science research in Britain', in E. Crawford and N. Perry (eds) *Demands for Social Knowledge*, London: Sage, pp. 61–90

Cherns, A.B. (1963) The development of the social sciences in Britain', *Social Science Information*, Vol. 2, No. 2, pp. 93–112

Clark, T.N. (1972) 'The stages of scientific institutionalisation', *International Social Science Journal*, Vol. 24, pp. 658–70

Cockburn, A. and Blackburn, R. (1969) *Student Power: Problems, Diagnosis, Action*, Harmondsworth, Middx.: Penguin

Cohen, S. (ed.) (1971) *Images of Deviance*, Harmondsworth, Middx.: Penguin

Collison, P. and Webber, S. (1971) 'British Sociology 1950–1970: a journal analysis', *Sociological Review*, Vol. 19, pp. 521–42

Corrigan, P. (1976) 'The crisis of applied sociology – a material answer', *Network*, Vol. 4, pp. 2–3

Costall, A. (2001) 'Pear and his peers', in G.C. Bunn, A.D. Lovie and G.D. Richards (eds) *Psychology in Britain*, Leicester: BPS, pp. 188–204

Coulson, M.A. *et al.* (1967) 'Towards a sociological theory of occupational choice – a critique', *Sociological Review*, Vol. 15, pp. 301–9

Cox, C., K. Jacka and J. Marks (1977) 'Marxism, knowledge and the academics', in C.B. Cox and R. Boyson (eds), *Black Paper 1977*, London: Temple Smith, pp. 117–26

Cradden, C. (1998) '"Old" university academic staff salary movement since 1949', *Higher Education Quarterly*, Vol. 52, pp. 394–412

Crouch, C. (1970) *The Student Revolt*, London: Bodley Head

Dahrendorf, R. (1995) *LSE: A History of the London School of Economics and Political Science, 1895–1995*, Oxford: Oxford University Press

David, M. (1977) 'Child care for colleagues?', *Network*, Vol. 8, p. 5

David, M. and Sharma, U. (1977), 'Equality of the sexes', *Network*, Vol. 7, p. 1

Deem, R. (1976) 'Sociology, sociologists and the BSA: a reply to Mike Rustin', *Network*, September/October, pp. 3–4

Demerath, N.J. (1981) 'ASAying the future: the profession vs. the discipline?', *The American Sociologist*, Vol. 16, pp. 87–90

Dicks, H.V. (1970) *Fifty Years of the Tavistock Clinic*, London: Routledge & Kegan Paul

Dingwall, R. (1997) Personal communication

Dix, A. (1992) Interview with Richard Brown

Dunning, E. and Hopper, E. (1966) 'Industrialisation and the problem of convergence: a critical note', *Sociological Review*, Vol. 14, pp. 63–86

Elston, M.A. (1976) 'Women's Caucus in Manchester', *Network*, Vol. 5, p. 3

EoS Committee (1983) 'Sex Equality committee report', *Network*, Vol. 26, p.11

EoS Committee (1986) 'Teaching gender: struggle and change in sociology', *Sociology*, Vol. 20, pp. 347–61

EoS Committee (1994) *Promoting Women and Research*, Durham: British Sociological Association

Evans, D.(1983) 'Le Play House and the Regional Survey Movement in British sociology', mimeo, Hall Green College Birmingham

Faris, R.E.L. (1981) 'Recollections of a half century of life in the ASA', *The American Sociologist*, Vol. 16, pp. 49–52

Farquharson, D. (1955) 'Dissolution of the Institute of Sociology', *Sociological Review* n.s., No. 3, pp. 165–73

Fenton, C.S. (1968) 'The myth of subjectivism as a special method in sociology', *Sociological Review*, Vol. 16, pp. 333–49

Fisher, D. (1980) 'American philanthropy and the social sciences in Britain, 1919–1939: the reproduction of a conservative ideology', *Sociological Review*, Vol. 28, pp. 277–315

Foundation for Science and Technology (1999) *Register of Learned and Professional Societies*, London: Foundation for Science and Technology

Galton, F. *et al.* (1904) *Sociological Papers 1903*, London: Macmillan

Gamarnikow, E. (1982) 'Sexual harassment at work', *Network*, Vol. 22, p. 7

Giddens, A. (1972) *Politics and Sociology in the Thought of Max Weber*, London: Macmillan

Giddens, A. (1968) '"Power" in the recent writings of Talcott Parsons', *Sociology*, Vol. 2, pp. 257–72

Ginsberg, M. (1929) 'Interchange between social classes', *Economic Journal*, Vol. 39, pp. 554–65

Ginsberg, M. (1956) 'The place of sociology', in *On the Diversity of Morals*, London: Heinemann

Gittus, E. (ed.) (1972) *Key Variables in Social Research*, Volume 1, London: Heinemann

Glass, D.V. and Gluckman, M. (1962) 'The social sciences in British universities', *Advancement of Science*, Vol. 19, pp. 54–60

Glass, D.V. (ed.) (1954) *Social Mobility in Britain*, London: Routledge & Kegan Paul

Goldthorpe, J.H. (1966) 'Attitudes and behaviour of car assembly workers: a deviant case and a theoretical critique', *British Journal of Sociology* 17, pp. 227–44

Goodman, R. (1951) Hon. General Secretary's interim report, October; LSE

Goodman, R. (1981) 'The First Post-War Decade', in J. Pinder (ed.) *Fifty Years of Political and Economic Planning*, London: Heinemann, pp. 97–116

Gould, J. (1977) *The Attack on Higher Education: Marxist and Radical Penetration*, London: Institute for the Study of Conflict

Gould, J. (1997) Interview with Platt

Gould, J. and Kolb, W.L. (eds) (1964) *A Dictionary of the Social Sciences*, London: Tavistock

Grebenik, E. (1986) 'Demographic research in Britain 1936–1986', paper presented to conference 'Population Research in Britain', mimeo; printed in Murphy, M. and Hobcraft J. (eds) (1991) *Population Research in Britain*, supplement to *Population Studies*, Vol. 45, pp. 3–30

Halliday, R.J. (1968) 'The sociological movement, society and genesis of academic sociology in Britain', *Sociological Review* n.s., No. 16, pp. 377–98

Halmos, P. (ed.) (1964) 'The Development of Industrial Societies', *Sociological Review Monograph* No. 8

Halsey, A.H. (1985) 'Provincials and professionals: the British post-war sociologists', in M. Bulmer (ed.) *Essays on the History of British Sociological Research*, Cambridge: Cambridge University Press, pp. 151–64

Halsey, A.H. and Trow, M. (1971) *The British Academics*, London: Faber & Faber

Hanmer, J. (1982) 'Gender trip', *Network*, Vol. 23, p. 1

Hawthorn, G. (1975) 'Why I resigned', *Network*, Vol. 1, p. 5

Hearn, J. and Morgan, D. (1989) 'Men, masculinity and social theory,' *Network*, Vol. 43, pp. 6–7

Heath, A. and Edmondson, R. (1981) 'Oxbridge sociology', in P. Abrams *et al.* (eds) *Practice and Progress: British Sociology 1950–1980*, London: Allen & Unwin, pp. 39–52

Heidensohn, F. (1989) *Crime and Society*, London: Macmillan

Hill, Mrs M. (1998) Conversation with Platt

Hindess, B. (1973) *The Use of Official Statistics in Sociology*, London: Macmillan

Hirst, P. (1973) 'Some problems of explaining student militancy', in R. Brown (ed.) *Knowledge, Education and Cultural Change*, London: Tavistock, pp. 219–48

Hoch, P. and Schoenbach, V. (1969) *LSE: the Natives are Restless*, London: Sheed & Ward

Hoy, J. (1997) Interview with Platt

Hughes, H.M. *et al.* (1973) *The Status of Women in Sociology 1968–1972*, Washington, DC: American Sociolgical Association

Jacka, K., Cox, C. and Marks, J. (1975) *The Rape of Reason: the Corruption of the Polytechnic of North London*, London: Churchill Press

Jary, D. (1979) *The Development of Sociology in the Polytechnics, SIP Paper 6*, Oxford: SIP

Johnson, M. (1974) 'Editorial', *Medical Sociology Group Newsletter*, Vol. 2, No. 1, p. 1

Joint Working Party of Social Science Societies and Associations (1974) *Social Science Societies in the UK*, London: Social Science Research Council

Jones, D.C. (ed.) (1934) *The Social Survey of Merseyside*, Liverpool: University of Liverpool Press

Kelly. T. (1981) *For Advancement of Learning: the University of Liverpool 1881–1981*, Liverpool: Liverpool University Press

Kent, R.A. (1981) *A History of British Empirical Sociology*, Aldershot: Gower

Kuper, A. (1983) *Anthropology and Anthropologists*, London: Routledge

Lakatos, I. (1969) 'A letter to the Director of the London School of Economics', in C.B. Cox and A.E. Dyson (eds) *Fight for Education: a Black Paper*, London: Critical Quarterly Society, pp. 27–31

Lassman, P. (ed.) (1988) *Politics and Social Theory*, London: Routledge

Law, L. (1976) 'A View of Sociology from "The Lower Levels"', mimeo, paper given to 1976 SIP conference. (LSE)

Lewis, J. (1992) 'Report from the President for 1991–2', *Social Science Report*, Vol. 7, pp. 8–11

Lindsay, K. (1981) 'PEP through the 1930s', in J. Pinder (ed.) *Fifty Years of Political and Economic Planning*, London: Heinemann, pp. 9–31

Lipset, S.M. (1994) 'The state of American sociology', *Sociological Forum*, Vol. 9, pp. 199–220

Lipset, S.M. and Ladd, E.C. (1972) 'The politics of American sociologists', *American Journal of Sociology*, Vol. 78, pp. 67–104

Lovie, S. (2001) 'Three steps to heaven: how the British Psychological Society attained its place in the sun', in G.C. Bunn, A.D. Lovie and G.D. Richards (eds) *Psychology in Britain*, Leicester: BPS, pp. 95–114

Lukes, S. (1974) *Power*, London: Macmillan

Lukes, S. and Westergaard, J. (1971) *The Atkinson Affair*, Council for Academic Freedom and Democracy

Macdonald, K. (1975) Letter to R. Moore, 27 January; on file

Macdonald, K.M. (1995) *The Sociology of the Professions*, London: Sage

Macleod, R. and Collins, P. (1981) *The Parliament of Science*, Northwood, Middx.: Science Reviews

Madge, C. and Harrisson, T. (1939) *Britain by Mass-Observation*, Harmondsworth, Middx.: Penguin

Mann, M. (1973) *Consciousness and Action among the Western Working Class*, London: Macmillan

Marshall, T.H. (1936) 'Report on the teaching of the social sciences in British universities', in *Institute of Sociology, The Social Sciences: Their Relations in Theory and Teaching*, London: Le Play House, pp. 29–51

Marshall, T.H. (ed.) (1938) *Class Conflict and Social Stratification*, London: Le Play House Press

Marsland, D. (1985) *Neglect and Betrayal: War and Violence in Modern Sociology, Occasional Paper* 14, London: Institute for European Defence and Strategic Studies

Marsland, D. (1988) *Seeds of Bankruptcy: Sociological Bias against Business and Freedom*, London: Claridge Press

Marsland, D. (1997) Interview with Platt

Martin, D. (ed.) (1969) *Anarchy and Culture: the Problem of the Contemporary University*, London: Routledge & Kegan Paul

Mass-Observation (1943) *War Factory*, London: Gollancz

Maynard, M. (1990) 'The re-shaping of sociology? Trends in the study of gender', *Sociology*, Vol. 24, pp. 269–90

Mazumdar, P.M.H. (1992) *Eugenics, Human Genetics and Human Failings*, London: Routledge

McNeil, M. (1985) 'Gender teaching survey', *Network*, Vol. 33, pp. 3–4

Meller, H. (1990) *Patrick Geddes: Social Evolutionist and City Planner*, London: Routledge

Mess, H.A. (1928) *Industrial Tyneside: a Social Survey*, London: Benn

Middleton, C. *et al.* (eds) (1993) *Sociology Teaching Handbook*, Sheffield: Sociology Teaching Handbook Group

Miller, H. (1976) 'On the impossibility of a profession', *Network*, April/May, pp. 8–9

Millerson, G. (1964) *The Qualifying Associations*, London: Routledge & Kegan Paul

Mills, D. (2001) '"We'll show them a real discipline": anthropology, sociology and the politics of academic identity', *Anthropology in Action*, Vol. 8, No. 1, pp. 34–41

Mogey, J. (2000) Personal communication

Moore, D.G. (1987) 'University financing1979–1986', *Higher Education Quarterly*, Vol. 41, pp. 25–42

Morgan, D. and Stanley, L. (1993) *Debates in Sociology*, Manchester: Manchester University Press

Moss, L. (1991) *The Government Social Survey: A History*, London: HMSO

Mulkay, M. (1972) *The Social Process of Innovation*, London: Macmillan

Nicol, A. (2000) *The Social Sciences Arrive*, Swindon: Economic and Social Research Council

Nisbet, R. (1972) 'Radicalism as therapy', *Encounter*, Vol. 38, No. 3, pp. 53–64

Paterson, T.T. (1955) *Morale in War and Work*, London: Max Parrish

Peel, J. (ed.) (1967) 'Details of Courses Mainly Concerned with Sociological Theory and Methods', 15th Conference of the Sociology Teachers' Section, mimeo

Perris, G.H. (1913) 'The record of the Social Science Association', *Sociological Review*, Vol. 6, pp. 161–4

Platt, J. (1971) *Social Research in Bethnal Green*, London: Macmillan

Platt, J. (1986) 'Qualitative research for the state', *Quarterly Journal of Social Affairs*, Vol. 2, pp. 87–108

Platt, J. (1988) 'Research policy in British higher education and its sociological assumptions', *Sociology*, Vol. 22, pp. 513–29

Platt, J. (1991) 'Anglo-American contacts in the development of research methods before 1945', in M. Bulmer, K. Bales and K. Sklar (eds) *The Social Survey in Historical Perspective 1880–1940*, Cambridge: Cambridge University Press, pp. 340–58

Platt, J. (1998) *A Brief History of the ISA: 1948–1997*, IMadrid: International Sociological Association

Platt, J. (2000) 'Women in the British sociological labour market 1960–1995', *Sociological Research Online*, Vol. 4, No. 4, 16 pp.: <http://www.socresonline.org.uk/4/4/platt, html>

Platt, J. (2002) Guest-edited issue on National Sociological Associations, *International Sociology*, Vol. 17, No. 2

Pope, C. and Ziebland, S. (1993) 'The BSA Medical Sociology Group: 25 years on', *Medical Sociology News*, Vol. 19, No. 1, pp. 12–16

Rayment, T. (1991) '40 years of the 'ology we all love to hate', *Sunday Times*, 17 February

Reid, I. (1974) 'The Sociology Section of the Association of teachers in colleges and departments of education', paper prepared for 'Which Way for the BSA' meeting

Reid, I. (1977) Letter to Hoy, 26 May; LSE, Subcommittees box

Revolutionary Socialist Students' Federation (1969) 'Manifesto', *New Left Review*, Vol. 53, pp. 21–2

Rex, J. (1997) Interview with Platt

Riley, M.W. (ed.) (1988) *Sociological Lives*, Newbury Park, CA: Sage

Rinde, E. and Rokkan, S. (eds) (1951) *First International Working Conference on Social Stratification and Social Mobility*, Oslo: ISA, mimeo

Robbins, L. (1963) *Report of the Committee on Higher Education*, Cmnd 2154, London: HMSO

Roberts, H. (ed.) (1981) *Doing Feminist Research*, London: Routledge & Kegan Paul

Rowntree, B.S. (1941) *Poverty and Progress*, London: Longman

Rowntree, B.S. and Lasker, B. (1911) *Unemployment: A Social Study*, London: Macmillan

Royal Statistical Society (1934) *Annals of the Royal Statistical Society 1834–1934*, London, Royal Statistical Society

Rustin, M. (1976) 'Sociology as a profession', *SIP Occasional Paper* 1 [an abbreviated version of this appeared in *Network*, Vol. 5, pp. 6–8]

Rustin, M. (1997) Interview with Platt

Sapper, L. (1972) Letter to A.H. Marks, Secretary of BSA, 23 August

Scharf, B. (1999) Interview with Platt

Schlesinger, P. (1976) Letter for a meeting of BSA study group convenors, April; LSE

Scott, S. (1984) 'The personable and the powerful: gender and status in sociological research', in C. Bell and H. Roberts (eds) *Social Researching: Politics, Problems, Practice*, London: Routledge & Kegan Paul, pp. 165–78

Scott, W.H. and Mays, J.B. (1960) 'Department of Social Science, University of Liverpool', *Sociological Review*, Vol. 8, pp. 109–17

Sewell, W.H. (1992) 'Some observations and reflections on the role of women and minorities in the democratization of the American Sociological Association 1905–1990', *The American Sociologist*, Vol. 23, pp. 56–62

Shaw, M. (1974) *Marxism Versus Sociology: A Guide to Reading*, London: Pluto Press

Simpson, I.H. (1988) *Fifty Years of the Southern Sociological Society*, Athens, GA: University of Georgia Press

Simpson, I.H. and Simpson, R.L. (1994) 'The transformation of the American Sociological Association', *Sociological Forum*, Vol. 9, pp. 259–78

Sklair, L. (1981) 'Sociologies and Marxisms: the Odd Couples', in P. Abrams *et al.* (eds) *Practice and Progress: British Sociology 1950–1980*, London: Allen & Unwin, pp. 151–71

Smith, C.S. (1975) 'The employment of sociologists in research occupations in Britain in 1973', *Sociology*, Vol. 9, pp. 309–16

Smith, H.L. (1930–5) *The New Survey of London Life and Labour*, London: P.S. King

Smith, J.H. (1961) *The University Teaching of Social Sciences: Industrial Sociology*, Paris: UNESCO

Sociology Club (1923–53) *Minute Book, Sociology Club*; Archives, British Library of Political and Economic Science, LSE Small Deposits 3

Solomos, J. and Back, L. (1996) *Racism and Society*, London: Macmillan

Stacey, M. (ed.) (1969) *Comparability in Social Research*, London: Heinemann

Stacey, M. (1993) 'Interview with Margaret Stacey', *Women's Caucus Newsletter*, p. 9

Stacey, M. (1997) Interview with Platt

Stansfield, R.G. (1981) 'Operational research and sociology ... ', *Science and Public Policy*, August, pp. 262–80

Stewart, W.A.C. (1989) *Higher Education in Postwar Britain*, London: Macmillan

Strong, P. M. (1973–4) 'York conference report', *Medical Sociology Group Newsletter*, Vol. 1, Winter, pp. 3–5

Strong, P.M. (1983) 'The rivals: an essay on the sociological trades', in R. Dingwall and P. Lewis (eds) *The Sociology of the Professions*, London: Macmillan, pp. 59–77

Sulek, A. (2002) 'The multifamous and changing functions of the Polish Sociological Association', *International Sociology*, Vol. 17, pp. 213–31

Taylor, B. (1976) 'One man's Manchester', *Network*, Vol. 5, p. 2

Taylor, B. (1994) 'The Anglican clergy and the early development of British sociology', *Sociological Review* n.s., No. 42, pp. 438–51

Thompson, E.P. (ed.) (1960) *Out of Apathy*, London, Stevens

Tropp, A. (1956) 'The present state and development of professional sociology in Great Britain', in *Transactions of the Third World Congress of Sociology*, Section VII, London: International Sociological Association, pp. 291–4

Tropp, A. (1956) 'The present state and development of professional sociology', *Bulletin* [BSA, mimeo], Vol. 1, pp. 1–7

Tuke, M.J. (1939) *A History of Bedford College for Women 1849–1936*, Oxford: Oxford University Press

UNESCO (1953) 'The teaching of sociology, social anthropology and social psychology', in *The Teaching of the Social Sciences in the UK*, UNESCO: Paris, pp. 75–92

University Grants Committee (1989) *Report of the Review Committee on Sociology*, London: University Grants Committee, mimeo

Wakeford, J. (1963) 'Courses in social structure and comparative social institutions', paper given at the 4th Conference of University Teachers of Sociology, mimeo

Wakeford, J. (1975) Letter to R. Moore, 10 January; on file

Webb, B. and Webb, S. (1932) *Methods of Social Study*, London: Longman

Webb, D.R. (1972) 'The employment of 1970 sociology graduates: a preliminary report.', *Sociology*, Vol. 6, pp. 433–42

Webster, F. (1992) *Science, Technology and Society*, London: Macmillan

Wells, A.F. (1935) *The Local Social Survey in Great Britain*, London: Allen & Unwin

Westergaard, J. and Pahl, R. (1989) 'Looking backwards and forwards: the UGC's review of sociology', *British Journal of Sociology*, Vol. 40, pp. 374–92

Wilkins, L.T. (1987) Interview with Platt

Wilkins, L.T. (2001) *Unofficial Aspects of a Life in Policy Research*, Cambridge, 'published' by his family

Williams, G. and Blackstone, T. (1983) *Response to Adversity, Society for Research into Higher Education Monograph 53*, Guildford: SRHE

Williams, G., Blackstone, T. and Metcalf, D. (1974) *The Academic Labour Market*, Amsterdam: Elsevier

Wilson, B. (1967) 'Establishment, sectarianism and partisanship', *Sociological Review*, Vol. 15, pp. 213–20

Wilson, B. (1969) 'Youth culture, the universities and student unrest', in C.B. Cox and A.E. Dyson (eds) *Fight for Education: a Black Paper*, London: Critical Quarterly Society, pp. 70–80

Wolfenden, J. (1957) *Report of the Committee on Homosexual Offences and Prostitution*, Cmnd 247

Woodward, D. (1977) 'One Lecturer's week', *Network*, Vol. 8, p. 10

Wootton, B. (1967) *In a World I Never Made*, London: Allen & Unwin

Worsley, P. (1973) 'An open letter to the Executive', LSE A12 Box 96–108

Young, M and P. Willmott (1961) 'Institute of Community Studies, Bethnal Green', *Sociological Review*, Vol. 9, pp. 203–13

Zubaida, S. (ed.) (1970) *Race and Racialism*, London: Tavistock

Zubaida, S. (1997) Interview with Platt

Zueblin, C. (1899) 'The world's first sociological laboratory', *American Journal of Sociology*, Vol. 4, pp. 577–92

Index to content

This index covers all material except references to sources, including the names of individuals mentioned in the text for reasons other than authorship of references. References to published sources appear in the separate Index to references.

Abbott, Joan   149

Abrams, Mark   26, 162

Acton Society Trust   30

Adams, Walter   109

Albrow, Martin   59, 141, 158

Allen, Sheila   39, 89, 91, 106, 156

American Sociological Association 86, 88, 90,106, 161, 170, 171, 172

Anderson, Digby   123

Andreski, S.   68

anthropology, anthropologists   20, 29, 31, 33, 36, 45, 63, 149, 170 *see also* Association of Social Anthropologists

Arber, Sara   156

Archer, Margaret   89, 141, 142, 158

Association/Academy of Learned Societies in the Social Sciences   39, 127, 154–5

Association for the Teaching of the Social Sciences   45, 135, 149–52

Association of Social Anthropologists 21, 36, 143, 153

Association of Social Research Organisations   154

Association of Teachers in Colleges and Departments of Education, Sociology Section   36, 148–51

Association of University Teachers 95, 116, 120, 126, 167

Atkinson, Dick *see* British Sociological Association and Atkinson affair

Attlee, Clement   16

Ayers, Gwen   31, 125, 131

Baldamus, Gi   113, 115–6

Banks, Joe   29, 34, 46, 77, 116, 157

Bartlett, Frederick   20

Bauman, Zygmunt   59

Beckford, James   141

Bedford College   13, 27

Birmingham, University of   12, 27, 112–7, 162

Bishop, T. J.   30

Blackburn, Robin   109–12, 118, 122

Booth, Charles   6

Bottomore, Tom   82, 141, 142, 143, 145, 158

Bouchier, David   99–100

Branford, V.   8

British Academy   155

British Association for the Advancement of Science   5, 31, 150, 155, 158

British Journal of Sociology   17, 23, 60–61, 63–5

British Medical Association   9

British Population Society   10

British Psychological Society   21, 57, 170

British Society for Social Responsibility in Science   118

British Sociological Association:
    Abrams Prize   131
    and academic freedom   108, 114, 116, 120–1
    and Atkinson affair   37, 112–8
    and Blackburn affair   37, 72, 109–12
    Book Club   41, 128, 130, 132, 138, 154

Bulletin 29
Business Manager 133
and charities legislation 43, 134
committee structure 32, 38, 42,
44, 134–7
conferences 23, 29, 30, 37, 38,
47–54, 125
    Sexual Divisions conference
    38, 41, 89–91
    child care 96
Cuts Bulletin 39
democratisation 52, 79, 140
Development Officer 38, 88, 126,
127, 132
disciplinary representation 19, 22
see also membership by discipline
Disputes Officer 131
Durham office 43, 128, 133
EC recruitment and composition
21, 29, 38, 44–5, 76–86, 177–85
    age 80–81
    becoming involved 82–84
    BSA careers 80, 82
    departments 84–86
    elections 78–9
    gender 80–81, 103
    polytechnics 78, 80–81
    rank 79–80
Equality of the Sexes Subcommittee
39, 92–9
ethics
    ethical codes 34, 162
    Professional Ethics Committee
    92, 99, 106, 116, 119
and exam boards 36, 149, 152
finances 19, 21, 31, 41, 46, 124–
131, 191–2
founding meeting 18–19
and government 154–5
guidelines 40, 43, 95, 97, 98
ISA, relations with *see* International
Sociological Association
as learned society 1, 31, 39, 135
London meetings 22, 47
membership 21–2, 29, 33, 41–2,
44, 69–77
    admission to 87
    at LSE 72
    by department 75–7, 87
    by discipline 21–2, 69–70
    by employment 150
    by gender 29, 44, 75–6
    by rank 71, 87

continuity 74
    reasons for belonging 74, 131
    reasons for resignation 72–3
office accommodation 125–6,
128, 133, 154
personal cases 131
provisional executive committee
19–21
Postgraduate Forum 51, 131
as professional association 136,
166–71
public issues, putting views on
30–31
publications 37, 40, 54, 60–7,
125, 134
    books 41, 54, 66–7
    journals 60–66, 98
    *see also Sociology, Work
    Employment and Society,
    Sociological Research Online.*
Publications Officer 132–3
Scottish branch 29, 47, 88
services to members 130–1
Sociology without Sexism 98
staff 19, 31, 131–4
Staff and Premises Committee
128, 133
Standing Committee of Sociologists
150–1
and student unrest 111
study groups 29–30, 36–7, 39,
44, 54–60, 68, 98, 187–90
    Asia 36, 54
    Auto/Biography 56
    Class Formation and the Third
    World 55
    Computers in Survey Analysis
    55
    Deviance 55, 56
    Ethnography 55
    Family 89
    Fatherhood Research 39
    Figurational Sociology 55
    HIV and AIDS 56
    Industrial Sociology 15, 29,
    30, 47, 54
    Leisure and Recreation/Sports
    and Games 56, 60, 68
    Lesbian Studies 39, 56, 97
    Medical Sociology 37, 56, 60,
    138
    Military Sociology 37
    Political Economy 37, 55

Political Sociology   37, 60
Race Relations   37, 57–8
Religion   58
Sexual Divisions and Society
39, 91, 94
Sexuality   39, 56
Social Policy   54
Social Psychology   57
Socialist Societies   37
Sociology of Art   37
Sociology of Design   36, 54
Sociology of Development   37,
60
Sociology of Education   29,
30, 47–8, 54
Sociology of Language/
Communication   36, 54
Sociology of Reproduction   39,
56
Sociology of Sociology and
Social Research   59
Theoretical and Comparative
Sociology/Theory   29, 30, 47,
54, 59, 97–8, 100
Urban Poverty and the Labour
Process   55, 60
Urban Sociology   29, 54
Uses of Mathematics and
Computing   37
Violence Against Women   39,
55, 97
Weber   55, 59
subscriptions   31, 38, 41, 124–8
summer school   35, 67, 97, 157
Support Fund   94, 127, 128, 130
Teachers' Section   34–5, 38, 48–9,
77, 113, 136, 149, 157, 161, 162,
171
and teaching and curricula   36,
42, 98, 99
Web site   44
women in   38–9, 63–4, 68, 161
Women's Caucus   38, 44, 51, 78,
80, 89–107
Working Party on the Position of
Women in the Profession   91–2
Working Party on Social Relations
Associated with Sex and Gender in
Sociology and Social Policy courses
91–2

Brown, Frederick   15

Brown, Sibyl Clement   15

Burgess, Bob   136, 156
Burt, Cyril   20

Campaign for Nuclear Disarmament
32
Cannon, Charmian   149
Carr–Saunders, Alexander   10, 20,
21, 25
Centre for Environmental Studies
126
Charity Organisation Society   7
Childe, Gordon   20
Christian sociology   24
Clegg, Sue   98
Cohen, Percy   59
Cole, G. D. H.   20
Colleges of Advanced Technology
27, 32
Council for Academic Freedom and
Democracy   114, 118, 122, 123
Council for National Academic Awards
36, 83, 87, 148, 167
Cox, Caroline   123
Coxon, Tony   156
Crozier, M.   51

Department of Scientific and Industrial
Research   16, 28
Deutsche Gesellschaft für Soziologie
171
Dix, Anne   31, 43, 125, 128, 130,
131, 133, 135, 137, 138
Durkheim, E.   9

Economic and Social Research Council
16, 31, 34, 39, 40–41, 45, 51, 109,
121, 154, 155–7
Economy and Society   62, 77
Eldridge, John   154
Elias, Norbert   59, 115
employment of sociologists   24, 32
Erikson, R.   51
Essex University   112
ethnomethodology   37, 62

Eugenics Education Society   9, 25
Eugenics Society   10–11, 19
Eugenics Review   9
European Sociological Association 145–6

Fabian Society   6, 7
Farquharson, Alexander   23
feminism *see* women's movement
feminist theory   59
Field, G. C.   20
Firth, Raymond   20
Florence, P. Sargant   20, 26
Ford, Percy   20
Fortes, Meyer   20
Frankenberg, Ron   118
Freedman, Maurice   29

Gaitskell, Hugh   11
Geddes, Patrick   8, 24
Gellner, Ernest   59
geography
   associations   170
   and Sociological Society   10
   and *Sociological Review*   63
Gilbert, Nigel   155
Ginsberg, Morris   10, 11, 13, 17, 20, 21, 24, 25, 68, 140, 141, 143
Glass, David   11, 17, 20, 25, 30, 56, 140, 141, 143, 158
Glass, Ruth   21, 54
Goldthorpe, John H.   31, 33, 61
Goodman, Raymond   12, 18, 20, 21, 28
Gould, Julius   40, 72, 118–9, 123, 143
Government Social Survey   15, 19, 24
Grimond, Jo   116

Habakkuk, H. J.   20
Hall, Stuart   82
Halsey, A. H.   29

Hamilton, Henry   20
Harrisson, Tom   11
Hatfield Polytechnic   148
Hawthorn, Geoffrey   164
Heads of Departments   43, 51, 152–3
Hetherington, Sir Hector   20
Hill, Reuben   145
Himmelstrand, U.   51
Hirst, Paul   118
History Man   96, 109
Hobhouse, Leonard T.   7, 9, 11, 13
Hoy, Jane *see* Development Officer
Hull University   118
Human Factors Panel   16
Human Relations   16

Illsley, Raymond   156
industrial sociology   15, 16
Institute for the Study of Conflict 123
Institute of Community Studies   16, 28
Institute of Race Relations   57
Institute of Sociology   10, 17, 19, 23
International Library of Sociology and Social Reconstruction   25
International Sociological Association 18, 23, 56, 90, 139–146

Jahoda, Marie   13, 15
Jaques, Elliot   16
Jennings, Humphrey   11
Johnston, Ron   170
Joseph, Sir Keith   39
Joseph Rowntree Memorial Trust/ Foundation   28, 30

Kandiyoti, Deniz   141, 142
Keele   63
Kelsall, Keith   91, 116
Korpi, W.   51

Labour Party/government   11, 12, 16

Lancaster University   84–85

Lazarsfeld, P. F.   13

Le Play, F.   8

Le Play House   10

Left Book Club   11

Leicester University   27, 31, 87

Leonard (née Barker), Diana   89

Lindgren, Ethel   14

Liverpool University 13, 25, 27, 28

London, representation of   11, 22–3, 29, 36, 50–1, 86

London School of Economics and Political Science   6–7, 15, 17, 19, 36, 45, 109–12, 128, 142–3
    Department of Social Biology   25
    Department of Social Science   8, 16, 153
    Department of Sociology   8, 11, 31, 85–86

London School of Ethics and Social Philosophy   7

London School of Sociology and Social Economics   7

London University see also Bedford College, Goldsmiths, London School of Economics and Political Science   13, 19

Lukes, Steven   114

Mace, C. A.   20

MacRae, Donald   17, 60–61, 143, 167

Madge, Charles   11, 12, 21, 141, 144

Madge, John   21

Mannheim, Karl   13, 16

market research   13

Marks, Tony   141

Marks and Spencer's   28

Marshall Plan   16

Marshall, T. H.   13, 17, 20, 21, 140, 141, 156

Marsland, David   40, 119, 123

Martin, D.   123

Mass–Observation   11–12, 13

Medical Research Council   28

medical sociology   9, 49

Mess, Henry   25

methods of research, this book
    documentary   2–3
    interviews   3
    sample   3
    sources   173–6
    use of own experience   4

Miller, Emmanuel   25

Mogey, John   21, 28

Moss, Louis   15

Myrdal, Gunnar   23

National Association for the Promotion of Social Science   6

National Council for Voluntary Organisations   134

National Deviancy Conference/ Symposium   49, 62

National Foundation for Educational Research   19

National Institute of Economic and Social Research   12, 19

National Institute of Industrial Psychology   19

Network   40, 68, 130

Neustadt, Ilya   28

New Left Review   32, 105

Newfield, Gabriel   116

North East London Polytechnic   150

Nuffield Foundation   21, 26, 28, 31, 35, 124, 157

Open University   118

operational research   15

Outhwaite, William   141

Outlook Tower   8

Pahl, Ray   40

Parsons, Talcott   59

Pear, T. H.   20, 26

Peart–Binns, John   58

Pilgrim Trust 13

Platt, Jennifer 141, 142, 156

Poggi, Gianfranco 59

Polish Sociological Association 145, 158

Political and Economic Planning 10, 12, 16, 18, 21, 26, 45

Political Studies Association 21, 29, 154

Polytechnic of North London 123

Polytechnics 32, 88, 148

Population Investigation Committee 10, 25

Posner, Michael 109

'professional sociology', professionalism 30, 35, 161–6

Research Assessment Exercise 41, 87, 88

research funding 28

Revolutionary Socialist Students' Federation 111

Rex, John 57, 118, 163–4

Rice, A. K. 16

Rock, Paul 156

Rockefeller Foundation 28, 131

Rose, Hilary 91, 118

Rowntree, B. S. 13
see also Joseph Rowntree Memorial Trust/Foundation

Royal Anthropological Institute 19

Royal Economic Society 21, 73

Royal Society 155

Royal Statistical Society 5–6, 9

Rustin, Mike 150–1

Save British Science 155

Scharf, Betty 26

Shils, Edward 16, 123

Sieff, Israel 45

Simey, T. S. 20, 25

Smart, Barry 118

Smith, Cyril 159

Smith, John H. 24, 143

Smith, W. O. Lester 20

Social Administration Association see Social Policy Association

Social Affairs Unit 123

Social Policy Association 22, 154, 159

Social Research Association 154

Social Science Research Council see Economic and Social Research Council

Social Survey of Merseyside 25

social surveys 8, 14

social work training 8, 13

Sociological Papers 9

Sociological Research Online 44, 66

Sociological Review 9, 10, 17, 23, 61, 63–5

Sociological Society 6, 8–10, 25

sociologists
    political attitudes 40
    professional 30, 34–5
    qualifications of 27–8, 33, 35, 163

Sociologists in Polytechnics 136, 138, 147–8, 150–1

Sociology 36, 41, 62–5, 125, 126, 127, 186

Sociology Club 11, 22, 25

SociologyPress 44, 67

Southern Sociological Society 161

Sprott, W. J. H. 20, 141

Stacey, Margaret 33, 91, 104, 138, 154

Standing Conference of Arts and Social Sciences 159

Stansfield, Ronald 21, 22

student unrest 37, 109–118

Tavistock Clinic 16

teacher training colleges 27, 32, 36

Thatcher government 39, 81

Therborn, G. 51

Thomas, Brinley 20

Thomas, W. I. 9

Thomson, Godfrey   20
Titmuss, Richard   20, 21, 29
Tönnies, F.   9
Touraine, A.   51
town planning and Sociological Society
10
Toynbee Hall   8, 24
Trist, Eric   16
Tropp, Asher   29, 30, 34, 46, 150,
152, 162

UNESCO   16, 17, 139, 140
university
    cuts in funding   39, 42
    expansion   27, 32
    new universities   27, 32
    sociology   13, 14–15, 32–3
University Grants Committee   24, 26,
27
    Review of sociology   40
Urwick, L.   7

von Wiese, L.   10

Wakeford, J.   157
Ward, Joyce   133
Ward, Robin   133, 138

Wartime Social Survey   15
Webb, Sidney and Beatrice   6
welfare state   16, 23
Westergaard, John   114, 118
Westermarck, Edward A.   7, 9, 13,
14
White, Martin   6, 7, 8, 24
Wilkins, Leslie   12, 15
Willener, A.   51
Wiliams, W. M.   63
Wilson, Roger   20
women's movement   38, 49, 68, 70,
90
    roles for men   99–102
Wootton, Barbara   13, 20
Work, Employment and Society   44,
46, 65, 127, 186
Worsley, Peter   116

Young, Kimball   16
Young, M. F. D.   118
Young, Michael   12, 16, 156

Znaniecki, F.   10
Zubaida, S.   142, 144

Index to references

This index includes all references made in the text to publications; it does not include references to archival sources, interviews, less formal conversations, or personal communications.

Abbott, J. (1969)   26

Abrams, P. (1968)   6, 9

Albrow, M. (1970)   166

Allen, S. and D. Leonard (1996)   68

Anon. (1962)   158

Anon (1970)   157

Atkinson, D. (1971)   122

Atkinson, P. (1974)   57

Bakke, E. W. (1933)   13

Banks, J. A. (1958)   24, 27

Banks, J. A. (1967)   30, 35, 161

Banks, J. A. (1974)   157

Banks, J. A. (1989)   13

Banks, J. A. and D. Webb (1977)   66, 169

Banks, O., R. Deem and S. Earnshaw (1980)   106

Barnes, J. A. (1981)   167

Barrett, M. (1986)   101

Bartlett, F. C. et al. eds. (1939)   14, 15

Bell, C. and H. Newby (1977)   103

Berger, B. M. ed. (1990)   106

Bhopal, K. (1997)   102

Bibby, J. (1972)   32

Blackburn, R. (1969)   110

Blackstone, T., K. Gales, R. Hadley and W. Lewis (1970)   37, 102

Bott, E. (1957)   16

Bottomore, T. B. (1962)   143

Bouchier, D. (1983) 90, 100

Boyne, N., C. Emslie, L. McKee, C. New, J. Quinn and C. Williams (1999)   98

Bradbury, M. (1975)   96, 109

Branford, V. (1928)   7, 24

Brown, R. K. (1967)   61

Bryce, J. (1904)   8

Bulmer, M., K. Bales & K. K. Sklar eds. (1991)   24

Burgess, R. G. ed. (1986)   66

Burgess, R. G. ed. (1989)   67

Calder, A. (1985)   25

Canaan, J. and C.Griffin (1989)   102.

Carr–Saunders and Jones (1937)   25

Chamberlain, M. K. ed. (1988)   106

Cherns, A. (1963)   28

Cherns, A. and N. Perry (1976)   16, 28

Cockburn, A. and Blackburn, R. (1969)   37

Cohen, S. (1971)   59

Collison, P. and S. Webber (1971)   38

Corrigan, P. (1976)   105

Costall, A. (2001)   26

Coulson, M. A. et al. (1967)   61

Cox, C., K. Jacka and J. Marks (1977)   123

Cradden, C. (1998)   126

Crouch, C. (1970)   121, 122

Dahrendorf, R. (1995)   7, 8, 25, 110

David, M. (1977)   96

David, M. and Sharma, U. (1977)   93

Deem, R. (1976)   151

Demerath, N. J. (1981)   161, 172

Dicks, H. V. (1970)   16

Dunning, E. and E. Hopper (1966)   61

Elston, M. A. (1976)   91, 105
EoS Committee (1983)   94, 96
EoS Committee (1986)   99
EoS Committee (1994)   98
Evans, David (1983)   25

Faris, R. E. L. (1981)   88
Farquharson, D. (1955)   10
Fenton, C. S. (1968)   61
Fisher, D. (1980)   28

Galton, F. et al. (1904)   9
Gamarnikow, E. (1982)   96
Giddens, A. (1972)   66
Giddens, A. (1968)   61
Ginsberg, M. (1929)   25
Ginsberg, M. (1956)   14
Gittus, E. ed. (1972)   66
Glass, D.V. ed. (1954)   25, 143
Glass, D. V. and M. Gluckman (1962)
28
Goldthorpe, J. H. (1966)   61
Goodman, R. (1981)   12
Gould, J. (1977)   40, 118
Gould, J. and W. L. Kolb eds. (1964)
143
Grebenik, E. (1986)   10, 25

Halliday, R. J. (1968)   10, 13
Halmos, P. ed. (1964)   46
Halsey, A. H. (1985)   17
Halsey and Trow 1971   122
Hanmer, J. (1982)   101
Hawthorn, G. (1975)   164
Hearn, J. and D. Morgan (1989)   102
Heidensohn, F. (1989)   67
Hindess, B. (1973)   66
Hirst, P. (1973)   123
Hoch, P. and V. Schoenbach (1969)
122
Hughes, H. M. et al. (1973)   106

Jacka, K., C. Cox and J. Marks (1975)
123
Jary, D. (1979)   158
Johnson, M. (1974)   57
Joint Working Party of Social Science
Societies and Associations (1974)
154
Jones, D. C. ed. (1934)   25

Kelly. T. (1981)   25
Kent, R. A. (1981)   5

Lassman, P. ed. (1988)   59
Law, L. (1976)   159
Lewis, J. (1992)   155
Lindsay, K. (1981)   12
Lipset, S. M. (1994)   88
Lipset, S. M. and Ladd (1972)   122
Lovie, S. (2001)   172
Lukes, S. (1974)   66
Lukes, S. and J. Westergaard (1971)
114

Macdonald, K. (1975)   126
Macdonald, K. M. (1995)   169
Macleod, R. and P. Collins (1981)
31
Madge, C. and Harrisson, T. (1939)
12
Mann, M. (1973)   66
Marshall, T. H. (1936)   10, 13
Marshall, T. H. ed. (1938)   10
Marsland, D. (1985)   119
Marsland, D. (1988)   119
Martin, D. (1969)   37
Mass–Observation (1943)   12
Maynard, M. (1990)   107
Mazumdar, P. M. H. (1992)   10
McNeil, M. (1985)   99
Meller, H. (1990)   24
Mess, H. A. (1928)   25
Middleton, C. et al. (eds). (1993)   67

Miller, H. (1976)   151
Millerson, G. (1964)   167–8
Mills, David   (2001)   46, 170
Moore, D. G. (1987)   39
Morgan, D. and L. Stanley (1993) 62, 65
Moss, L. (1991)   15
Mulkay, M. (1972) 66

Nicol, A. (2000)   16, 28
Nisbet, R. (1972)   122

Paterson, T. T. (1955)   15
Peel, J. ed. (1967)   34
PEP, Director (1950)   18
Perris, G. H. (1913)   6
Platt, J. (1971)   45
Platt, J. (1986)   15
Platt, J. (1988)   40
Platt, J. (1991)   13
Platt, J. (1998)   18, 158
Platt, J. (2000)   27, 38, 45, 69, 74, 96, 122, 127, 151
Platt, J. (2002)   1
Pope, C. and S. Ziebland (1993)   56

Rayment, T. (1991)   121
Reid, I. (1974)   34, 148
Revolutionary Socialist Students' Federation (1969)   111
Riley, M. W. ed. (1988)   106
Rinde, E. and S. Rokkan eds. (1951) 143
Robbins, L. (1963)   33
Roberts, H. ed. (1981)   107
Rowntree, B. S. (1941)   13
Rowntree, B. S. and B. Lasker (1911) 13
Royal Statistical Society (1934)   6
Rustin, M. (1976)   151

Sapper, L. (1972)   116
Scott, S.(1984)   157
Scott, W. H. and J. B. Mays (1960) 28
Sewell, W. H. (1992)   39, 106
Shaw, M. (1974)   120
Simpson, I. H. (1988)   161
Simpson, I. H. and R. L. Simpson (1994)   86, 161, 171, 172
Sklair, L. (1981)   46
Smith, C. S. (1975)   34
Smith, H. L. (1930–5)   25
Smith, J. H. (1961)   143
Solomos, J. and L. Back (1996)   67
Stacey, M. ed. (1969)   37, 66, 125
Stacey, M. (1993)   91
Stansfield, R. G. (1981)   15
Stewart, W.A.C. (1989)   27, 32, 148, 149
Strong, Phil (1973–4)   56
Strong, P. M. (1983)   171
Sulek, A. (2002)   158

Taylor, B. (1976)   101
Taylor, B. (1994)   24
Thompson, E. P. ed. (1960)   32
Tropp, A. (1956)   30, 162
Tuke, M. J. (1939)   1

UNESCO (1953)   17, 143
University Grants Committee (1989) 40

Wakeford, J. (1963)   34
Webb, B. and S. Webb (1932)   25
Webb, D. R. (1972)   26, 157
Webster, F. (1992)   67
Wells, A. F. (1935)   14
Westergaard, J. and R. Pahl (1989) 46
Wilkins, L. T. (2001)   16

Williams, G. and T. Blackstone (1983) 34

Williams, G., T. Blackstone & D. Metcalf (1974)   34, 45

Wilson, B. (1967)   61

Wilson, B. (1969)   112, 123

Wolfenden, J. (1957)   30

Woodward, D. (1977)   103

Wootton, B. (1967)   14

Young, M and P. Willmott (1961)   28

Zubaida, S. (1970)   37

Zueblin, C. (1899)   8